THE
PLAYGROUP
HANDBOOK

THE PLAYGROUP HANDBOOK

Revised and Updated Edition

Laura Peabody Broad

Nancy Towner Butterworth

St. Martin's Press ◆ New York

Book Design by Anne Scatto
Illustrations by Bill Charmatz

Library of Congress Cataloging-in-Publication Data
Broad, Laura Peabody.
    The playgroup handbook / Laura Peabody Broad and Nancy Towner
Butterworth.—Rev. and updated ed.
        p.   cm.
    Includes index.
    ISBN 0-312-05494-7 (pbk.)
    1. Play groups—Handbooks, manuals, etc.   2. Creative activities
and seat work—Handbooks, manuals, etc.   I. Butterworth, Nancy
Towner. II. Title.
HQ782.B75   1991
649'.5—dc20   90-19115
                                                                                CIP

Second Edition: April 1991
10 9 8 7 6 5 4 3 2 1

Note to readers: The pronouns "he" and "she" are used interchangeably
throughout this book, but the information refers to both sexes.

CONTENTS

◆

PART TWO: ACTIVITIES THROUGH THE YEAR

ACKNOWLEDGMENTS

◆

To the people who helped us in a multitude of different ways, we say "thank you." Special appreciation goes to Larry White and other staff members at the Needham Science Center; Harriet Hair, Professor of Music at the University of Georgia; Ginny Mullahy, The Learning Tree, Danvers, Massachusetts; Jean Lindblad, Director of Needham Congregational Nursery School; Louis Demosthenous of Louis and Clark Pharmacies in Wilbraham and Springfield, Massachusetts; Sandra Gellert of the National Association of Family Day Care (NAFDC); Dee Rabehl of the National Association of Child Care (NAC-CRRA); Pat Seigel of the California Child Care Resource and Referral Network; Marjorie Kopp of the Child Welfare League of America (CWLA); Suzanne Garber, Research Librarian at Western New England College in Springfield, Massachusetts, Wilbraham and Springfield Public Libraries; Doug Graybill of IBM; Jack Ampuja, Steve and Lisa Nelson, Doug Broad, Ginny Swallow, Valerie Thompson, Shari Walder, and most importantly our editor, Anne Savarese, who cheerfully waded with us through the avalanche of details.

To our own and other families
who have shared with us their ideas,
support, and enthusiasm for this revision.

INTRODUCTION

◆

If you are holding this book in your hand we know you must have a concern about the important preschoolers in your life. You may be a parent juggling myriad obligations that include career, child care, and leisure time. Whether your preschooler is in your care full time or spends part of his day with others, you want to know that he is in a safe atmosphere, having lots of fun in creative, educational ways. Most of all, you would like to have a part in planning and sharing his experiences. These pages are meant to help you do this.

The Playgroup Handbook speaks directly to people who want to help their children play and learn with a small group of other children in the home setting. The book can also be used as a treasure trove of ideas for a parent, grandparent, babysitter or friend looking for age appropriate ways to spend time with a single child. In addition, the book provides guidelines for the person seeking to run a small day care operation for profit, and is full of ideas for the early childhood teacher.

We want to give you the things we were looking for as we planned playgroups and shared time with our own children and their friends. Back when we first tried to find printed material to help us we found very little. Desperation was often our teacher; we invented new projects and games in our kitchens minutes before our children's friends arrived at the door. We soon realized that watching the children work and play gave us many new ideas to incorporate in our plans. We talked with other parents about everything from the changes we'd seen in our two-year-olds to our favorite kinds of outings and spur-of-the-moment math games. Working in nursery school settings, we acquired lots of simple techniques to expand the mind, capture the imagination, and build the self-esteem of young children. We learned ways to help children become more independent in solving the problems that confronted them as they experimented with new materials or coped with personal situations.

Playgroup is one of the child care options that worked best for us. At its simplest level, playgroup involves several parents who trade off taking care of each other's children in the home. We wanted our children to have more than unstructured play hours together, so the parents planned activities that drew on their own special talents. Unlike a formal nursery school, the playgroup allows parents to have a direct impact on what is going on with their children. The most wonderful element is the plan's flexibility. You can choose the structure that best suits the schedules and other needs of your children and yourselves.

Playgroup can be anything from casual playtime you share with the children to something as sophisticated as a professional nursery school, encompassing many hours, days of the week, and even sleep time. You might even choose to rent space outside the home for the children's regular meeting times and combine your own playgroup time with that of a paid caregiver.

Whatever arrangement you choose for the learning and play times of your preschooler, *The Playgroup Handbook* can help you. The book takes you step by step through the organization of the simplest kind of home-based playgroup. It shows you how to work with small groups of children and moves through the months with you as you plan your days with the children. The collection and use of different materials are discussed, and there is a sample plan for a playgroup day. Most important, there are many activities, both seasonal and nonseasonal, from which to choose. These activities are arranged in a progression through the months of the year. While many can be used at any time, they are set forth in this manner simply so you will have at your fingertips practical guidelines that you can put to use in a flexible way.

You will find activities in a number of subject areas designed to fit the children's capabilities and your own talents and training. There are helpful hints on how to adapt the activities to different situations and settings or to different ages and stages. You will find support in areas in which you feel less secure. In some cases we even suggest words to use when dealing with the children. We also include advice on how to take advantage of the toys, materials, and environment you already have without spending large sums of money.

This new edition of *The Playgroup Handbook* reflects recent changes in teaching techniques and philosophy. Activities are set up in minimally directed, open-ended ways that encourage children to experiment with materials and come up with their own unique solutions to problems. The emphasis is on the child's positive experience with the process rather than on the outcome.

This edition also incorporates up-to-date materials and equipment available to you, wholesome foods to use when cooking with preschoolers, and expanded health and safety guidelines.

We hope you will reap the benefits of our trials and errors as you walk in the world of your preschoolers. We want you to enjoy the experience as much as we have.

A. PRELIMINARIES

◆

WHY PLAYGROUP?

Practical Considerations

There are many different reasons for choosing the home playgroup as a child care option. Perhaps you are a parent looking for a sociable way to share time with other parents and their preschoolers after work. Combining the children's playtime with your break time may suit your needs.

You may be looking for the perfect bridge between your child's infant days at home and the days he or she will spend in a formal preschool. A small playgroup, intimate in character, can be a low-key preparation for the complexities of school life. It could also be your child's primary source of interaction with others near his or her age, especially important if playmates do not live nearby.

A playgroup might also turn out to be a good supplement to the nursery school experience. It could fill a period of time when you must be absent because of your own work or recreational requirements. Your child will look forward to his own special group, while you will feel comfortable knowing he is happily and productively occupied. In every case a playgroup is a wonderful way to share a special time in your child's life with other parents and children.

Playgroup—Good for Your Child

Playgroup gives children so many ways to grow. It will be one of the first places that they make friends. At its best it will provide a safe, secure niche for them to share experiences and toys with others close to their age. You will know your child is feeling better and better about herself when she enjoys just plain fun with the others in the group and runs home, eyes shining, to show you some treasured item culled from her playgroup day.

Both you and she will begin to feel good about how well she can manage at times when you are not around. In this close situation you can get lots of direct feedback from the other parents, and she will feel as if she has new brothers, sisters, cousins, aunts, and uncles as the playgroup takes on the shape of a warm family.

She will begin to build relationships with other adults while she learns the slightly different sets of house rules that they may impose upon her. It is important for her growth that she find her fears wiped away when others create safe limits, free from harsh discipline, in places other than her own home.

You will watch while she stretches intellectually as the children experiment with new materials, learn new skills, and become better at following directions. Her confidence and yours will flourish as she is given lots of we-knew-you-could-do-it messages. These are just a few of the fringe benefits of the playgroup experience.

Playgroup—Good for You

Playgroup can give you the support you need in the demanding business of your job as caregiver. No parent—and that includes you—can be everything to a child. To do your best for your child you need to share him with others. In playgroup you will benefit from a new kind of extended family as you hear about your child from the other parents' caring perspective. You will come to know that your parenting skills are just fine when you find that your child is not so different from the other children. As you learn about the preschoolers from the other adults you will become more secure about what to expect from your own child, and when you watch his interaction with others you will come to have whole new understandings about him.

Sharing in playgroup is not an abdication of your responsibility. It is a practical way to achieve some sense of equilibrium in your nonstop balancing act of managing child care, career, home, and social life. Feeling run ragged is not the hallmark of a job well done. In fact, it is a warning message to you that it is time to regroup and look at some of your choices so your family benefits from more than a harried you. Playgroup is an option that will give you special time for sharing creatively in your child's expanding world, and time away from him when you can feel comfortable because you have had a direct hand in planning the hours he spends away from you. Playgroup is also an option that allows some much needed time for restoring yourself.

Choosing Participants

Who will join you in the formation of your group? Jane, who has seven years of teaching experience? George, the single parent who works for an insurance company? What matters is not so much their previous child care experience but the mutual desire to form the group and a few similar ideas about its goals. There is absolutely no substitute for enthusiastic parents motivated by the love of doing things with and for their own children.

We remember an exuberant mother who bundled a group of four-year-olds into her car and set off for, of all things in New England, a buffalo farm! En route she stopped at a filling station, asking the startled attendant to please fill up the buffalo bus with buffalo gas—much to the delight of the children. Everyone caught the spirit. It was clearly a pleasure to the mother to have it be "her day."

Avoid the parents who are so overextended socially or professionally that they cannot commit themselves to the importance of playgroup. Their time with the children will be a nuisance to them and the little ones will feel it. They are not likely to plan ahead and are less likely to provide a very happy, relaxed atmosphere for the children. They will be the ones to cancel out on their turn at the slightest provocation. If you should find you have parents who refuse to do their share when the group is underway, the wisest move, difficult though it may be, is to politely eliminate them as participants.

Like-minded people with similar needs are the ones you want for your group. Check around the places where people you like are generally found—your workplace, library story hour, church, ski group. Do you think you have spotted a likely prospect or two? Spend time exchanging ideas about child care. You will soon see whether their attitudes and philosophies live comfortably with yours. Watch how they manage with their own children. Is it an easy-does-it relationship, balancing a firm hand and warm flexibility?

The parents in your group will have different abilities and interests. Some may even be trained or experienced in a particular field, but this is certainly not necessary. Each individual should capitalize on his or her own interests—enthusiasm will be contagious.

A playgroup mother we know loves to walk through the garden of a nearby estate and tramp in the snow by a lake. Her own love for what she is doing makes the children simply glow with the shared experience.

If you are lucky, grandparents or other relatives may figure into your playgroup. One playgroup child has his grandfather living with him. Time with Grandpa in the garden has become a real treat for the children, especially when they are sent home with ripe tomatoes they have picked right from the vine. In some cases grandparents can serve as wonderful substitutes for playgroup leaders who have been confronted with occasional last-minute emergencies.

Do not discount doing a playgroup just because practical considerations mean that you cannot arrange time to be a participant yourself. Maybe the other parents who want the special playgroup experience for their youngsters have similar problems. Think about hiring a caring person to work with the children in your place. It might be one parent who is free to lead the playgroup all of the time. If you are available part time, then paying a regular substitute to fill in the gaps also can work very well. The advantage of this kind of arrangement over a larger day care situation is that it remains very personal. Parents can stay in close touch with what is happening and take part in the overall planning for the group.

If you do choose to call on outside help, you might take another look at the choice of meeting places for the group. Options might include having the preschoolers gather at the caregiver's home or shifting the scene from home to home among the children. Make a decision that best suits your unique demands while still addressing the needs of the children in a comfortable and happy way.

Take a look at the work and play patterns of your prospective playgroup parents. Make sure a cursory inventory indicates you will be able to juggle your mutual time constraints. Worry about fine-tuning the details later as you move into serious planning sessions.

Ages of Group Members

What ages should the children be? Emphatically the ideal is to have them the same age. The year between a two-year-old and a three-year-old or a three and a four makes a great difference in both interests and attention span. A two-year-old is most content just playing beside a friend. The three is preoccupied with "me" and "mine" and her attention is diverted very quickly. The four can devote herself to an activity with a companion for quite some time. Anyone who has had the same playgroup over a period of three years knows how independent and reliable four-year-olds are in comparison with the threes, who simply fall apart in a group if left unsupervised for a few minutes. Most threes can work at a task only a short time before becoming interested in something else, while the four can tackle a project with some degree of persistence. A ten-minute directed art activity is plenty for many three-year-old groups, but a four-year-old group might be intrigued with some creative undertaking for twenty minutes. Needless to say, there are enormous differences among children. You will get to know your own group and will gear your activities according to their particular needs.

The same age group ideal is not always possible. There are dozens of reasons for needing to mix the ages of the children. You may find that the parents who will work best with you have children of assorted ages. Perhaps there are some younger brothers and sisters to be dealt with. Whatever the reasons for mixing, go with it and adapt accordingly.

Becoming more flexible about age saved the day on one occasion when a normally excluded two-year-old was allowed to join his four-year-old brother and playgroup buddies. Neil watched at the edge of things as his brother and friends cut and pasted some paper bag puppets. He first cried because he wanted some materials. Denied them, he went quietly into another room where he reduced the binding and pages of his brother's *Winnie the Pooh* to shreds and threw them at his mother's feet, waiting for a reaction. He had reached his peak of frustration and acted accordingly. A few minutes later he was happily hooked into his highchair beside the other children, armed with blunt scissors, a crayon, and paper, where he stayed content for the next half-hour. How much simpler and happier for everyone if he had been included in the first place.

Two-year-olds deserve a special word or two, because there really is a much wider gap between twos and threes than between threes and fours. To begin with, many two-year-olds are still in diapers, so they are much more demanding in terms of physical needs. When you are planning trips it is probably easier to find another alternative for the two-year-old. Otherwise you must take extra precautions to know where toilet facilities are and to build in more frequent potty stops.

Safety, already a top priority with preschoolers, becomes even more of an issue. Extra vigilance is necessary because the two-year-old can be a notorious wanderer. She knows no fear and is at an unselfconscious stage where she wants to try all sort of things. She may still be in the phase of testing everything in the mouth first.

Anyone who has spent time with a two-year-old is acquainted with the mood swings that go with the age. Given the materials she wanted so badly to use one minute, she may experiment for a second or two, then dash off to do something else; or she may want very much to try a task but be unable to muster the physical skill needed to accomplish it. Another time, the skill may be well developed but the desire lacking.

If you understand the behavior characteristics of your two-year-olds, you can make the necessary adjustments. Focus on solutions, not the problem. Your job in all this is to keep a balanced cool while she swings. Be ready for anything.

One parent was startled speechless when, after unlocking the door to the house, she turned to see one playgrouper, Claire, fling herself to the ground in high tantrum. What brought it on? Claire wanted to unlock the door herself—a task she was unable to do and previously had shown no interest in doing.

The positive side to all this is that two-year-old children are often quite content to simply follow the leadership of an older child, at least for a while. Being with "the big kids" sparks an enthusiasm in two-year-olds to give any activity a try. When they lose interest they are equally happy to entertain themselves with something else at hand. In some cases, age may not be as much of an issue as development. One of your three- or four-year-olds may be following the script we've just written for twos.

If you had a group made up entirely of two-year-olds, you would be hard put to find a leader for activities. Without the presence of older children you would need to limit projects to the simplest kind and spend much more of the day in free play.

Since we assume you will be addressing the needs of different ages and stages, many of the activities in this book include hints for adapting the project to suit greater interest and ability, or scaling it down for the younger, more limited group members.

If you keep your projects simple and open-ended and try not to overdirect, you will keep everyone in your group, including yourself, excited with the process of exploring and learning.

Size of Group

In the enthusiasm of planning a group you may find a number of parents wishing to have their child join. Small numbers are a *must*. Not only is space a factor to consider but the average parent will be busy, indeed, with just a small group. For three-year-olds, a group of four is large enough. Remember—four easily distracted people are easier to control than six who have begun to get a little wild in a moment of your divided attention. The bedlam that can ensue while you answer the phone or chat with a neighbor who has unexpectedly dropped by is amazing. Even with a small group in tow, the playgroup parent must learn to tell a caller, "I have a playgroup here now. I'll call you back later."

While four in a group is a good number for the younger ones, the four-year-old, with his greater independence and longer attention span, is easy to manage in a slightly larger group. If there is space available and all the parents are willing, five or six is a good number.

For a group of mixed ages, choose what seems practical in regard to what you can manage and what you need. Four to six would be a reasonable number. This is the range often suggested in various state home daycare guidelines. Try to include at least two of any one sex.

A determining factor may be the space you have available. A general standard suggested by Massachusetts day care guidelines is 150 square feet for one to two children, 225 for three to six.

FACILITIES

Now where should all this productive activity be taking place? Although renting outside space is certainly one of your options, the playgroup setting most likely is your home. It really makes no difference whether you are an apartment dweller with no garden or a suburbanite with some yard space available. There is no specific house or yard requirement. It is simply a matter of establishing a workable pattern for your space. A backyard is great to have, equipped or not, but city streets and parks provide endless possibilities for excursions and discoveries.

Define Areas of Play

You don't want to turn household furnishings upside down and inside out to accommodate the group, and you certainly do not need to. However, defining areas of play is important. This is a way of providing clear boundaries for the children about what can go on and where it is acceptable to do it. Arranging the space instead of the play allows the children to make choices free of constant direction from you. This, in turn, frees you to watch the children and to respond to their special enthusiasms and demands.

Look over the categories of activities that are listed in this book. Think about where it would be easiest to carry them out in your playgroup facility. Decide which room or rooms will be used by the children, then do the necessary arranging. When the children arrive, is there a place for their sweaters or coats? A plan as simple as using doorknobs down a hallway will do. Where is the snack table or counter? What area is best for blocks, toys, and games? Which room or corner is good for pretending and storing the "dress-up" clothes? Art can be messy. What space is best for those sorts of projects? It should be where you are not fearful of spills and near water for cleanup. If you have more than one bathroom, which one is for the preschoolers? When they come, let them know you are happy to help them with any problem they encounter in using it. Is all your space planning being done so that you will be able to keep track of the whereabouts of the children at all times? If naps are part of the playgroup day, have you provided the necessary sleeping facilities? Is there quiet space for alone time or reading?

Shift a few strategic pieces of furniture. Perhaps the coffee table can be pushed aside to allow more space for movement. Block off areas that are out of bounds. Make outdoor play boundaries equally clear.

Decide which pieces of furniture are for the children's use and which are off limits. Provide pillows and mats for easy moving and regrouping in a creative use of space. Then when the children arrive, introduce them to the plan. They are counting on you to let them know the limits.

Be sure to see to it that there is a special place for the children's belongings and all the playthings, and that when the day begins as well as when it ends, everything is tidily in place. Though there may be dozens of toys in a messy room, disarray confuses young children, and they cannot find anything to do. At the end of a play day it can be a matter of pride and learning for them, and a help to you, if everyone pitches in to put things back in order. Clearly designate the tasks: "Phillip, put the blocks in this box." "Mary, line up the dolls on that bench." It will be surprising what a good job little ones will do.

Equipment

It should not be necessary to buy a great amount of equipment for the group. Each home becomes a special attraction because of what it has: a slide at one, a hobby horse at another, a doll house somewhere else. The playgroup parent need not try to create the perfectly equipped professional nursery school. The emphasis should be on making the most of what is already there. Of course, it will be necessary to purchase some materials, as the need arises, for special activities such as arts and crafts.

If you have written permission from each parent for walking or car excursions, the playgroup does not always need to meet at your home on your day. Wherever you live there are endless possibilities for trips and outings: a picnic in the park or woods, a visit to a museum that has something of special interest for your group, a morning at the local library for story hour—but more about this later.

WHEN TO MEET

The Group's First Encounters

Some of the children in the group may not know all of the other children and parents or playgroup leaders. While it is impractical to have meetings of all the parents with their children at each individual house, some effort should be made so the children have at least met all the people who will be involved. Such an effort is necessary for each child to feel secure as he ventures into new surroundings with new faces in what may be his first experience away from his family.

One solution is to have a special outing for all the families. One group spent a sunny day picnicking at a nearby beach. After a few hours of splashing and munching sandwiches together, the little ones, as well as the parents, felt like longtime friends. Your group's outing could be as elaborate as that one or simply a get-together for refreshments and playtime at someone's house or apartment.

Another approach is to have the children circulate among one another's homes for short playtimes. This way there is an opportunity for becoming acquainted with the group members and different settings in a gradual way.

The Regular Schedule

The regular playgroup calendar will be dictated largely by your needs—and that means operating around people's work schedules. You will have chosen participants whose timetables mesh well with one another.

The alternatives are as many as the minutes in a day. Will you operate in weekly blocks of time, alternate days, mornings and afternoons? Are any evening hours to be included? Sleeptime? Are weekends considered? Are you thinking of flex time with a different combination of children participating on different days? What about a "drop-in" playgroup?

Make the final arrangement clear. Print up schedules. Come to a mutual agreement about penalties for dropped responsibilities, sickness, lateness, and how to work around emergencies.

Special Times

Holidays can present problems. Older children in your families may be out of school on days when you are working. Trading off times and a new, temporary set of responsibilities may sort out the situation. If you are lucky, parental members of your group may celebrate different holidays. With a little negotiation you might trade off your playgroup hours so you can celebrate with your children at your special time. Vacation periods can be similarly exchanged.

Select some reliable substitutes who can fill in for you if an emergency arises and exchanging with the other group leaders is not possible. Give the children opportunities to become acquainted with any substitutes before the substitutes are called to lead the group.

SPECIAL CONCERNS

The year will be happier for everyone if the playgroup parents come to some agreement ahead of time about what they expect of one another and what the group's goals should be.

One parent may envision a playgroup as a morning of general free play for the children. Another may desire a structured program in which every parent must plan balanced days with a sample activity from every subject area and designated times for naps and juice. Both of these views represent extremes. You and the other parents can discuss what kind of day you want your children to have and agree to plan your days accordingly. You may settle on a basic plan that all of you will follow, or you may decide to leave the decision about each day's activities to each individual. The object is to suit the desires and needs of your particular group. Planning a Day (page 30) is a point from which to work. You can discuss some of the ideas in that section and adjust them to suit your own needs. A little planning together will save misunderstandings later on.

Facing the Issues

All kinds of special issues surface when you deal with children in a group. It is well worth your time to discuss some of these with your playgroup parents, so everyone can have an idea of the sorts of things that come up and some notion of how to deal with them.

It is important to know at the outset that different people have different styles of handling situations. You can come to a consensus on generalities, but in the end you will need to accept and trust in the variances of approach from person to person.

However, you need to be in accord about certain basics. The first is that no one will ever lay an angry hand on a child. Establish that the focus in all situations will be on the positive—the do's instead of the don't's. The general atmosphere should be noncritical but safe. The objective is to accept each child as she is and help her develop the best of herself. Talk about how important it is for each adult to observe the children closely in order to anticipate and avoid problems.

All parents should be aware that the adult's attitude will have everything to do with the children's response. In any situation where the children might have doubts about appropriate behavior, it is vital that the grownup convey a sense of certainty. The words you speak must be definite and any action you take should match the words. An uncertain tone of voice or hesitancy in body language has a greater impact than any words you choose. Sound convincing and move as if you mean business.

In a circumstance where danger is involved, take immediate, physical action. If there is no direct safety problem but you are doubtful about what to do, pay attention to your instincts. Your inner voice is an honest voice.

You and Your Child

The bravest person blanches at the thought of having to cope with an uncooperative, overactive, or overly aggressive child. It may come as a shock, but this child will probably turn out to be your own. Relax! She will not behave at someone else's house in such a fashion. She will store it up and save it just for you.

She is excited to a pitch that the group will be at *her* house and *her* mom or dad will be "teacher." The other children descend, and she is distressed to find that all this glory includes their being able to use all *her* things. All of her belongings suddenly become important treasures and she is more than reluctant to relinquish them. Of course, learning to share is part of what playgroup is about, but you can help soften the harsh reality of this. One way is to suggest that the other children bring a toy. This initially gives them a sense of security, and then as they become interested in your child's toys, she has their toys to examine and play with for some new interest.

Most difficult of all for your child, however, is the fact that she finds she must share *you* with all these people. She may feel called upon to do all sorts of negative things to capture your attention.

Never mind. That same child is going to come home from someone else's playgroup day with the announcement, "David was so naughty that his mommy had to send him to his room." Maybe she even had to carry him there kicking and screaming!

Separation

Children suffer varying degrees of uncertainty about early forays away from home. It can be an uncomfortable time for parents, too. A father or mother faced with saying goodbye to a child who has been concerned about leave-taking may feel an almost physical pull, preventing smooth departure. This is one of those times when mustering the sure tone of voice, the reassuring words, and the certain walk is in order. If the parent seems positive that the child will be just fine, the child is more likely to be convinced. "We know you can do it" is the message of self-esteem. This is a time, too, where other people can be of help. The adult who is in charge for the day can both encourage and distract the child. Another child may be enlisted to help the unhappy preschooler over the hump.

Strangely enough, some children who breeze through early preschool days on a happy "high" may be overtaken by gloom a month or so into the group's operation. The fresh experience carries him for a while, but with the evaporation of newness, this sort of child will need the same help that others were given earlier on.

Overdependence

Some children show many signs of overdependence. This is a real self-esteem issue. It becomes the playgroup parents' job to gently guide such youngsters toward the kind of independence that is appropriate for their ages.

First you have to be able to recognize the problem. Detect it by paying attention to a variety of clues. The hallmark is attention-getting behavior of one sort or other. There is the child who is forever running to the teacher with tales ("Suzanne just spilled the paint") or the person who continually seeks approval ("Is this right?" "Do you like it?"). Another is the preschooler who is always uncertain about how to do something even when it has been clearly explained and done before—"How do I do it?" Of course, constant clinging is another clear-cut sign of overdependence. Many other bids for your attention will become recognizable to you as indications of the problem.

The child who is so concerned about how to do things the right way may be accustomed to a great deal of direction from the people around him. For someone worried about the right way to paint, for instance, you might say, "Let's look at Johanna. Watch how she is holding the brush. Maybe you can look at how some of the others are doing it." You are pulling his focus away from you to the other children who are busy with the process. The child begins to see reminders of how to do it all by himself. Another time he might look around and find the solution without coming to you.

For the child who is attracting attention by minding other people's business, you can help him focus on himself. Assure him that Suzanne and the paint problem is between you and Suzanne. Steer him to the task at hand that belongs to him.

When you hear the approval-seeking, people-pleasing, do-you-like-it questions, talk about how the child himself likes it, how he feels about it. Let him know that his own assessment and feeling is really important.

Whenever a child has a problem, help him find his own solution. Aid him in seeing various possibilities for resolution. Have *him* choose one of the acceptable answers. When children learn that the solution to problems is in their own hands they are on the road to independence and feeling terrific about themselves.

Aggression

Occasionally a child may confront you with some highly aggressive behavior. The rule is clear here. You cannot allow destructive behavior or any acting out that threatens the safety of anyone, including the aggressor.

The first strategy is to divert the preschooler. If she is simply fury bent on her objective, this approach will not work. You have to rescue her from herself more decisively. Give her "time out" to pull herself together. Sound matter-of-fact. Steer her to a quiet space where she can sit alone and perhaps look at a book or pick up a toy. Give her neutral time to recover from the feelings that were overwhelming her and endangering the surroundings.

When you are involved with this kind of situation, keep your own voice firm but neutral. Steer away from messages that convince the child she is a bad person. Stay as free from negative judgment and punishment as possible. Remember, this is a special kind of rescue operation. You want to keep the child's self-esteem intact, let her know what is acceptable and unacceptable, and assure her that she is in a place where an adult will keep her safe.

TRANSPORTATION

Whether you are using mass transportation, cabs, or private cars, work out all the details of arrival and departure carefully. If car pools are involved, discuss the use of seat belts and infant restraints. Time needs to be addressed again with an emphasis on punctuality and the need for everyone's cooperation.

Think about distance between the children's homes. If each is an only child and there is no one else to consider, then long drives are not necessarily a problem. For maximum convenience, however, the closer the better. Each group of parents will have its own feeling about whether each family should provide transportation on the day the group comes to their home or on other days. Often just planning and overseeing the activities of the day is enough responsibility without the additional task of ferrying people about.

Many working parents prefer to drive their own children to playgroup if it is convenient to their job location and time schedule. This allows for shared time between parent and child, and often can make the difference in how a preschooler feels about his or her day.

HEALTH AND SAFETY

Safety requires careful planning so that the management of activities and the materials used ensure a safe experience. It also means that you should prepare for the unexpected.

One group of preschoolers may be hyperactive, so you find yourself automatically on guard for the climber, who is continually investigating beyond playgroup boundaries, or the daredevil who will attempt anything and winds up needing the bandage treatment. Some groups are low-keyed and easygoing, but this does not mean you can feel completely at ease. Often the quiet ones are wanderers who get lost if left for a minute during outdoor play or experimenters who sample inedible activity ingredients without calling attention to their act.

If you have found it necessary to have a child's younger sibling on the scene, the challenge becomes greater. You must be sure of that child's well-being before you become involved with group activities. You need to be aware of what each person is up to at all times. Small children can easily sense the "best" moment for trying the unusual.

Whatever the makeup of your group, avoid mishaps by screening materials for safety, planning ahead so you do not have to leave your preschoolers unattended, establishing appropriate limitations and rules for the group at your home, and reviewing how you would handle a serious emergency.

Remember that in an emergency situation you have a *dual* responsibility. You must take care of the child in trouble *and* see to it that the other children are not left unsupervised. There are two questions to ask yourself before each playgroup day: Is there someone nearby to call on for help? Is transportation available?

To enable you to handle the unexpected:

1. Have these numbers by your telephone:

+ Your doctor or local hospital
+ Poison control center
+ Police
+ Fire department
+ Children's parents or parent substitute
+ Person to take charge of the group for you

2. Have a file for each child which contains the following:

+ Written permission from parents or guardian to get medical attention
+ Record of medical problems, including allergies
+ Special instructions regarding medication, including permission to administer nonprescription medication (such as antiseptic)
+ Name and phone number of child's doctor
+ Plan to be carried out in case of illness or accident

3. Be first-aid ready with these materials:

+ A first aid booklet in a handy spot
+ Basic first aid equipment on hand, including:

  2- by 2-inch, 3- by 3-inch, 4- by 4-inch sterile gauze dressings, nonstick, individually wrapped, for cleaning and covering wounds
  roll of gauze
  4- by 4-inch topper sponges (to absorb blood)
  roll ½-inch-wide adhesive tape
  box of assorted adhesive bandages
  small bottle mild antiseptic such as Betadine
  meat tenderizer or After Bite for insect bites
  tweezers (for splinters)
  needles (for splinters)
  eye wash
  2 bottles syrup of Ipecac (to induce vomiting after swallowing poisons other than caustics; call a poison control center before using)
  reusable or disposable cold packs (for sprains)
  scissors

- Thermometer
- Extra shirts, hats, and (with parent's permission) sunscreen and bug repellent

4. Take a CPR and/or first aid course, and know the Heimlich maneuver.

Childproofing Indoors and Out

A key to the good health and safety of the children is a childproof environment. The indoor and outdoor areas where playgroupers spend time need to be as hazard free as you can make them. It is impossible to anticipate every problem, but here are some simple things you can do to protect your group. Many of these steps are recommended in various states' guidelines for day care safety.

INDOORS

- Keep all areas clutter free and sanitary (remove breakables and valuables, put trash and garbage out of the way).
- Remove and store dangerous articles (sharp objects; weapons; plastic bags; tiny, easily swallowed objects; insect killers; toxic plants; household cleaners; medications; and all other poisons) out of children's reach.
- Put safe childproof locks or latches on doors.
- Hook extension cords and electrical wires out of the way.
- Install smoke detectors and a fire extinguisher.
- Avoid use of electric heaters.
- Mark glass doors.
- Cover locks on closet, bathroom, and other doors to prevent children from locking themselves in.
- Barricade stairs.
- Barricade coal or woodburning stoves.
- Cover radiators and electrical outlets.
- Keep fans and cooking equipment out of children's way.
- Keep furniture and equipment in safe repair. Use nonslip pads under rugs.
- Confine pets.
- Make sure toys and materials are play safe.
- Test drinking water for safety.
- Remove lead paint.

OUTDOORS

- Keep play area free of trash, tools, construction work, open drainage ditches, animal waste, glass, wells and water holes.
- Fence or otherwise protect the playground.
- Remove rusty nails.
- Bar access to bodies of water. Fence pools.

BUSINESS MATTERS

How you manage the business matters will be unique to your situation. The two general areas to explore and act on are operating expenses and insurance.

In many informal situations parents have seen fit simply to let each household carry the cost of the playgroup time spent there, with the exception of special outings or trips. Others have chosen to open a bank account and contribute in equal parts to an ongoing "kitty." The latter arrangement requires a treasurer to oversee the cash flow. If you have hired substitutes or a regular caregiver, you'll need to work out a satisfactory means for salary payment.

All of you need to check your insurance coverage. Liability is an issue today, so review the policies you have for home and car. In addition to homeowner's and car insurance, you may want an umbrella liability policy which picks up expenses beyond regular coverage in other policies. Ask your insurance company for information.

B. GATHERING MATERIALS AND PLANNING

◆

The parents have agreed on all the ground rules for the group. The schedule has been decided upon and the transportation worked out. Now it is up to you to carry out plans when your day comes. You are on your own!

Attention turns to collecting materials to have on hand for various projects. It will be helpful to know what basic items to purchase and what to save for future use. You will also welcome a few hints on how to plan effectively for the children.

MATERIALS

Basic Items to Consider Purchasing

There are a few items you will need to purchase in order for the playgroup to function. Most of these are for art activities. Some may be bought or borrowed as you choose the activities for a new playgroup day. Certain items will be used so frequently that it would be wise to purchase them at the outset. You will find most of the materials you need at hobby or art shops, stationery stores, discount department stores or pharmacies.

Art Materials

PAINTING
powdered tempera (least expensive)
tempera, ready mixed (convenient, more expensive)
　Add 1 teaspoon of liquid detergent to 1 pint of tempera paint to make paint-soiled clothes easier to wash.

finger paint, ready mixed, or liquid starch with powdered tempera
watercolors (small sets are great for fine-motor painting)
slick paint—(water-soluble fabric paint in tube)

BRUSHES

large easel brushes, long or short handles (½- or ¾-inch width)
1-inch hardware brushes (less expensive)
foam disposable brushes
sponges for cleanup, sponge painting

PAPER

manila: buy 1 ream (500 sheets) for economy, divide among parents
newsprint: buy 1 ream, 9- by 12-inch or 18- by 24-inch standard
    easel size
shelf paper or finger-paint paper with coated surface
colored construction paper: 50-sheet package, assorted solid colors
aluminum foil
colored tissue paper (Art Tissue, available at art supply stores,
    bleeds easily for experimenting with colors)
colored cellophane
colored plastic wrap
posterboard for signs, portable teaching board
oaktag (easy to cut, best for nametags and flannel board figures)
brown paper bags (cut open)

DRAWING

crayons (jumbo, antiroll are best)
primary pencils
felt-tip markers, wide and thin tips, primary or pastel colors
soft chalk (dip in liquid starch before drawing to eliminate chalk
    dust)
Cray-Pas chubbies—special crayons with brilliance
Caran D'Ache crayons—water soluble, perfect for face makeup

CUTTING

right- and left-handed plastic scissors with steel shank for cutting of
    all materials (Kingshead brand is inexpensive and safe)

PASTING

white glue (to make glue glaze, add water to glue until the mixture
    has consistency of light cream)
containers
paste
paste brushes (or Popsicle sticks)
glue stick, 1 per child (no mess)

FASTENING

stapler (larger size less apt to jam)

brass fasteners
paper clips
cellophane tape (easiest for children to use from large dispenser)
clear Contact paper

MODELING: Best-Ever Clay Recipe

3 cups flour	3 cups water
1½ cups salt	3 tablespoons cooking oil
6 teaspoons cream of tartar	food coloring

In a small bowl, mix together flour, salt, and cream of tartar. In a separate bowl, mix water, oil, and food coloring. Combine contents of both bowls in a saucepan and cook over low heat until thick. Knead while warm. Keeps well for long periods of time in an airtight container. This clay can be made successfully with the children using an electric fry pan.

commercial playdough
plasticine, solid colors (stiff, works best with clay tools and for older
    children)
self-hardening clay, porous (can be painted but not glazed)
potter's clay, gray or red (bake to harden; nonporous, so can be
    glazed)

SPECIAL ART ITEMS

glitter in shaker container
doilies
craft sticks
pipe cleaners
small wooden rolling pin (to use with clay)
stamp pads with variety of stamps (a roller stamp is fun for a
    change)
peel-and-stick stickers
marbles
felt, white and assorted colors
shaving cream
Ivory Snow soap flakes
food coloring
spring clip clothespins
paper plates, small and medium sizes
quick-drying plaster

Cooking

If you have all the items on this list you will be able to do just about all of the recipes in this book and most other cooking projects that you might choose to do with preschoolers.

mixing bowl
measuring cups
mixing spoon
sharp knife
eating utensils (knives, forks, spoons)
spatula
baking dish or pan
saucepan
cookie cutters
cookie sheets (2)
rolling pin
strainers
food brush
apple corer/sectioner
food grinder
grater (grinding type)
chopper (chopper sits on cutting board with blade and food inside.
   Children pump handle to bring blade down and cut food.)
french fry cutter (for alternate way of cutting vegetables and fruits)
potato peeler
juicer
small cutting board (1 for each child if possible)
pitcher
tray
colander
serrated plastic knives (picnic knives safe for children to use)
paper plates, cups, bowls*
plastic bags (sandwich, food, and trash sizes)*
electric frying pan (nonstick)
hand-held electric mixer (for your use only)

Handy extras:
  electric slow cooker
  blender or food processor
  microwave oven

Dramatic Play

Many props and items of clothing can be donated or loaned by parents
who work in different professions. The rest can be found in closets,
attics, or (if you are not a saver) at garage sales.
  puppets
  dolls and accompanying clothes, blankets, carriage, bed, highchair

---

* Consider the environment. Use washable, reuseable plates, cups and cutlery as often as
  possible. Find alternatives to plastic bags. Save plastic bags to reuse.

housekeeping materials—small table, chairs, dishes, pots and pans,
broom, telephone (Improvise with boxes if you do not have play
stove, sink, refrigerator.)
mirror—nonbreakable, full-length size
dress-up clothes—shoes, hats, pocketbooks, jewelry, ties, crowns,
veil, simple clothing
cash register—play money
attaché case
kits—fill from the science list (page 26) to encourage doctor,
carpenter, and other pretend play
doll house, with furniture and people

Music

record or tape player
records or tapes—be familiar with before using
musical stories
simple songs
nursery rhymes
music for movement
classical music of all cultures
popular artists: Hap Palmer, Ella Jenkins, Bev Bos, Rosenshontz,
and Raffi
rhythm band instruments
purchased: bells, drum, maracas, tambourine, triangles, rhythm
sticks
homemade: see page 258
music books:
American Folk Songs for Children, Ruth Seeger (New York:
Doubleday & Co., 1948).
Songs to Grow On and *More Songs to Grow On,* Beatrice Landeck
(New York: William Sloane Associates, Inc., 1950, 1954).
Eye Winker, Tom Tinker, Chin Chopper: Fifty Musical Fingerplays, Tom
Glazer (New York: Doubleday & Co., 1973).
Animal Folk Songs for Children, Ruth Seeger (New York: Doubleday
& Co., 1950).
120 Singing Games and Dances for Elementary School, Lois Chosky and
David Brummitt (Englewood Cliffs, N.J.: Prentice Hall, 1987).
A Song is a Rainbow, Patty Zeitlin (Glenview, IL: Scott, Foresman &
Co., 1982).
Sharon, Lois & Bram: The All-New Elephant Jam, Sharon, Lois &
Bram (New York: Crown, 1989). Elephant records and tapes also
are available.
American Favorite Ballads, Pete Seeger (New York: Oak/Music Sales,
1961).

special instruments:
  autoharp
  xylophone

Physical Exercise

INDOORS
  soft foam or rubber balls
  bean bags
  scarves
  balance beam
  mattresses or mats for tumbling
  blocks (use as bowling pins)
  hopscotch grid (vinyl sets available, or make your own with tape)

OUTDOORS
  any special equipment you already have—slides, swings, climbing
    set, sandbox, hoppity hop, Hula Hoops
  kickballs, soccer balls, beach balls
  equipment at local parks and playgrounds

Science

Use what you have or can borrow to give children the thrill and experience of using scientific equipment. They will gain a sense of
accomplishment as they master the use of suggested items and become
involved in the scientific approach to learning by trial and error.

GENERAL EQUIPMENT
  mirrors—reflections
  magnifying glass—collections, inspections
  lighted magnifier
  flashlight—circuit fix-it, investigations, shadows
  magnets (horseshoe, bar)—classifying by differences
  tweezers, tongs—fine-motor control
  sieves, sifters, funnels—sandbox, water table play, melting projects
    (page 136)
  eye droppers—color mixing
  meat baster—water play
  thermometer—to measure air temperature indoors and outdoors
  retractable tape measure
  scales—balance scales are especially fun for experimenting
  tuning fork
  color paddles—set of three transparent paddles in primary colors

(child looks through paddle to change color of surroundings. Overlapping paddles create additional colors—red and yellow, for example, make orange.)

MORE SPECIALIZED EQUIPMENT

cages—bug catchers, aquariums, wire enclosures
small aquarium
bird feeders
binoculars
microscope or water lens (see water lens activity on page 300)
stethoscope
kaleidoscope
garden tools—spade, hoe, rake, trowel and other hand tools (child-size tools are available, but most children can manage and prefer the regular size).
prism
windsock
pet ball
pulley and wheels

Storytelling

PUPPETS—simple, homemade or purchased. Elaborate puppets are not comfortable for preschoolers who often see puppets as companions, not performers.

FINGERPLAYS—one helpful book on this activity is *Finger Frolics: Fingerplays for Young Children, Revised Edition,* Liz Cromwell and Dixie Hibner (Livonia, MI: Partner Press, 1976). Children follow you as you designate each finger to tell a simple story that often involves counting. It is important to allow children to improvise and create their own fingerplays.

FLANNEL BOARDS—easiest flannel board can be made using *foam core* (purchased in art supply or framing stores) cut to size to slip inside a *standard-size flannel pillowcase.* Use purchased flannel-backed story sets or make your own using medium-weight *pellon* (sold in fabric stores as interfacing) to trace pictures, then color and cut. Children can also draw on pellon with markers and create their own original stories.

STORYBOOK AND TAPE SETS—a wonderful way for children to enjoy storytelling independently. Public libraries or book clubs have excellent selections. *Rumplestiltskin, Sleeping Beauty* and *The Wizard of Oz* are a few classic favorites.

VIDEOTAPES—preschoolers exposed to these have more familiarity with classics such as *Charlotte's Web,* an excellent favorite. Video stores offer listings appropriate for this age level.

Woodworking

For the most part you will be using items from the home workbench. The following list is meant as an aid if you need to purchase some equipment and want a guide to the ideal tools. Woodworking requires close supervision and is best when extra adults are available to lend a watchful eye and helping hand.

HAMMER—12- or 18-ounce claw hammer (also pulls out nails)

HACKSAW—type for 10- or 12-inch blade. Buy blades with 14 or 18 teeth per inch. We think this is the best saw for small children: it is sturdy, offers maximum safety, is easier to cut a straight line with, and can be used with both hands if desired.

VISE—3½-inch light duty with swivel base, if available (or use C-clamp)

COPING SAW—6- to 6½-inch blades, 15 teeth per inch. Though commonly used with small children, this saw presents the safety hazard of blades snapping. It is also more difficult than the hacksaw to guide in a straight line.

SCREWDRIVER—short, stubby one preferable, standard size or ¼-inch blade, 6 to 8 inches long, to fit screws. If children have difficulty with a conventional screwdriver, use a Phillips-head screwdriver. The Phillips head doesn't slip as easily.

NAILS—2d 1-inch and 4d 1½-inch common nails, 1-inch or 1½-inch galvanized roofing nails

SCREWS—¾-inch and 1-inch # 9 steel flathead

SANDPAPER—medium or coarse

FILE—10-inch combination shoe rasp

HAND DRILL—eggbeater type with #9 screw bit and/or ¹⁄₁₆-inch twist drill

RULER

PENCIL

SOFT WOOD SCRAPS—nail or glue together

Materials to Collect and Recycle

JUICE CANS—marker and pencil holders

BABY FOOD JARS—paint containers, butter making

CARDBOARD TUBES, VARIETY OF SIZES—stamp painting, bubble blowing, message sending

NEWSPAPERS—easel painting, covering work areas to minimize cleanup

COMPUTER PAPER—drawing, collages, stamp pad storybooks

OLD SHIRTS—cut to size, decorate for smocks

BROWN PAPER BAGS—kites, collecting treasures, puppets

MICROWAVE FROZEN-FOOD CONTAINERS—paints or sorting items

FOAM MEAT TRAYS—collage base, paint container
SHELLS—sorting, gluing, sand castings (broken shells are fine)
CARBON PAPER—drawing
RIBBON—collage, decoration
TWIST TIES—fasteners
OLD WALLPAPER BOOKS—variety of paper for painting, gluing, cutting. Free from many paint or wallpaper stores.
ONION BAGS—suet bird feeder, storing water toys
MATERIAL SCRAPS—collages, puppets, wind art, flannel board figures
BUTTONS—sorting, collage
COFFEE TINS (1 POUND)—gift containers, storing supplies
TRIMS (OLD JEWELRY, LACE, RIBBON, BRAID)—collage, decorations
YARN REMNANTS—stringing, collage, masks, puppets
CLOTHESPINS, REGULAR OR SPRING CLIP—clothesline art, sponge paintings, sailboats
EGG CARTONS—sorting, shaker, monsters, glue container
SPICE CONTAINERS—musical shakers
RUBBER BANDS—box guitar, nail board
POPSICLE STICKS—glue sticks, mask or puppet handles
STRAWS—paper puppet handles, collage, bubble making
LARGE BLUNT-END NEEDLE—stringing
SNAPSHOTS—memory tray, special cards
SQUEEZE BOTTLES—water play
PINE CONES—bird feeder, holiday decoration
BOX COVERS WITH 1-INCH SIDES—marble art, shadow box
ROCKS, STONES—sorting, collecting, painting
FLOWERS, PRESSED OR DRIED—arrangements, Contact paper designs
MARGARINE TUBS—art containers for paint, glue, etc.
FOAM CUPS—bells, planting bulb or seeds
GOLF TEES—use with Styrofoam for sculptures, counting
FLORAL FOAM—arrangements
CLOTHESLINE—tent, art show, drying paintings
MISCELLANEOUS ITEMS (CURLER, CASTER, MASHER, OTHER INTERESTING OBJECTS)—stamp painting, imprinting clay, memory game

PLANNING A DAY

In the most rewarding playgroups we know the key to success has been planning, planning, and overplanning—which your little ones should never be pressured by or aware of. The planning is a matter of having ideas and materials at your fingertips, to be used on a given playgroup day or set aside for another. The choice depends on the immediate needs and moods of the children.

Materials for projects should be prepared and easily accessible. One parent we know lines her things up on trays ready to whisk on the scene when needed. If you are using a record player or other special equipment, have it set up and ready to go. Make sure it is in working order. Balls or other playthings for which you have planned a special game should be assembled so you need not leave the children while you scramble about trying to retrieve the items. If you are an inveterate listmaker you will, perhaps, make out a proposed schedule for the day or just list the different ideas you have.

Why all this? After all, it is not a military campaign you are planning. But remember that brief attention span of your three-year-olds . . . ten minutes, maybe? You need to be ready to move into some new activity quickly if their interest flags. Your four-year-olds are expected to be interested longer, but what if the project you planned just doesn't strike a chord or takes less time than you expected? You need something else in its place. More planning means more flexibility.

Flexibility is the key word. Your group may be low-keyed one day, quite equal to listening and to doing quiet activities. The same group may have switched into high gear another day and more time outside is in order, or if that is not possible, then some moving-around activities inside are necessary. Be ready to switch the order of activities to suit the day or the moment. Be prepared to spring into a little aerobics in the middle of an art project before returning to it.

It will be helpful if you take your cue from exponents of the schools of education. They preach an activity rule of thumb—"quiet followed by noise; still followed by movement." One automatically sets the stage for the other. After running about, a child is ready to sit quietly and listen to a story; after drawing a picture he is all set to use some of his larger muscles and excess energy.

For a basic idea of what might be included in your day, consider the following: free play, arts and crafts, music, group time, story, juice time, nature or science project, games, outdoor time. That list sounds more intimidating than it is in practice. You would not, of course, do all of those things every time. The idea of having to set up anything scientific or musical may overwhelm you, but overcoming such apparent difficulties is what this book is for. It includes very simple activities, right for the preschooler and right for the average parent to tackle with the group.

Group time is a chance for the children to relax with you as they listen, participate, and observe in more directed group activity. This quiet provides a nice transition between activity time, lunch, and outside play.

SAMPLE PLAYGROUP PLAN

You may want a concrete plan of attack for setting up your half day. Here is a sample plan to give you something from which to work. Essentially all it amounts to is a simple list of ideas of what the parent hopes to do—a list such as you might scribble in abbreviated form on a piece of scrap paper. Opposite the list is spelled out what preparation is necessary. You might go over your own plans for preparation by making mental notes as you look at your list of ideas—or you might like to jot down a companion list of things you need to do ahead of time in a fashion similar to that shown here.

Following the well-laid plans is an interpretation of how the day actually may have gone. It is important to realize how successful a *rearranged* day can be and that the thoughtful planning and preparation remains the basis for a wonderful playgroup experience.

SAMPLE PLAYGROUP PLAN

(activities drawn from different months)

Children's Activities	Preparation by Adult
1. Neighborhood walk or Hike in the house	1. Assemble treasure bags, picnic snack.
2. Car tracks in paint	2. Assemble small toy cars, paint, foam tray containers, large paper.
Clean-up *Quiet time* 3. Music—loud and soft sounds	3. Collect instruments.
4. Shaking butter	4. Set out small jar with lid, heavy cream.

Lunch
5. Menu: cheese
        bread and butter
        carrot strips
        milk
        fruit kabobs
Cut day-old bread and cheese with cookie cutters.
Assemble as sandwich.
Make fruit kabobs.
	5. Collect sandwich ingredients (bread and cheese, butter).
	Prepare carrots.
	Cut fruit.
	Set out napkins, milk, cups, plates, cookie cutters, kabob skewers.

SAMPLE PLAYGROUP PLAN

(activities drawn from different months)

Children's Activities	Preparation by Adult
Ending	
6. Flannel board story	6. Set out flannel board, story figures.
7. Fill-in activities (in case children cannot play outdoors before they leave)	7. Be ready with fingerplays.

As we have pointed out, plans do not always materialize as you had intended.

WHAT MIGHT HAPPEN

It's stormy, so your anticipated trip is canceled. The children are at loose ends. Redirect their energies to play travel, offering a chance to make car tracks in paint. The special trip snack can be used as planned for a hike in the house, creating a nice departure from the usual snack routine. The rest of the schedule goes pretty much as planned, but one child is more interested in putting together a puzzle than in the music activity. She is allowed to go her own way, since she is not distracting others.

or

The day is beautiful and the planned trip is a huge success. You return home later than anticipated, filled with the children's enthusiastic conversation about what they have seen and done. Everyone is hungry, so you set aside group time and concentrate on setting out lunch ingredients for the children to assemble. Once they have eaten and cleaned up, enjoy a flannel board story with them and do fingerplays together until their rides arrive.

In both instances the playgroup half day has been a success. The parent has been well prepared, but flexible enough to rearrange the schedule to fit the weather and the moods of the children. As a result, the children have had a relaxed, unpressured, happy day while learning from a few well-planned activities.

C. PLAYTIME WITH THE CHILDREN

◆

PLAN SO THE CHILDREN CAN EXPRESS THEMSELVES FREELY

Armed with a few materials and your plans for the day's activities, you are ready to begin working with the children. Within the framework of your plans, your young visitors will have the facility to express themselves. Your reserve of ideas and materials is prepared in advance. You are ready to stand by as a guide and helper for the busy children. You have not created a rigid situation; you have merely set the scene so that the children can express themselves freely in a creative way and have an enormous amount of fun doing it. If you are inadequately prepared or if you leave your group of preschoolers on its own, you will soon be confronted with decidedly noncreative chaos.

SET UP MATERIALS SO THE CHILDREN CAN BE INDEPENDENT

Plan special activities so that the children can be as independent as possible. If the materials have been set up ahead of time, the children can do an activity on their own and follow right through the cleanup. Once the project is under way, the children are eager. Any distraction—such as that of finding additional supplies—divides attention, mars enthusiasm, and spoils results.

Let us look at an art project as an example. The children are to do finger painting on a plastic tabletop. Each child is supplied with a small plastic squirt bottle filled with liquid starch, a shaker of powdered paint, and a wet sponge. They are now ready to proceed independently.

As the children experiment with varying proportions of starch to paint, they have the fun of trying out different designs, enjoying the smooth feel of the paint as their fingers slip over the tabletop. When they are finished they may reach for the sponge to wipe up the mess, with a little help from the playgroup parent. The understanding of how to use the paint has grown, the results are individual, and each child has done the whole project from the creative beginning to the tidy end.

SHOWING THE CHILDREN HOW

It is important to spend time introducing a technique or material being used for the first time at playgroup even if you know the children have been exposed to it somewhere else. Certain skills require actual demonstration. For example, children cannot experiment with cutting until they know the proper way to hold a pair of scissors. Helpful hints are in order on how to throw a ball or how to stir the Jell-O mixture without flipping it out of the bowl. You can ask a child who has already mastered a skill to show others how he does it. He will be proud to oblige, and his peers will learn most effectively from his demonstration.

Some techniques lend themselves to individual interpretation and experimentation. An assortment of ideas here is more important than a set way of using tools or media. The way a child manipulates clay, the number of sprinkles he puts on a cookie, or the way he moves as he acts the part of a bunny rabbit are purely individual. Rather than acting as a director, you can work beside the children in such situations. Each person absorbs himself in trying out his own way of testing a new experience. One person might copy entirely another's approach, but he is more likely to make his own discoveries while incorporating some ideas from the work of others.

BEGIN WITH SIMPLE THINGS

When working with three- and four-year-olds, simplicity proves to be the best approach in any area. Generally, it is not wise to try more than one new idea at a time. Another day you can reuse the same technique or activity at a more advanced level. For example, the first time the children use scissors the main job will be learning to hold the scissors and trying to make some kind of cut on paper. After a little practice the youngsters will be able to cut across a small piece of paper to make scraps. In time, the children can follow a simple outline—circles first, then squares, rectangles, or triangles. Once the cutting of simple shapes has been mastered, they can try more difficult cutting projects.

You might introduce a technique by doing a one-step activity on playgroup day. The next time the children come you might do the same thing but add other steps. An illustration of this is cookie making. For the first venture, the group might just frost and decorate ready-made cookies. If this undertaking proves to be appealing to them, then during the next session they might cut the shapes from ready-made dough in addition to decorating the cookies. An older group might even be ready to tackle the whole process—mixing dough, cutting, and decorating.

WORKING WITH YOUR GROUP

You will soon become aware of your group's individual needs, interests, and abilities. If it seems necessary, make sure there is an alternate way for different children to accomplish similar results. What one child can do with ease, another child may find much too difficult. You might give group members each a page from a sticker book and suggest that they punch out and match pictures of farm animals to an outlined form. One child in the group finds the matching beyond her capabilities. Sticking the figures on a blank sheet of paper would be easier and more fun for her. She might even enjoy adding a few details with crayon.

Your plans for the group may be complicated by a wide difference in the rate various children tackle and complete an activity. It is impossible to make three children continually wait for a methodical and deliberate worker who always takes twice as long. Yet it clearly is important to that child to feel the satisfaction of finishing. A reasonable amount of time should be provided for each activity. Make sure the child who is unusually slow accomplishes enough of the activity and has sufficient materials so she can easily finish it at home on her own.

Every child can contribute to the group in his own special way. As you begin to know what your preschoolers' abilities are, you can choose activities and assign roles accordingly. In a mural project, one child might cut, while someone else pastes, another draws, and an imaginative nonartist tells a story to accompany the completed picture.

As the playgroup day is planned, you include everyone in most activities without forcing a child to do something she strongly disfavors. Most often the role of the observer is taken at music or dramatic play time by the self-conscious child who wants to join in but needs time to watch and know how to go about it comfortably. She has interest and gradually will become involved in the activity, but in the meantime she will appreciate fringe jobs you find for her.

Sometimes a child just wants to play with the toys and rejects most suggested activities. This is natural at the start and time should be given just to playing and getting to know each other. However, as most of the children become more interested in activities, it is important that an individual not be a distraction to the group while she is allowed to play with appealing alternatives. Two children busily engaged in running racing cars over a network of speedways might find it impossible to work up any enthusiasm for making cinnamon toast. Let them continue to play while those interested in cooking make the toast. Perhaps the kitchen crew will share their toast and add to everyone's good time.

Sometimes a simple matter of interest determines whether a child wishes to take part in a given activity. Someone may never be inspired by artsy-craftsy pursuits. It is far better that a person be allowed to choose another kind of activity while the others do the planned project, but be sure to let her know she is welcome to join in if she has a change of heart.

Certain activities like singing require group cooperation, and here an observer can be important as a listener. But to play nearby, even quietly, would be a distraction and unfair at a time when it is important for the group to be a unit.

Many children at this age have an assortment of colorful individual fears which help to govern the degree of their participation. One play-group mother had armed her children with collecting bags and set out for a woodland walk. A small girl in the group, hanging a bit behind, ventured no more than several yards into the woods and resisted going one foot farther. Who knows the reason why? The mother responded by taking the group into the field at the edge of the woods. The adventurous among them were allowed to go a short way into the woods, while the girl happily played and collected where she felt more secure. The mother positioned herself where she could see all of the children.

Another playgroup child became convinced, with the help of his imaginative friends, that there was a monstrous creature lurking in the basement playroom of one house. No logic could shake his firm belief. The parent arranged to have the planned activities take place upstairs. Free play was allowed both in the playroom and upstairs so that each child could be where he was most comfortable. By the next visit, the fearful boy had completely forgotten the awesome dangers of the downstairs room.

Do not be startled when one of your little ones displays some very unique sort of anxiety. Do what you can to make her feel happy. Adapt the activity to the situation and rearrange your plans around her fears.

KNOWING YOUR OWN ABILITIES AND LIMITATIONS

You, too, have your own special needs and abilities. Consider this fact, a distinct advantage. Remember to draw on your own natural interests and talents. You are counting on the other parents to do the same. The result will be a surprising balance in the kind of experiences the children have during the year. You may be discounting the fact that you are a whiz in the kitchen, for example. Cooking projects with the children might become your forte.

Every parent has certain limitations. Do not be afraid to accept them in yourself. There will be days when you find your plans are entirely too ambitious. Neither you nor the children are in tune with your original ideas for the day. The children are overexcited, and you feel irritable. Feel free to readjust your plans. Simplify. Set aside more involved projects such as paper-bag puppets or sand castings. They are better for congenial, relaxed days because they are the kind of activity more likely to stretch patience.

There will come a day when you don't feel physically or mentally up to par, but not sick enough to cancel the playgroup activities. Rearrange your plans so that the day does not require so much energy. Likewise, if a visitor appears and the rhythm of the day is thrown off balance, just choose another activity less demanding of your attention.

HAVE FUN

The most important element in the successful playgroup day is a feeling of plain, old-fashioned fun. Without that, you and your little people might just as well have forgone the day. All of the earlier mentioned suggestions on working with the children do contribute toward this end, but more elusive qualities can be equally important in making "fun" happen.

Your attitude is a major factor. Treat yourself to happy absorption in the children. Try to set aside the other details of your daily living. Nothing will build your own confidence more readily than your immersion in the spirit of fun.

Do you feel a need to show the other parents you are doing your part by seeing to it that every child has some product to show for his time with you? If a special holiday is coming up, do you feel pressured to center your planning around that time?

So many activities are entertaining and accomplish real learning whether or not they result in tangible products. Remember those children "squishing" paint to produce their own patterns on the laminate tabletop surface? Nothing remained to take home after cleanup. The children's delight was in the experimenting, and surely they left the project with a new confidence about finger-painting which they would bring to later trials on paper.

Enjoy the freedom to depart from traditional seasonal activities. In midwinter, when the children have been essentially housebound, break free from snowtime-centered activities for a change. Bring good-weather activities inside with a swing hung from a doorway, a slide hitched to set tubs, or a makeshift basement sandbox. In summer, a target contest using snowballs stashed away in the freezer last February can be an unexpected treat. Don't be afraid to be simple and original in working with the children. Above all, HAVE A GOOD TIME!

HINTS FOR WORKING IN SPECIFIC AREAS

Art

You will understand the individual children much better as they communicate their emotions through art. They can express a mood of the moment or convey how they feel about the world around them in their manipulation of artistic materials. At the age of three or four, they are largely unable to express their feelings with the spoken word. They find enormous relief and satisfaction in working out their emotions with their hands. The *process* through which the child is going is of prime importance. The product itself does not really matter except as an expression of his feelings.

What you see being produced will bear little relationship to your adult, preconceived notions of what a picture or clay figure should be. It will be an enormous temptation to ask, "What is it?" To the child it is perfectly obvious what it is, because it is so much a part of him. He will find your question, phrased that way, hugely unsettling. Inquire instead, "Can you tell me about it?" and the child may take you into his world. In the explanation of his work he may reveal some of his deepest feelings.

If you were not aware of the place of art work in the child's life, you might unwittingly be responsible for a sad error similar to that of a mother who spent time helping in a cooperative nursery school.

Time after time she had seen Tommy come in, settle himself in front of the easel, carefully choose black paint and proceed to make circle after stark, black circle . . . clearly scribbling, clearly not developing artistically or any other way. Wanting to help him progress, she approached him and asked, "Why don't you try making something else? That is just scribbling."

Tommy did not make those big, black scribbles anymore, but he didn't try to make anything else either. Tommy stopped painting altogether. He didn't touch a brush for the rest of the school year.

What the mother did not know was that Tommy had gone with his family on a trip to New York City. They had driven through the Holland Tunnel, which, from Tommy's point of view, was the highlight of the family adventure. His picture was the picture of the tunnel. Each time he made those big black circles, he was reliving the happy excitement of the ride. If only the nursery mother had opened the way to sharing Tommy's experience! So much can be learned about a child through what he does in playgroup.

To the adult eye black was somber; repeated circles were nothing more than scribbling. You want to view the children's work through the eyes of a child, because in doing so you will encourage your preschoolers to express more of themselves. The development of skills in using materials and in creating realistic figures will evolve naturally and at each child's own pace.

It will help if you understand that there are three stages in the development of children's art. The first is the manipulative stage in which the children experiment with the media. This is the time when the children are pouring their concentration into the sensation of clay as it feels when squeezed through the fingers, the pleasure of watching pieces fall as the scissors snip off bits of paper, or the feel of the brush as it spreads paint across the page. Some members of your group will be in this phase when you begin getting together.

Later comes the symbolic stage. This is the phase in which many three- and four-year-olds find themselves. At this point the child draws, cuts, or models things that have meaning for him. People begin to resemble people, but key details such as feet or the nose may be lacking. The young artist exaggerates parts that he feels are important and eliminates others altogether.

Three-year-old Laurie, enthusiastic after the first encounter with ice skating, came home and filled a paper with faces and double lines drawn in various areas and positions to indicate bodies moving. Skates were missing in the picture, as were many other details, but the rhythm of the lines actually gave a wonderful feeling of people skating. To Laurie, the motion and the numbers of people were the important points, and she expressed them beautifully.

Representational art is the last stage. Figures are more nearly complete. They often stand on a base line. Sometimes both the inside and the outside of an object are shown. This last phase is unlikely to be very evident as you work with your young artists, for it is more characteristic of a kindergarten child or first-grader.

Drawing

The children's first experiences with art will probably have been with pencil or crayon. In your work with them it is better to leave the pencil for writing when they are older. Crayons provide a more satisfying means for creating. A page from a coloring book occasionally may be given to each child, to help develop the specific skill of controlling the crayon and staying within lines, but generally it is preferable to supply blank pieces of drawing paper. The pictures produced in this manner will be truly original.

Have the children tear the paper wrappers off the crayons and encourage using the side of the crayon for making wide, sweeping designs. Show them how the point of a crayon can produce dots or lines.

For variety give them chalk to test on colored paper or slate. And allow them some experience with soft-point marking pens—first the wide and then the thin-line type.

All of these artistic tools afford the easiest, quickest means of capturing a child's moment of enthusiasm for creating something.

Painting

Preparing for a painting session is a little more difficult, but the results are well worth the added effort. Painting presents the children with the opportunity to create in a larger, broader, freer way than they can with drawing materials.

After you have fortified each artist with a smock, rags, water, and newspaper, introduce the brush. Show how to hold it. Let the children demonstrate some of the ways to use it so the effect is different: split, tap, twist, press, roll, mix paints, paint color on color. Let them experiment in their own ways. Then let each child tell what his painting is about—if it has a "story." Provide a clothesline or table, counter, or floor space adequate for the drying of finished paintings. Make sure that the responsibility for cleanup is part of the art activity.

When you embark on any activity that is as untidy as painting, don't be surprised if you encounter a preschooler who becomes alarmed at the messiness of the project and is concerned about dirtying his hands. You may find ways to adjust the activity so it is acceptable to him or he may need to find something else to do.

It may be that you are the person who finds the enterprise upsetting. Maybe painting projects are not for you. Find other art outlets that keep you feeling balanced and good-humored.

What to Do with Completed Paintings and Drawings

Children put a good deal of heart and mind into producing a painting or drawing. You and the other playgroup parents should save an ample selection of such lovingly executed artwork. The children feel rewarded when you show your delight by hanging their work on a refrigerator door or wall for a while. If you like a tidier way to put up artwork, a bulletin board is an easy solution. Most effective of all is the use of a large picture frame hung in a room where the family often gathers. Children's work hung inside it can be regularly changed.

When the display period is over, the work can be stored for use at appropriate times as gift wrapping. Gift tags or cards for special occasions may be made by cutting drawings or paintings with regular scissors or pinking shears. A gift box wrapped in tissue paper can be dressed up in a personal way by gluing a picture or part of a painting to the top of a box.

The day that Grandpa is sick, and you know a child-made remembrance would help to brighten his room, may not be the day when the child is in the mood to make something. Treasures saved from playgroup projects done earlier will come in handy for such occasions.

Storage may seem a drawback. Simply purchase two large pieces of poster cardboard from the stationer's or hobby shop if you do not have a good substitute already in the house. Use four clamp-type paperclips to hold them together. Keep artwork pressed inside. If you feel extravagant, you might invest in an artist's portfolio. It will be used all through your child's years in elementary school.

Tearing and Cutting

Cutting is a small-muscle motor skill often difficult for three-year-olds. Let them start by tearing up old magazines and newspapers for appealing pictures. They'll love it! Encourage them to tear an enormous scrap—then a tiny one. At first this is more fun than making a definite shape. Eventually introduce scissors—the small blunt-end ones—but always allow the same result to be accomplished by tearing. This satisfies the child who is not quite ready to master the more difficult skill.

Once the children take up scissors you'll find them determined to conquer the skill. Don't worry about what they might destroy: It's difficult even for an adult to cut anything but paper with the small, blunt-point scissors you will provide for the children. Just provide a supply of small pieces of paper so they can test their progress. Initially you may need to hold the paper for them. They may not be able to coordinate the scissors and paper. Gradually they will begin snipping many nondescript shapes in free cutting activity. Another time give them large simple shapes to cut out. Once they have mastered simple shapes, the children will automatically undertake more difficult tasks.

Pasting

For many preschoolers the fun of paste is in spreading it everywhere. The youngsters are apt to plunge in with little concern for results, using the paste like finger paint, then peeling the dried paste off their fingers. Delightful! When they have succeeded in covering themselves as thoroughly as their paper they are at a loss to understand why objects are sticking everywhere but on the desired spot.

Since the initial joy is in the spreading, in early pasting experiences choose activities that allow the children to enjoy smearing away. For the young three-year-olds, actually tape the paper to the table so it doesn't slip about and use thick paper that will absorb extra moisture. The paste can be colored with a little vegetable dye for eye appeal. Cotton swabs, toothbrushes, or paste brushes can enhance the fun of manipulating the paste.

Enlarge the pasting experience by having paste-spreading sessions that include sprinkling, dropping, or placing materials onto the pasted surface. Such materials could include paper scraps, fabric, herbs, objects from nature, colored sand, or glitter. The possibilities are endless.

After much practice in this kind of activity, the children will be ready to attempt gluing materials of their choice to a surface. Make sure you have chosen amply large pieces for the youngsters' first trials at this skill. Big magazine cutouts or generous snippings of fabric would be good starter materials. Allow the children to choose the items they plan to use for their composition before they even touch the paste. Now they are ready to use fingers or brushes to smear paste on one of the pieces. Next they carefully stick it to the surface that they are decorating. The children should have many opportunities to use paste with large materials before trying to glue tiny bits. Remember—large pieces in small numbers will provide the best early experiences.

As always the ages and individual skills of your children will determine how complicated the activity can be. As a rule three-year-olds will need more time with the spreading skill first, whereas four-year-olds will soon be ready to attempt gluing individual objects.

Fastening

While pasting is the primary means children use for putting pieces together, there are other methods of fastening. Sometimes there is a more efficient or durable way of holding parts together. Other times a new means of hooking items to one another can provide an appealing change of pace. Some of the variations are tape, Contact paper, brass paper fasteners, large paper clips, and staples.

Tape is probably the most popular with the children. They love tearing tape off the roll, and they can stick it to almost anything except wallpaper without doing harm. Sometimes little hands have trouble tearing or cutting tape. In this case it is helpful if you cut off different size pieces and stick them lightly along the edge of the table or around the edge of a plate or pie pan in the center of the table. The children can then easily take pieces as they need them.

Initially tape-fastening activities should involve attaching flat surfaces. One mother happened on a wonderful two-dimensional activity.

Desperate for something to keep a sick child busy, she dumped in his room some masking tape, markers, and colored oaktag scraps left over from playgroup. The results were smashing—cars and trucks, letters, rockets, and so on, all a conglomerate of shapes and colors. The mother had solved the problems of entertaining her patient and of deciding what to do with playgroup next time in one fell swoop.

Tape lends itself to creative work that is not specifically fastening. It can be used as a medium for making designs on paper, forming letters on a background, or framing a picture. You might just give the children tape and see what ways they can invent to use it.

Brass paper fasteners can give children's art mobility. With early trials do not make the children conscious of creating anything specific. Start out with a quantity of paper scraps in which you have made holes with the fastener, a sharp implement, or a paper punch. The children will love hooking pieces together and moving the parts. Much later and more likely with four-year-olds, you can begin doing hinged figures that require designing, cutting, coloring, and fastening.

Don't forget that some children love to save pictures and make books. The simplest use for brass fasteners is securing together the pages and cover.

Large paper clips of various kinds are fun to use for holding small stacks of paper. Children immerse themselves in pretend 'office work' and other games.

Contact paper is expensive but the results of projects using it are so effective that it is worth considering it for at least one trial. A piece of clear Contact, sticky side up, provides a transparent background for collages and pictures composed of all manner of materials—leaves, sequins, paper, fabric. Covered with colored cellophane it is a see-through picture to hang in front of a window or lamp. Such an activity is perfect for children who find pasting pictures too messy or complicated for their liking. For economy's sake, save Contact paper scraps. Small bits can be used for making attractive bookmarks or small window hangings.

The stapler is primarily for your use. Small staplers that children can handle easily break quickly, and the larger ones are sometimes difficult to use. Yet a stapler is often clearly the best means of attaching parts of the children's projects. In such cases, it is usually best for you to do the stapling for each child.

Modeling

Of all art activities, modeling is perhaps the most relaxing for children—a great starter for new groups still getting acquainted or a calming treat for children temporarily at odds with one another. Almost immediately they become absorbed in creating. There is no beginning or end. Attempts unsatisfactory to the artist are quickly demolished and tried again. Actually, for many the highlight lies in destroying one creation and starting again in a new direction. The children will often talk freely as they work, and here is another chance for you to become aware of their feelings and thoughts.

The first time you use clay or playdough, just leave it on a table without any accessory tools and see how the children use their hands. After they have experimented on their own, sit down with them and talk about the different ways they have found to change the shape of clay. Ask them if they can find some new ways: pound, twist, fold, roll around to make a ball, or work the clay back and forth to make a snake. If it seems appropriate, give other ideas. For example, you might show how an arm or head grows out of a body by squeezing the shape from the side or top of the lump of clay.

Another time the youngsters might enjoy using rolling pins and a blunt knife to cut clay shapes. Cookie cutters work well on firm clay. Fork tongs and spoon handles make interesting imprints in flattened clay. Set out toy pans and dishes and you'll be amazed at the muffins, cakes, and pancakes the children produce.

Cooking

What child doesn't enjoy munching a special culinary treat? The pleasure of snack time or lunch is increased tenfold when the goodies are made by the children themselves. There are many kitchen projects that preschoolers can do, from making creative sandwich fillings to decorating cookies, with nibbling and sampling as part of the plan.

Part of the joy in cooking is sharing what you make. The children love preparing some treat, then inviting a special guest, such as an elderly neighbor or the driver of the day, for "tea."

Keep It Simple should be your motto. In planning your kitchen fun, choose an activity that is short enough that the children will see the results promptly. You can facilitate this by doing part of the work ahead of time. Premeasure ingredients. Wash and partially cut fruits or vegetables. Have the equipment set out ahead of time. Whenever possible, give each child her own set of materials to minimize long waits for turns.

Do several steps of a longish recipe, leaving the last part for the children to complete. For example, if you decide to give them the experience of baking bread, mix the dough and let it rise before the children come. They can do the kneading, watch it rise, and bake a small loaf to take home.

Sometimes you will have each child do the same activity at the same time to practice a specific skill. For instance, everyone may chop vegetables for soup to practice handling and using chopping tools. You chose the recipe that best suits your group. Skills that everyone can practice together include peeling, sifting, cracking an egg, crushing crumbs, or slicing.

On other occasions you may organize a joint activity in which each child is assigned a different task. One example is making Cranberry Relish (page 110). Here, one person puts oranges and cranberries into a grinder, another grinds, while a third child stirs in sugar and a fourth fills the jars.

With all this fun you will be building a foundation for a healthy future. The way the children do things today will stay with them a lifetime. Your planning will include wholesome ways of handling food—washing fresh fruits and vegetables, scrubbing hands, tasting with clean spoons.

Choose the foods carefully with good nutrition in mind. Think of what is most wholesome within each of the basic food groups (meat, dairy, vegetables and fruits, grain). For example, settle on chicken or tuna more frequently than bologna or hot dogs. Poultry and fish contain less fat and salt than prepared meats do. In choosing dairy products, low-fat items such as 2 percent milk or yogurt are good selections. Breads made with whole grains are tastier and more nutritious than white bread. When you are choosing drinks, read labels to find pure juices that are not heavily watered down and sugared up.

The word "treat" does not need to mean sweet and gooey with no nutritional value. Ice cream and cookies are fun, but popcorn and pretzels are fun too, and better for you. The way food is presented can make it a special treat. Children love to dunk raw vegetables in a dip or eat chunks of fruit from skewers. Food in fanciful shapes or a colorful, eye-catching arrangement make any occasion special.

You might choose to look outside the kitchen for ways to broaden the children's experiences with food. Today all manner of food takeout is available from fast-food establishments, specialty stores, and even the supermarket.

It can be a real adventure to experiment with ethnic foods on special occasions. Venture into the realm of Asian, Mideastern, European, and other tastes with your preschoolers. They probably already have some family favorite they would like to share with their friends. As food suppliers feel more pressure to promote sound dietary practice, you will be able to find an increasing variety of foods that are nutritionally acceptable and fun to eat.

A little planning—a little work—a lot of fun. *Bon appétit* with the children!

Dramatic Play

When the children are left to their own devices, you will often find them immersed in imaginative play. Make-believe is so natural a part of play that sometimes the lines between fantasy and reality blur. Using body movements and language—with or without toys, props, or costumes—children love to be someone else. They draw ideas from what they know of the real world. They will plunge into what seems to be pure fantasy, but even this is rooted in their own experiences. These adventures in pretending are what largely constitute the dramatic play experiences of the preschooler. After many of these extemporaneous acting-out sessions they are ready for more formal, directed activities.

Children pretend about what happens inside their own homes and what happens in the outside world. They become adults, taking the role of Daddy, Mommy, or some other person important in their lives. Dramatic playtime gives them the opportunity to become nurses, astronauts, or garage mechanics. Or they revert to baby times to handle their fears about a visit to the doctor, a move, divorce, sibling rivalry, or to express hidden wishes. Hero play allows them to be all-powerful and in control.

Sometimes children lose themselves in the world of fantasy—a world peopled by witches, queens, cowboys, and superheroes. The simplest of props—a toy, a pillow, even the kitchen sink may inspire a trip into the world of "let's pretend."

Keep in mind that some youngsters prefer to become involved in dramatic play by themselves, while others require stimulation from members of their group or from a few props. You can encourage uninhibited, unstructured dramatic play by setting the scene informally. A box of old clothes, different kinds of hats, or a covered card table playhouse are all examples of things you can make available.

While pretending is instinctive with the very young, dramatic activities can become gradually more sophisticated. As the children get older it is both fun and successful to have the group act out a story in a slightly more formal way. You might read a story that is simple enough for the youngsters to act out later. You could trigger their imaginations by supplying props, assigning parts, and suggesting they dramatize a familiar situation such as a trip to the dentist or a shopping spree. Sometimes you can use a narrative tape or record so the preschoolers can act out a favorite story while listening to the recording. On another occasion, follow a puppet-making project with a little performance. Let an unusually creative group of children create their own fantasy play complete with plans for who will be monster or hero and what props will be used.

In such directed dramatic play, some children may be more self-conscious than others. Let the shy child gradually become absorbed, contributing first as an audience, then as "prop manager," "sound expert," and finally "actor."

Age makes a difference in the way children will use their imaginations. While a four-year-old friend may pretend that a block is anything from a flashlight to a baby kangaroo, a two-year-old will see the block only as a block. If the older child is assigning a new role to some object, the younger preschooler may copy the action but would be unlikely to initiate such play.

In general, the preschooler at any age feels more self-conscious when she is asked to perform alone. Doing things in unison comes more naturally. At times a child feels more relaxed by taking a turn at something everyone is trying, such as imitating a motion, rather than having a spotlight placed on her single performance.

The dramatic play activities chosen for this book take into account age and personality differences of the children in your group. We have tried to give you a broad variety of possibilities. Some are very much adult directed and specific—for example, fingerplays or a game like Animal Walk (page 152). Some guide the pretending with a specific setting or props. Others, like the box play suggested in Box Train (page 296) allow children to improvise freely with various objects.

Whether you choose purely spontaneous or planned and directed dramatic activity, you will find this kind of play a particularly rich opportunity to become more familiar with the children as individuals. A child's pretending reveals so much about her knowledge, needs, strengths, and emotions.

Music and You

Music is an area in which many people often feel inadequate. If you don't play a musical instrument and you can't sing unwaveringly on key, then you are sure that you are totally unqualified to be involved in helping others learn anything about music. Remember that you have at least three important skills at your fingertips: you can put on a record or tape; you know a few nursery rhymes; and you can clap your hands. If you can add guitar playing or some other talent to those three skills, consider it an extra bonus. If you don't have a cassette player or a few appropriate tapes, you can borrow the player from a friend for the day, and the desired music from the library.

Perhaps you entertain some doubts about the nursery rhymes. This book supplies you with a list of familiar ones along with a list of songs you are likely to know. Glance over these and you will be surprised at how many you recollect. The appendix will aid you in recalling words to the songs. If you worry about your singing talents, look confident and cheerful and the children will think you equal anything on television. Most important is that you share pleasure in music with the children. Once you begin a song there may be a child in your group who will "take the lead" and guide the melody of songs he knows, or you can use bells, records, or piano in teaching new tunes.

When you lack the proper record or song to sing, use your two hands. Clap to provide a wonderful source of music. The children can fill in during a start-and-stop music game, and they can provide all sorts of sounds and rhythms. Best of all, the children have the same "instrument." They will love clapping with you.

*Tunes You Already Know**

NURSERY RHYMES

1. "Baa Baa Black Sheep"
2. "Do You Know the Muffin Man"
3. "Farmer in the Dell"
4. "Here We Go 'Round the Mulberry Bush"
5. "Hickory Dickory Dock"
6. "Hot Cross Buns"
7. "Humpty Dumpty"
8. "I'm a Little Teapot"
9. "Jack and Jill"
10. "Little Jack Horner"
11. "Little Miss Muffet"
12. "London Bridge"
13. "Mary Had a Little Lamb"
14. "Old King Cole"
15. "Old MacDonald Had a Farm"
16. "Pop Goes the Weasel"
17. "Rain, Rain Go Away"
18. "Ring Around the Rosie"
19. "Rock-a-Bye Baby"
20. "See-saw, Margery Daw"
21. "Sing a Song of Sixpence"
22. "Teensy Weensy Spider"
23. "Twinkle, Twinkle, Little Star"

*See Appendix 2 (page 311) for words to most of these songs

ROUNDS (TO SING IN UNISON)

1. "Are You Sleeping?" ("Frere Jacques")
2. "Row, Row, Row Your Boat"
3. "Sweetly Sings the Donkey"
4. "Three Blind Mice"

OTHER FAMILIAR SONGS

1. "Down by the Station"
2. "I See the Moon"
3. "If You're Happy and You Know It Clap Your Hands"
4. "I've Been Working on the Railroad"
5. "Jingle Bells"
6. "Oh, Susanna"
7. "Pick a Bale of Cotton"
8. "Punchinello"
9. "Skip to My Lou"
10. "Ten Little Indians"
11. "This Old Man"
12. "Yankee Doodle"

How to Choose a Song

A new song can be a delight if it has been chosen carefully. Most preschoolers favor nursery rhymes or other songs that are similarly catchy and uncomplicated, short and repetitious. Learning will be particularly rapid if the song ties in with an activity or experience they have shared.

There are several things to keep in mind about the children's abilities when you select a song. First, a preschooler has a limited singing range. Folk songs are particularly appropriate as most limit scale range to a few different notes.

Second, the young child cannot remember a great deal at one time, so the song needs to have a refrain or sequence of words that is very easy to remember. The more repetitious the words and melody, the easier it will be for your playgroupers to learn. A song like "Farmer in the Dell" is ideal. It has the same words repeated over and over again with only a simple change or two for each verse.

Third, when a child sings, her pitch will be higher than her talking voice, so when you introduce a song by singing it yourself, remember to pitch it higher than you normally would.

Two kinds of songs work particularly well with this age group. Folk songs that reflect the music of the various people in our culture are especially appealing. The other kind most successfully taught is the song that lends itself to improvisation—with children replacing pieces of the original lyrics or tunes with two or three simple words or sounds of their own choosing (see "Halloween Farmer in the Dell," page 94).

Whenever possible, present a new song through experiences familiar to the children. For instance: "Just before you go to bed at night, do you ever look out the window and see the moon watching you? Have you thought about someone special and wondered if they were looking at the same moon?" Then you could begin to teach "I See the Moon, the Moon Sees Me" (page 317).

How to Teach a Song
Here are a few helpful hints for you to use when you are ready to teach the song you have chosen.

1. Sing the song once or twice so the children will hear how it sounds. (If it is on a record, play it.) Longer songs can be broken down into smaller parts.
2. *Chant* the words without the music but with much rhythm so it is still fun to listen to. You might clap as you chant or have the children join you in clapping. You could even use bells or other instruments in place of clapping.
3. Sing the song again, letting the children join in as they are able.
4. Invite everyone who knows the song to join in again. The music is contagious and soon others will join with body movement, clapping, humming, and words.

Creating Songs
Remember that children love to improvise by adding their own words to songs or creating entirely new lyrics and melodies. A child's composition may amount to only a snippet. You might say, "Sing me a song about how you feel today." Ask questions like, "How would you sound if you were tired . . . angry . . . frightened . . . silly?" A preschooler will spontaneously sing a handful of simple words. Other sing-about ideas might include a song about what you did this morning, about Mommy or Daddy, or about someone in the group. Encourage the child to make her own music.

Music and the Children
What is music in the world of a child? It is many different kinds of sounds: high, low; fast, slow; loud, soft. It is rhythmic movement. The child finds with delight that he can move with the music, imitating the sounds and rhythms and reacting to the moods. Music is also a means of expression. A child can create new songs about his daily experiences.

A first awareness of music comes from the child's everyday experiences with sound. He is conscious of the wind in the trees, a plane roaring overhead, or a hammer being wielded by a carpenter. If you are encouraging the children to listen to the sounds around them, you are teaching something about music. An activity as simple as tapping wood, metal, and glass with a stick helps them to be mindful of different kinds of sounds. Using their own voices to say something in a high squeaky way or in a deep scary voice will help them to understand something about pitch and mood.

Rhythm is in the children's own movements. It is in their hopping, jumping, and running. It is the sound of a heart thudding as a child lies still after moving very fast. By letting the children move in the ways so natural to them—slowly, quickly—they will even come to know something about tempo.

Children have a natural feeling for music and love to use it as a means of expression. The three-year-old often conveys something of how he feels by singing an impromptu original song about himself as he plays. Children can reveal emotions such as happiness or anger as they move spontaneously to the sound of a record or tape or join the group in song.

Using music to tell a story is a favorite children's activity. Children love to take the parts of different characters in a musical record. You will enjoy choosing an appealing story for them to dramatize.

The use of musical instruments provides another opportunity for self-expression. You can help the children construct simple instruments so they can learn how to make many different kinds of sound stories.

Like adults, children enjoy hearing music in the background. You can relate the mood of the music to different colors or the flow of melody to line drawing—jagged, round, smooth, dotted, and so on. Putting on a record while the children have a snack or eat lunch can help maintain a low-key atmosphere. Playing a merry melody for cleanup can make a game of that task.

Music Time

Music time can be a warm, happy time—a special time for the group to come together. Assemble in a small circle to sing a song; make the circle larger for musical games that require broad movement. Often, beginning in the circle will enable the children to slip into a relaxed and confident mood, setting the stage for later open, free expression on their part. Having begun in this secure way they soon begin to feel uninhibited enough to move away from the boundaries of the circle, dancing, being imaginary beasts, or whatever the moment suggests.

In helping the children enjoy music keep in mind outside sources that you can draw upon. You may have a friend who can come and play an accordion or some other instrument one morning. Would the organist of a nearby church let you visit during practice hours? There are a number of possibilities.

See Appendix 1 (page 303) to refresh your memory on the words to many musical rhymes, rounds, and other favorite songs. If you have trouble recalling the melodies, remember that virtually all of the songs are easy to find on records.

Physical Exercise

Specific physical exercise activities may occupy a small percentage of your playgroup time, but they are a key to its success and are important for the total development of the children. Our ideas for these are planned so that quick, enjoyable releases of energy are sandwiched between two relatively quiet activities. Sometimes the need for motion arises in the middle of a long project as the children begin to show signs of restlessness. An active game such as Mr. Rubber Man gives them a chance to stretch their muscles. After they have exercised they are ready to finish the quiet work, spirits much renewed.

A few minutes of very active exercise like an aerobics workout can help pace a morning and gives an opportunity for the development of large-muscle control and eye-hand-foot coordination. If the weather is good and play equipment available, the children will enjoy the freedom to exercise in their own way, pumping, climbing, and jumping. Whether you have or haven't any swings, jungle gym, or the like, the ball remains the cheapest and most versatile of all equipment. Make sure you have a big one for ease in handling. It will provide the perfect outlet for energy and muscle development.

When weather is poor, games such as a beanbag toss can be good indoor physical activity. Just aiming and throwing will give the children pleasure and at the same time will develop their eye-hand coordination. As they become more skilled at making "baskets" in some of the toss games, the children will naturally become more interested in scoring. You do not want to emphasize the competitive aspect with two-, three-, and four-year-olds. Remember this both in physical and other types of games that your group plays. There is nothing more discouraging than never being the winner. Stress the fun of trying and developing a skill. Defining the degree of success is unimportant. Plan activities so each child has a chance to excel sometimes and help the children to enjoy a wide variety of physical exercise. The important point is the fun and relaxation they experience as they exercise.

Both indoor and outdoor creative "story" games provide a wonderful means of using many muscles without focusing on competition. Let the children help you make up stories about where they might be going—hopping on stones, climbing a tree, jumping over a brook—and let everyone make the motions as you tell the story. Not a bit of equipment is required, but the variety is endless. There is plenty of opportunity for moving, and everyone has a marvelous time.

Science

Children are always full of curiosity about the things around them. Many of their questions are about nature. Many are related to their experiences with the senses of smell, sight, touch, hearing, and taste. If you had not planned to include these in your playgroup activities, you will find they just naturally become part of your experience together. The children are *aware* of the seasons changing and want to know why. They *collect* caterpillars in a jar and wonder what happens to these creatures when they let them free again. They *observe* that big puddles gradually disappear once the sun comes out and want to know where they have gone. They begin to understand how things grow as they *experiment* with seeds, soil, water and sunlight. They have an immense sense of satisfaction as they watch grass that they planted indoors in late November sprout on a winter day.

Nature provides the perfect background for scientific discovery. You will find the children approaching nature through their senses. They touch the dandelion and then pull it apart to see how it is made. They watch birds building a nest or sit by a pond and listen to peepers and bullfrogs. They smell pines in the woods and find pleasure in touching the different kinds of tree bark from rough pine to smooth birch. Children find great pleasure in exploring objects in detail.

Nature activities for the very young child are difficult to program in detail or rush through quickly. It is more a matter of timely exposure and letting each child ask questions about and absorb facts about things he is interested in and able to understand. Taking walks is a favorite playgroup activity and a wonderful way for preschoolers to experience and appreciate nature. Bags for collecting, a big magnifying glass, and a pocketknife for you to use are excellent aids for investigating. You are not limited to sunny days. A windy day with lovely moving clouds, or a dull, damp day—each has its special sights and smells. Even on a snowy winter day it is worth the challenge of boots, ski pants, and mittens for a time outside. If you walk a familiar route, the children will notice landmarks and the changes that come with different seasons.

Nature-oriented walks are like treasure hunts. Who can find the first new plant growth hiding under the last snow? Walk along a beach and see how many sea creatures you can capture with a pail or net. Spread a sheet out in an autumn field and come back later to see what has collected on it. Go out in a snowstorm and catch different-shaped flakes on a piece of black construction paper. The treasures collected and sights seen can become an integral part of your next art project. You will find it a relaxing time for yourself, and the children will delight in exploring, collecting, experimenting, and observing individually and together.

On days when outdoor activities are impossible, you can provide a number of indoor activities that involve the senses—objects of different textures to feel, foods of various tastes, things to smell. A careful selection of library books can expand what you all saw on the sunny day when you found the caterpillar or picked leaves of changing color.

Your role is to set the stage for the outdoor or indoor activity. Plan where you will go on your special walk, or set up a simple experiment. Help the children to interpret what they are experiencing. Provide the name for something that is new to your little ones. Give a brief explanation when interest is high. Ask the children questions that lead them to new discovery. Be ready to change your objectives as a nature walk turns into an observation of sewer installation. You will find yourself developing a keener awareness of the things around you as you help your preschoolers.

Storytelling

Story time is a favorite time for three- and four-year-olds. A hush will settle over normally rambunctious youngsters as they hang on every word of your tale. A story you tell the children can be retold by them in any number of ways—each as much fun as the first listening. Preschoolers even enjoy creating their own original poems and narratives.

Whether you are telling or reading your story, careful choice is essential. A shorter, simpler story is required for a group than for a single listener. If possible, relate the piece to a recent experience of one or all of the children. For example, if a baby is born to a playgroup mother or neighbor, others enjoy hearing a story about the family's new addition. Find authors like Mercer Mayer who address children's feelings.

Use a story to give more meaning to an art project or science walk. Read about the coming seasons before giving your preschoolers appropriate colors to express on paper their ideas about the time of year. A tale about a caterpillar might expand their understanding of the creatures they have found and examined outdoors.

You may enjoy simply having the group settle around you as you read a story or poem, sharing the illustrations as you go. Keep in mind, however, that there are other ways for the children to enjoy hearing someone read. You might take the group to the local library for story hour or have another member of the household lead story time with the youngsters. There are many excellent records and tapes that come with story books. These can be borrowed from friends or the library if your own collection lacks the selection you need for your group. You might combine ideas. For example, read aloud a story of "Little Red Riding Hood," play a recorded version, and finish by having one or all of the children tell it in their own words. For a wonderful guide to age-appropriate storybook selections, see *The Read Aloud Handbook* by Jim Trelease (New York: Penguin Books, 1979; revised 1984).

Storytelling rather than story reading is often more effective with a group of preschoolers. You will find that telling the story in your own words and with lots of eye contact is fun for you and fun for your group. If the story is a part of you the children will readily sense the humor, beauty, or wonder you find in it.

A good storyteller must not depend on memorizing words. It is not just the words but the way they are put together that is the key to the progression of a story. You would not want to change the essential nature of the story, but certainly there will be times when you'll wish to alter it to suit different circumstances or audiences. You'll want to build a reserve of words, choosing sometimes for sound, other times for meaning.

Tell the story simply, directly, and sincerely. Storytelling is a shared experience. You will communicate the anger, sorrow, or joy of the tale to your listeners by the tone of your voice, some body movement, or your facial expression. No two tellings will be alike.

Sometimes you may need or want props for your storytelling. The lion hunt is a favorite one that can be enhanced by special sound effects. The presentation of nursery tales, favorite short books, story songs, and poems can be nicely reinforced with a flannel board (see page 117). Puppets can also help to bring a story to life for the children.

If the children love to dramatize, let them first enjoy a series of very familiar tales such as those about Peter Rabbit, and then take parts of different characters. Favorites such as "Three Billy Goats Gruff," and "The Tortoise and the Hare" have sufficient repetition to make them easy for the group to retell by dramatizing.

Preschoolers have lively imaginations, and creating stories comes easily for many. They might enjoy devising a continuing story, with each child adding his part where another has left off. If there are five in a group, one begins and another ends the story and the three others supply the middle. This idea can also be used in the retelling of familiar stories. If three of the children cover a whole story, let the next child begin a new one.

Books are special treats, and often the best-loved ones are home-made. Children can make books on a variety of topics (see page 198) and add pages to them throughout the year.

Be adventurous and try a variety of approaches to storytelling and reading. You and your little group will find the experience an enriching one.

Trips

Preschoolers tire easily, especially when they are doing something unfamiliar in a group. This is why short trips are best: a picnic by a duck pond only five minutes away by car, a visit to a florist around the corner where you can walk for a breath of spring in midwinter, or a trip to the bakery or pet shop in your town. Some libraries have midmorning story hours for preschoolers—a special treat for your group. Avoid the spectacular all-day trip with more than one excitement, and try to plan the visit at a time that is not rushed for the florist, post office, or poultry farm.

Try not to duplicate trips you know the children will be taking in nursery school and kindergarten. Always be aware of individuals nearby who have a hobby they might enjoy sharing with small children. Film developing, gardening, ceramics, and woodworking are all examples of hobbies children would love to observe.

Most simple trips can be handled by one playgroup parent, but if you have a grandparent or neighbor who would find it a treat to join you, all the better. An extra pair of hands for dealing with the unexpected is always welcome.

The trips that you plan will add fun and variety to your program and give both the children and yourself happy experiences to remember.

Woodworking

Few things generate as much excitement in a group of preschoolers as wood scraps, a hammer, and nails. You do not need to be a master carpenter to give a three-year-old a few hints about how to wield a hammer and acquire a few other basic woodworking skills. You don't even need a special workbench.

Simply choose a convenient corner somewhere in your home where you can set out a few wood pieces, a tool or two, and nails. A wooden box or old table would make a dandy workbench, but your initial attempts can be made right on the floor. When you see how enthusiastically your preschoolers respond to the activity, you might want to set up a more permanent work area.

If wood scraps are not right at hand, a trip to the local lumber store is in order. Many such places allow children to clean out scrap barrels free of charge or sell sacks of scraps for a small charge.

While you are in the store, pick up any tools you have decided to acquire. You should avoid toy tool sets for children. Most of these are flimsily made and lead to frustration. Often they are also too small. Since children handle big objects more easily than little ones, they will have the greatest success by developing a few basic skills with *real* tools. Have on hand such items as a tack hammer and small nails with big heads. As you expand woodworking skills add a short screwdriver with a large, stubby handle, a hacksaw, and a C-clamp or vise to your collection. (For more detailed information on what tools work best in the hands of children see pages 29. Specific skills such as hammering and sawing are described in individual activity instructions.)

At home gather your group in your chosen "carpenter corner" with the wood pieces and tools. The variety of wooden shapes will stir imagination and the children will set about creating their own clusters. The final product is not as important as the satisfaction of hammering a nail. For added flair, supply a few bits of wire, string, or old door fixtures for use as accessories to the objects made.

As the children work, be on hand to oversee the situation. Point out simple directions for safety, and be firm about the children's using tools in the proper manner. If there is any flagrant misuse, just remove the tools, saying that only people who use them properly will be allowed to work with them. And then try the activity again later.

When you meet with an enthusiastic response to that first woodworking session, you may want to undertake some of the simple woodcrafting projects described in the activities section of this book. You will feel fully as proud as the children, as they create special objects.

SEPTEMBER

September Contents

◆

SEPTEMBER GUIDEPOSTS

♦

THINGS YOU CAN COLLECT

Each month of the year has its own special flavor. The season will auto-matically suggest "treasures" that you can gather outdoors to set aside for future projects. You might embark on a solitary walk or on a family outing and find time to pick up a few appealing items along the way. A walk with your own children or with your whole playgroup may pres-ent the perfect opportunity for collecting items that you can use in a special way another day or take home to use right away.

If you are a parent, you already know that children are born collec-tors. You have probably been called upon to muster up enthusiasm for a great chunk of stone presented to you in one of your child's tender moments. It may, even now, be sitting amid perfume bottles or framed photos atop a dresser.

You may have watched a paradise of fishing bait materialize in mo-ments as a cluster of enthusiastic diggers conquered their "worm mine," a wood-chip pile in the corner of the garden. Harness this en-ergy to achieve your own ends. Set the children about the task of look-ing for materials that will lend themselves to future use indoors.

Don't forget that your group does not hold exclusive claim to these collectibles. They can be a resource for rainy-day activities. Hand some to Grandpa or the babysitter to keep little hands busy.

September is one of the most ideal times for collecting. The weather still beckons you outdoors. Here are some items that you can set off to find and a few hints about what to do with them later.

Shells

On that last trip to the beach fill a pail or two with shells. Remember, blemished shells patterned by the work of a sea worm or broken pieces shaped by shifting sand and tides can be as interesting to look at and effective to use as a perfect specimen.

Set them aside for sand casting, decorating boxes or cans, or painting with small brushes and watercolor paint sets.

Soak the shells in a strong solution of an enzyme wash product (found beside laundry detergents in stores) for a few days. The enzyme will remove odors caused by the residue of once living organisms. To remove shell creatures without creating sea odors, bag the shell and put it in the freezer for 10 to 20 minutes. The creature will be removed from the shell easily, and the shine and markings on the shell will be perfectly preserved.

Stones

Add a few stones from the beach to your pail of shells. Look for diversity in colors, shapes, and textures. Expand the collection later at a quarry, along a roadside, or at a building site.

Use them for counting and size games or for hide and find.

Let the children fill tiny jars with pebbles. For variety add a few marbles, shells, or sea glass. Fill with water and screw on the lid. Lovely to look at!

Have a session of painting larger stones with watercolor designs or crayoning funny faces onto them.

Make paperweights by gluing shells, plastic beads, and other pretties onto stones. Elmer's glue is good for this.

Flowers

Pluck flowers to press in waxed paper or between pieces of clear Contact paper. To make print designs, dip pressed flowers into poster paint, lay on newspaper, and gently press paper on top to make an imprint.

Dry a few for creating little arrangements later. Mix two parts cornmeal to one part borax. Pour a layer of the mixture in a box. Spread out the flowers (zinnias are particularly good) after pulling off the leaves. Pour the rest of the mixture carefully over the flowers to cover each separate petal. Leave in the covered box at room temperature for seven to ten days.

Let your energetic preschool diggers take up your geraniums, roots and all, to "put them to bed" for winter. Place in pots to keep in the house (a corner of the cellar is fine). Forget them until spring when the children can help you set them out again where they will revive.

Give everyone a turn with real clippers to cut a sprig of impatiens or begonia. Put the cuttings in small jars of water and in a week or so the children will see roots sprouting. You can help them with the potting of the new plants later on.

Leaves

Pick leaves of different sizes and shapes. Don't neglect the pretty lacy ones nibbled by hungry caterpillars. Press them in a book for later projects or put between a sheet of Contact paper and a sheet of plain or colored cellophane to make a window hanging or bookmark. (What a pretty gift!)

Pine Cones

Send everyone scurrying for pine cones in some pine-scented grove. Use the finds later for bird feeders, wreaths, or holiday ornaments.

Acorns, Horse Chestnuts

Acorns, chestnuts, and other gifts of nature may present themselves as you scour the ground. Take some for collages or counting games.

Feathers

An Indian headband sporting real feathers is a four-year-old's prize. Not enough feathers after your hunt? Alternate with homemade paper feathers or use the real feathers in the acorn and leaf collage.

Cocoons

Someone may come upon a cocoon or two. Put them in a jar or terrarium where it is moist and wait for changes.

REMEMBER THE FAMILIAR

Sometimes in our quest for the original or the unusual, we bypass the familiar. Just because something has been done before is no reason to neglect it. What is "old hat" to you may be brand new to your little people. Even if it is not totally new to the children, you can keep in mind that children love to do over and over again anything that is fun. They take exuberant pride and pleasure in showing off what they already know.

Show and Tell

So when September rolls around remember the simple things—let the children tell about their summer adventures. A teacher finds this a wonderful exercise in language arts. Let the children show and tell about a prized possession.

Family Celebrations

Remember the warmth of a family celebrating a holiday together. September holds Jewish holy days. Perhaps a child can share something of Rosh Hashana with you. Share birthdays, christenings, and other special days.

The Autumn Sky

This is the month of migrations and fluffy clouds in an autumn sky. Talk together about where the birds or butterflies are going and why. Lie on the ground, gaze at the heavens, and find pictures in the changing clouds.

Familiar things, simple things can be the making of gentle adventures shared.

SEPTEMBER ACTIVITIES

◆

ARTS AND CRAFTS

◆ Fun with Scissors

Ages 2 and up

YOU WILL NEED:
small plastic bags, 1 per child
scissors, 1 per child
paper (colored for variety; scraps are fine)

METHOD:
Give the children paper in several colors cut to moderate size for easy handling and to avoid waste. Each child cuts pieces to put into his bag. This is simply practice in cutting skill. (Two-year-olds can practice tearing instead.) Some children will fill their bags with nondescript clipped pieces. The more advanced might be encouraged to try some specific shapes like circles or squares. The fun is in the simple doing and having the bag of bits to take home.

SUGGESTIONS:
Save bags of torn and cut bits to use in a gluing project later.

◆ Star of David

Ages 2 and up

YOU WILL NEED:
paper, blue and white, 9 by 12 inches, 1 sheet of each color per child
scissors, 1 per child
paste and brushes

METHOD:

> *Ahead of time:* Draw large triangles on each sheet. Make sure all the sides of the triangle are the same length.
>
> *With the children:* Each child cuts out her two triangles and glues one onto the other to make a blue and white star. If any children have difficulty cutting, cut the triangles for them, and they can just form and glue the star.

◆ Mixing Colors with Paint   *Ages 2 and up*

YOU WILL NEED:

> finger paint
>
> shelf or finger-paint paper, 1 piece per child

METHOD:

> The first time you do this project, use *two* colors only (a limited selection helps avoid confusion). Let the children mix the colors on their paper to discover what will happen. Name the colors they started with and the new color being made. Try another color combination another time.
>
> *Paint Combinations:*
>   Red and yellow make orange.
>   Blue and yellow make green.
>   Blue and red make purple.
>   Black and white make gray.
>   Red and white make pink.
>   Red, yellow, and blue make brown.

SUGGESTION:

> Children ages 3 and up can use poster paint and brushes.

◆ Clay Play Guess   *Ages 2 and up*

This comfortable play brings children closer together during their first playgroup encounters.

YOU WILL NEED:

> Best Ever Clay Recipe (page 24) or Granny's Dabblin' Dough (ask your art or toy store for playdough that does not crumble)

METHOD:

> Sit down with the children and work the clay in different ways. Introduce the game idea of making shapes and asking the others to guess what it is. Starting ideas can include making a clay ball and

using your finger to poke a hole in the center. It could be a lifesaver, tire, Cheerio, or doughnut. Another familiar favorite starts with a skinny clay shape that can be made into a pretzel, wound around to create a nest, or coiled to become a boa constrictor. Children quickly catch on and enjoy the guessing game without feeling pressured to produce. Clay is a relaxing way for preschoolers to enjoy individual play in a group activity. Clay play is important to preschoolers and should be offered regularly.

COOKING

◆ Bag-a-Snack   *Ages 2 and up*

YOU WILL NEED:
Choose a combination from:
- assorted cold cereals (Chex, Cheerios, and so on)
- chow mein noodles
- raisins
- goldfish crackers
- M & M candies
- pretzel sticks
- popcorn

small paper cups or sandwich bags
mixing bowl
mixing spoon

METHOD:
The children take turns scooping cupfuls of ingredients into a large bowl and stirring. Then each child can fill a cup with the mixture to munch, or toss the mixture into a sandwich bag for a snack time treat during outdoor play. You could mix a batch just before a trip to a nearby playground or a walk in the woods. Children should sit while eating this snack.

◆ Peeling Carrots   *Ages 3 and up*

Children have a field day with this one. "Look, Ma, no carrot!"

YOU WILL NEED:
carrots
knife
potato peelers (See if you can borrow extras so everyone can work together.)
optional: plain yogurt with choice of herb seasonings

METHOD:

Before passing out materials, show everyone how to peel carrots. When each child has a peeler and carrot, move from child to child helping each to hold the tool correctly.

SUGGESTIONS:

When carrots are peeled, cut them into strips. The children dip carrot strips in yogurt and munch. Carrots disappear. Or, shred away until carrots shrink. Use shreds for *Crazy Carrot Mixup:* Mix with spoonfuls of yogurt or cottage cheese and a sprinkling of raisins, apple chunks, or chopped nuts.

VARIATION:

Use candles or soap instead of carrots for peeling practice.

✦ Pocket Soup   *Ages 2½ and up*

A harvest treat! Each child brings a vegetable from the backyard garden or chooses a favorite from the supermarket. Talk about some of the possibilities ahead of time: string beans, carrots, tomatoes, zucchini, leeks, celery, broccoli, onions, and more. Tell parents when the vegetables will be needed.

YOU WILL NEED:

vegetables
chicken, beef, or vegetable broth (canned, or bouillon cubes
   dissolved in water), about ¾ cup per child
electric slow cooker or other large pot with lid
serrated plastic knives (for the children)
cutting knife
cutting board

METHOD:

Ahead of time: Put the broth in the pot. Peel and partially cut up vegetables that are hard to handle.
With the children: Let the children chop up the prepared pieces and other vegetables. Scoop up the chopped ingredients and add to the broth. Cook until vegetables are soft.

DRAMATIC PLAY

◆ Tune in on Station Playgroup

Ages 2 and up

YOU WILL NEED:
toy microphone made with ½-inch dowel about 9 inches long
6-inch Styrofoam ball
twine
tape

METHOD:
Ahead of time: Stick one end of the dowel into the center of the Styrofoam ball. Tape the twine to the other end of the dowel to make the power line.
With the children: Let the children take turns with the microphone giving news reports about playgroup friends. "Pete caught a toad." "Wendy visited her grandmother by train." Only the one holding the microphone speaks. Share feelings, songs from home, and silly fun. A weather report of the moment could close the program.

VARIATION (FOR AGES 4 AND UP):
To make the experience even more realistic, record the voices of your roving reporters' interviews on tape. Play back at snack time.

◆ Pretending

Ages 3 and up

YOU WILL NEED:
spirit of imagination
optional: background music

METHOD:

Choose two or three ideas at a time. Have children pretend they are:
a bowl of Jell-O ("shake, shake, shake")
a rag doll ("head and arms loose and floppy")
a rubber band ("stretch hard, go limp")
a sleeping seed in the ground ("curl up tight, then stretch hard and long")
a tired puppy ("yawn and stretch on your mat")
a balloon ("start on the floor—once you are blown up, begin to float in the air")

VARIATIONS:

Use seasonal pretend ideas, such as carving a big pumpkin, walking in deep snow, planting a garden.

GAMES

◆ What Is Gone from the Tray?   *Ages 3 and up*

This is a memory game.

YOU WILL NEED:

tray
5 or 6 familiar items

METHOD:

The children sit in a circle and view the items on the tray. Then they cover their eyes. Ask a child to remove one thing from the tray. The others open their eyes and try to guess what is missing. The game continues until each child has had a chance to remove an item.

SUGGESTION:

Increase the number of items as a game continues, or vary the items from turn to turn.

◆ Two Blackbirds   *Ages 2 and up*

YOU WILL NEED:
2 small chairs

METHOD:

Choose one child to be Jack and another to be Jill. They each sit on a chair and pretend it is a hill. All the children recite the verse with you.

VERSE:

Two little blackbirds sitting on a hill,
One named Jack, and one named Jill.
Fly away, Jack. Fly away, Jill. [Each child "flies" to a different place
  in the room.]
Come back, Jack. Come back, Jill. [Each returns to his chair—the
  "hill."]

After a while, substitute the names of children in your group for
Jack and Jill. Preschoolers love to hear their own names.

MUSIC

◆ Count and Sing
Ages 3 and up

METHOD:

Choose a song that has numbers in it.

Examples:
  "Ten Little Indians"
  "This Old Man"
  "Five People in My Family" (from "Sesame Street")
Count together (example: 1 to 10 "Ten Little Indians"). Sing the
song together.
(See How to Teach a Song, page 51.)

◆ Faster–Slower
Ages 3 and up

A circle rhythm game.

YOU WILL NEED:

masking tape or string (or chalk for hardtop)

METHOD:

Make a circle with tape, string, or chalk. Clap different rhythms:

1. even patterns for walking or running
2. uneven patterns for skipping

The children move in rhythm—slow walk, faster walk, running,
skipping, and so on around the circle to whatever pattern is clapped.

walk, walk, walk, walk =   ♩♩♩♩   or long, long, long, long

run, run, run, run	=	♪♪♪♪	or short, short, short, short
run, run, run, run		♪♪♪♪	short, short, short, short
ski-ip, ski-ip	=	♩♪♩♪	or long, short long, short
ski-ip, ski-ip		♩♪♩♪	long, short long, short

When they have the idea, the children can take turns clapping while the others move to the rhythm.

PHYSICAL EXERCISE

◆ Balance Beam

Ages 3 and up

YOU WILL NEED:

a long piece of wood (stud) 2 by 4 feet or any long, narrow piece of wood that seems suitable for the activity (special balancing beams are sold as gym equipment. If you already have one, fine).

METHOD:

Let the children practice walking on the beam. Let them suggest what else can be done on it. You can supplement their ideas: Be a tight rope walker; walk forward; move backward; hop over it; straddle it; jump off; play "follow the leader."

VARIATION:

Use chalk or tape to draw a long wide line on kitchen or basement floor or on driveway. Use as beam.

◆ Train Game

Ages 3 and up

YOU WILL NEED:

long rope or piece of string

METHOD:

The children line up to make a "train." Have the rope go along one side of the "train," across the front, and down the other side. The children hold the rope with each hand. Children take turns being engine, caboose, boxcar, coal car, oil car, flat car, and so on. Being engine is the most fun because the engine takes the rest of the "train" with it.

◆ Call Ball

Ages 4 and up

YOU WILL NEED:

large kickball

METHOD:

Form a circle. One person stands in the center with the ball. The person in the center tosses the ball up gently and calls the name of a group member. The child called tries to catch the ball before it bounces more than once.

SCIENCE

◆ Collecting Seeds   *Ages 2 and up*

YOU WILL NEED:
  serrated plastic knives
  small plastic bags
  a few of the following items for:

indoor projects:	*outdoor projects:*
apple	*Fall:*
orange	pine seeds
avocado	apples
acorn	milkweed
cherry	flowers going to seed
corn	*Spring:*
pear	maple seed
lemon	dandelions
pine cone seeds	
grape	
melon	
seed packets	

METHOD:
  Ask the children how the seeds can be used. Let them tell you what they know about planting seeds. Ask where they might find seeds.

Indoors:
  Set out a few items from the above list. Help the children slice the fruit samples and let them pull out the seeds. Notice color differences, size differences (big avocado seed, tiny pear seed), and so on. Let everyone put seed samples in a bag to take home. Limit choices for simplicity.

Outdoors:
  Armed with a bag for everyone and a serrated plastic knife for cutting samples, look outside for examples of seeds. Use the list above for help. When your group has found a few samples, talk about different sizes and colors. Let everyone keep samples to take home in a bag.

SUGGESTION:
  Supply cups filled with fertile soil. Help each child plant two or three seed samples to take home, with directions to keep them moist and in a sunny place. The first person whose seed sprouts can bring it to show on another playgroup day.

◆ **Explore the Neighborhood—What's Happening?**   *Ages 2 and up*

METHOD:

Take a walk around the immediate neighborhood. Look for:
road work
construction work
people doing jobs (street sweepers, road workers, mail carriers, delivery people, gardeners, and so on)
special buildings (shops, fire station, apartment house, library, and so on)
Talk about what is happening.

SUGGESTION:

Save planned, thorough visits to the fire station, police station, and so on for a later time. This is simply a walk to become acquainted with the general surroundings.

◆ **Our Special Tree**   *Ages 2 and up*

METHOD:

Together pick a nearby tree (not evergreen) to be your Special Tree for the year. See what discoveries the children make about the tree. Keep returning to the tree as the seasons pass and notice the changes.

Let everyone have one leaf from the tree. What color is it? Look at its shape next to another kind of leaf. Is its color different from the last time we looked? Are all the leaves gone? Are there buds on the branches?

STORYTELLING

◆ **Where-Have-You-Been, What-Did-You-Do? Map**   *Ages 3 and up*

YOU WILL NEED:

map (town, city, state, or country, depending on the boundaries of your group members' summer experiences)
name tag for each child
photograph of each child
portable board (bulletin board or posterboard large enough for map, photos, and name tags)
string
scissors
tape

METHOD:

Ahead of time: Talk with the children and their parents about each child's summertime travels and experiences. Put the map on a portable board, or tape it to the wall low enough for children to enjoy. Stick photos with name tags outside the edges of the map. Use string and tape to connect each name and photo to a place on the map that was important in the child's summer fun.

With the children: Let each child show and tell where he visited. Compare. "Jason traveled the farthest." "Leah and Jake went to the same place." You and the children will get to know the group by looking at the photos and following the strings.

TRIPS

◆ Visiting a Farm   *Ages 3 and up*

METHOD:

As the gardens begin to change, plan a trip to a nearby farm to watch the harvesting. Have the farmer explain how the garden and the farm animals are prepared for winter. Pack a picnic snack to have at the farm.

SUGGESTION:

The next time playgroup comes to your home, talk about frost and gardens. Let the children help you get your garden or window box ready for winter by bringing in geraniums, begonias, impatiens, and other plants that can be kept throughout the winter.

◆ Trip to See an Unusual Pet   *Ages 2½ and up*

Perhaps you know of someone who has an unusual pet—a talking mynah bird, land hermit crabs, a tame chipmunk, raccoon babies found living in the chimney, or another something out of the ordinary. Visiting a pet store offers an alternative.

METHOD:

Ask the animal's owner if he would be willing to let the playgroup visit his pet. On playgroup day go for your visit. Encourage the children to tell what they already know about the pet. Let the owner tell everything he knows about the animal—how he got it, its habits, care, and so on.

WOODWORKING

◆ Sanding   *Ages 2½ and up*

This activity uses a woodworking skill that also teaches the concepts "rough" and "smooth."

YOU WILL NEED:
scraps of wood
sandpaper of various grades

METHOD:
Show the children how to smooth rough edges with sandpaper. Let them feel the rough edges before you sand; then feel the smoothness after you sand.

Let the children experiment with sanding.

OCTOBER

October Contents

◆

OCTOBER GUIDEPOSTS

◆

THINGS YOU CAN COLLECT

Was September so busy with back-to-school shopping and those first-of-the-season meetings that time went by without a single glorious foray into the park or woods to collect acorns, leaves, and the variety of other items that you wanted to set aside for projects? October is equally ideal for gathering all the things mentioned on September's collecting list—with more to add.

Things from September's List

Play "how many can you find" as you send the children scurrying for acorns. Sit down together and enjoy the brisk autumn air as you count how many items each person has.

If there has not been a frost, there is still time to snip the impatiens for rooting and dig up the geraniums from your garden, pots, or window boxes to save for next spring. Take time to talk about why you are doing these things. Point out that cold weather is sneaking up. ("Feel the nip in the air? See? Douglas had to wear his baseball jacket today.") Explain how Jack Frost is about to put the flowers to rest.

Colored Leaves

Now the leaves are really changing their color and leaf collecting is at its best. Look to the city streets, a nearby park, your own backyard: there are samples all around you. Pick up especially pretty single leaves. If you are doing your gathering on your own property, let the children try your clippers all by themselves to cut a spray or two from bushes and tree branches to take home for an arrangement.

Twigs and Branches

Small twigs and delicate bits of branches can look like miniature trees in themselves. Have a hunt for "tiny trees." When there is one for each child, prop each into a clump of clay or small paper cup or pot filled with dirt. Each person can create her own autumn tree by tearing and cutting paper scrap leaves to glue or tape on the branches. Gwen's "tree" may have shed most of its leaves, so she puts on just a leaf or two. Neil, an enthusiastic paster, may produce a tree laden with many leaves of brilliant hue! You will be amazed at how each creation has its own distinct personality.

Seeds

Have you noticed that some of the squash, cucumbers, and other produce from your garden are "past it"? Are you about to serve your family the last of the season's luscious cantaloupe? Are there some fruits on your grocer's discard pile? Are flowers going to seed? Did you save the seeds from your jack-o'-lantern? Collect seeds and save for dropping onto glue on paper for an unusual abstract design. If you have plenty of pumpkin seeds, some could make a wonderful jack-o'-lantern. Help them to draw the outlines; children glue and drop seeds.

Try the June sunflower seed roasting recipe (page 250) with pumpkin seeds for a culinary treat.

Catalogs

Holiday mail-order catalogs have probably begun to overstuff your mailbox. Encourage your playgroupers to clean out the catalog clutter at their own homes and share the supply with you.

Everyone in the mood for shopping? Pull out the mail-order catalogs. Hand out scissors and a bag for each person. Tell everyone to go on a snip-and-bag-it shopping spree. Preschoolers snip out their favorite photos and pop them in the bag. This activity is perfect for early cutting practice, and fun to try again in December.

REMEMBER THE FAMILIAR

Year after year, October means pumpkins and costumes and trick or treat—and year after year these all produce the same sense of excitement.

Making Jack-o'-lanterns

What is October without a pumpkin? A trip to a farm stand or corner produce market can put everyone in the mood for Halloween. You may even know a spot where each child can harvest his own "jack." Whether each preschooler plucks or purchases his own special little pumpkin, you are all set for a spirited face-making session at home. Supply everyone with markers for the job, or set out pieces of vegetables to be affixed to the pumpkin with toothpicks. If your choice is one large pumpkin, the children can help in scooping it out and suggesting what shape eyes or what expression you should carve.

Costume Parade

If you are having the group near the time of The Big Night, have everyone don a costume for a costume parade. Find a willing audience—a stay-at-home neighbor, perhaps—and parade away! A marching record can enhance the atmosphere.

Trick-or-Treat Bag

A simple lunch or grocery bag can be transformed into the all-important trick-or-treat bag. Give each child orange and black crayons to make designs. Hand out sheets of orange and black paper to be snipped or torn into pieces and pasted on. You might have Halloween stickers handy to decorate the bags, or supply some precut seasonal shapes for pasting. Use these ideas in any set of combinations. By giving your imagination free rein you can come up with some of your own ideas for bedecking the bag.

Treasure Hunts and Other Games

A perennial favorite is the treasure hunt. You hide the booty; they dash about, bags in tow, to discover the hiding places of the goodies. At this already candy-drenched time of year, use inexpensive nonedible favors as treasure-trove.

Of course, any holiday can be an occasion for a variation of pin-the-tail-on-the-donkey. For October it can be pin-the-hat-on-the-witch, for example.

A smashing hit at one four-year-old's Halloween birthday party was bobbing for apples—with a new twist. The preschoolers fished for them instead! Attach string to sticks and put cup hooks on the end.

Screw cup hooks into apples floating in a bucket of water, then let the children take turns "fishing."

Songs

For every season there are songs. Borrow the record of an autumn tune or a melody with words about witches and ghosts from your local library. Everyone can learn it. Test your new accomplishment on the driver of the day, a grandparent, or someone from the neighborhood diaper set.

Columbus Day

The concept of someone's sailing around the world is pretty tough for a three- or four-year-old to grasp, but the exciting story of Columbus's trip told in a brief, simple way—maybe with three ships on a flannel board—can have appeal. Perhaps you can find a catchy poem or a colorfully illustrated book to help you tell the tale.

October is full of so much to do. Choose a little of the old, a little of the new, and you are bound to have fun with your preschoolers.

OCTOBER ACTIVITIES

◆

ARTS AND CRAFTS

◆ **Monoprint with Finger Paint** *Ages 2 and up*

YOU WILL NEED:
liquid starch (in discarded dishwashing detergent bottle or other
squeeze bottle for easy dispensing)
poster paint in powdered form (in flour shakers for best control)
manila (drawing) paper, 9 by 12 inches or larger
plastic laminate tabletop or other well-protected surface (individual
trays work well)

METHOD:
Either you or the children squeeze a small amount of starch on the
tabletop; shake on color and mix with hands. Children make designs
with fingers.

Help each child place a piece of paper over his design and rub to
make an imprint. Let children do a new design in another color. Use
the imprinted paper to pick up the second design in a different
color. The result is a superimposed picture with a silk screen appearance.

◆ **Paper Plate Masks** *Ages 3 and up*

YOU WILL NEED:
Popsicle sticks or tongue depressors, 1 per child
paper plates, 1 per child
crayons
paper, fabric, buttons, other materials
glue and brushes

METHOD:

Each child makes a face on a plate using some or all of the above materials (strips of paper for hair, button or crayon eyes, and so on). Then she glues a Popsicle stick on bottom, so she can hold the mask to her face.

Many small children do not like the kinds of masks that are worn over the face, so this type is a good solution. Older children may enjoy cutting eyes and nose holes through the plate and using string or large rubber bands to enable them to wear their masks.

◆ Foot Ghosts   *Ages 2 and up*

This project is quick and effective, and kids love it.

YOU WILL NEED:

crayons

shelf paper, long enough to include print of each child's foot

METHOD:

Use a crayon to trace an outline of each child's shoe on the paper. Have each person add a face and details to his foot shape. The preschoolers will have created a bevy of ghosts. They will enjoy talking about the differences in the ghost sizes and other ghost features. Each child's foot ghost may be cut from the long sheet to take home.

◆ Fuzzy Animals   *Ages 2 and up*

YOU WILL NEED:
   heavy pieces of paper, 9 by 12 inches, 1 per child
   scissors
   pencil
   variety of soft and fuzzy material scraps such as:
      yarn
      felt
      cotton balls
      pieces of carpet sample
      pieces of fake fur
   glue and brushes

METHOD:
   Ahead of time: You draw and cut a large animal shape from each piece of paper.
   With the children: Children select and glue the "fuzzies" to the animal shapes. For example: cotton body, yarn hair or tail, felt eyes. Let the children pick their own combinations.
   Variations: Make "feelies" using a variety of textures such as sandpaper, wet-look wallpaper, Styrofoam plates, and so on. These can be in a special shape or a collage.

COOKING

◆ "Walrus" Salad

Ages 2½ and up

YOU WILL NEED (for 4 children):
  ½ cup raisins
  Optional: ½ cup chopped walnuts
  ½ cup plain yogurt
  2 apples
  juice of 1 lemon
  2 stalks celery
  mixing bowl
  measuring cups
  plastic knives
  apple corer

METHOD:

Help the children measure the raisins, walnuts (if desired), and yogurt. You core and slice the apples in half. Children cut the apple slices into chunks, stir them with the juice in the bowl, then cut the celery into small pieces. Each child can add celery or one of the other ingredients to the apples and mix. Eat a "walrus" lunch!

◆ Cinnamon Snails

Ages 3 and up

YOU WILL NEED (for 4 to 6 children):
  1 slice soft whole wheat bread per child
  small tub soft cream cheese
  cinnamon mix (4 tablespoons sugar; 2 teaspoons cinnamon; ¾ stick
    margarine, melted)
  plastic knives
  cookie sheet

METHOD:

You make the cinnamon mix and preheat the oven to 350° F. Each child will spread cream cheese on a slice of bread. Roll up the bread with the cream cheese on the inside. Cut each roll into three pieces. Dip each "snail" into the cinnamon mix. Place "snails" seam down on the cookie sheet.

Bake at 350° F for 10 minutes.

SUGGESTION:

If your group is on the young side, have them work assembly-line fashion: one spreads, another rolls, and so on.

◆ Grilled Halloween Burger   *Ages 3 and up*

YOU WILL NEED:
cheese slices cut into hamburger-size circles
cooked hamburgers and buns
plastic knives

METHOD:
The children cut faces into the cheese circles and put them on top of cooked hamburgers. Place the burgers under the broiler just until the cheese melts.

DRAMATIC PLAY

◆ Trick or Treat Face Paint   *Ages 2 and up*

YOU WILL NEED:
hand mirror
makeup set or Caran D'Ache crayons (available from craft stores)
props: cowboy hat, bunny ears, princess crown, fairy wand, and so
    on
pillowcase
optional: video camera

METHOD:
Ahead of time: Collect enough simple props to give each child a disguise. Choose low-key disguises familiar to the children so their pretend play will come easily. Place props inside the pillowcase. Locate the mirror so the children can watch the make-up transformation.
With the children: Make the children up one at a time: A preschooler reaches into the pillowcase without looking and pulls out a prop. Decorate this child's face to suit the prop while he holds the mirror and watches the transformation. As you finish announce, "Now you are a real (cowboy, bunny, etc.). Allow time for pretend play.

SUGGESTION:
Use a video camera to record the children's pretend play. The videotape can be shared later with the other parents.

◆ Halloween Night Fingerplay   *Ages 2 and up*

Enjoy this fingerplay rhyme at Halloween time.

METHOD:

Using all the motions, say the following rhyme to the children. Have the children copy you with words and motions, line by line, as you repeat the rhyme a second time. Do the whole rhyme together in unison. Allow children to extend the rhyme with their own variations.

VERSE:

Witches in their pointed hats, [Form point over head with hands]
    rattling skeletons, [Shake arms, legs, and heads]
    noisy, scary cats. [Make fingers form whiskers, meow loudly.]
Ghosts dressed in sheets of white [Wave arms around in air]
    parade around on Halloween Night. [Children parade around in circle.]
Trick or Treat. Trick or Treat. [Place hands like megaphone on mouth.]
What goodies do you have for us to eat?" [Pretend to hold out treat bag.]

SUGGESTION:

Talk about Halloween safety. Ask children what costumes they are planning to wear. Create and act out other verses with motions to include everyone's Halloween disguise.

GAMES

◆ Witches Brew Treasure Hunt   *Ages 3 and up*

YOU WILL NEED:

paper bag or pail for each child
paper
glue
Choice of "brew" ingredients, such as:

acorn	pine cone
twig	seeds
leaf	pine needle
stone	pod

METHOD:

Ahead of time: Glue ingredients onto the paper so the children can "read" what they need to find.

With the children: Give the children bags or buckets and have them search outside for the listed "brew" ingredients. Emphasis should be on the fun and searching, *not* on competition. No winner, please.

◆ Simon Says

Ages 3 and up

This traditional game is always popular.

METHOD:

Take the part of Simon. Every time you say, "Simon says (*jump, hop,* and so on)," the children follow your directions. If you give a direction without first saying "Simon says," the children must try NOT to do it. If a child does, he has been "fooled." Encourage each child to take a turn as Simon.

This game is ideal for hopping, jumping, and doing other exercises to blow off steam when children are restless. For children this young, do not play the version in which a child is put "out" when he is "fooled." It is more fun for the children if they all can participate through the whole game. This way, being "fooled" is a joke everyone can enjoy.

VARIATION:

Children ages 4 and up enjoy the version where they move around the room following "Simon says" directions such as, "Simon says sit on a rectangle . . . find something smaller than a book . . . point to something living."

MUSIC

◆ Musical Sound Effects

Ages 2 and up

Here's a great activity for the nonmusical playgroup leader.

YOU WILL NEED:

musical instrument (autoharp, xylophone, ukelele, guitar)
story or poem

METHOD:

You do not need to be "accomplished" with the instrument. Strum it to make scary sounds, loud sounds, or quiet secret sounds appropriate to the telling of your story or poem. Children enjoy listening to music that emphasizes the mood of the tale being told.

◆ Halloween Farmer in the Dell   *Ages 2 and up*

METHOD:

Have the children help you to list all the Halloween characters they
know (goblin, cat, bat, skeleton, ghost, pumpkin, and so on). Then
make a circle with one child chosen to stand in the center as the
"goblin." Sing this song to the tune of "Farmer in the Dell":

> The goblin in the dark. The goblin in the dark.
> Hi-ho, it's Halloween, the goblin in the dark.
> The goblin takes the witch. The goblin takes the witch.
> Hi-ho, it's Halloween, the goblin takes the witch.

Continue according to the children's suggestions:

> The witch takes a cat. . . .
> The cat takes a bat. . . .
> The bat takes a pumpkin. . . .

PHYSICAL EXERCISE

◆ Ball Toss Practice   *Ages 2 and up*

YOU WILL NEED:

large ball

METHOD:

Get into a small circle with the children. Slowly pass the ball from
person to person around the circle. Gradually widen the circle as the
game goes on.

◆ High Jump   *Ages 3 and up*

YOU WILL NEED:

balloons (not helium)
string
scissors

METHOD:

Ahead of time: Blow up the balloons and knot the ends. Cut strings.
Attach a balloon to each string and hang from the ceiling, indoor
pipes, or a tree branch high enough so jumpers are challenged to
stretch.

With the children: Assign each child a place and have her jump to
make contact with and move the balloon. A child might bump the
balloon with the top of her head, use her nose, reach with her
hands, and so on.

SCIENCE

◆ Treasure Sorting
Ages 3 and up

This is good practice for waste recycling. It also presents a good opportunity to create awareness of this important environmental issue.

YOU WILL NEED:
  6 pieces heavy cardboard, shirt size
  marking pen
  masking tape
  sample piece of each of these materials:
     wood   rubber
     glass   plastic
     metal   leather
  collection of objects:
     wood—clothespin, spool, button, twig, Popsicle stick
     glass—mirror, beads, beach glass
     metal—soda can, paper clip, bottle cap, Band-Aid box
     rubber—gloves, balloon, ball
     plastic—straw, toy figures, spoon, food containers
     leather—belt, glove, shoe
  sorting containers—pie tins, shoe boxes

METHOD:
Ahead of time: Write a sign for each of the six categories (wood, glass, and so on). Glue an appropriate piece of sample material to each sign for visual identification. Tape the six cardboard signs together, accordion style. Place a container in front of each category sign.
With the children: Spread the collection of objects out for the children to handle. Encourage them to pick up each object and feel the material. Ask, "Do you know what it is made of? Can you match it to the sign, and place it in the proper container?" Help them discover similarities among objects in the same category.

◆ Surprise Bulb Planting
Ages 3 and up

YOU WILL NEED:
  bulbs (daffodil, tulip, crocus), 1 or 2 per child
  trowels
  popsicle sticks, 1 per bulb
  optional: fertilizer (bone meal works best)

METHOD:
Ahead of time: Divide the bulbs according to the number of children. If soil is really packed hard, loosen it with a shovel to make digging easier for the children.

With the children: If the garden has ample space for all children to plant at the same time, assign a designated area for each child. If the garden space is small, plant in relay fashion so each child gets a turn. Use a Popsicle stick as a marker once a bulb is planted so children will not redig the same space.

Planting bulbs is the most fun when you add the element of surprise. Choose a special spot in a friend or neighbor's yard and plant the bulbs while they are away from home. On the next holiday or birthday combine the empty bulb bag with an appropriate card and clues so the recipient can enjoy watching for his early spring surprise.

VARIATION:

Bulbs also can be planted in pots or terrarium containers indoors. Check bulb directions for growing time, as it varies with each type. Enjoy an early sign of spring, or give the planted bulbs as gifts.

◆ Real Work   *Ages 3 and up*

Engaging in grownup tasks is fun and feels oh-so-important.

METHOD:

Encourage your preschoolers' natural willingness to be helpful. They can be quite good at what they set out to do and are able to perform many jobs. Some favorites are large muscle activities:

pumping up bike tires, inner tubes, or inflatable beach toys
sweeping, indoors and out
watering gardens or potted plants with an old-fashioned watering can
pushing a grocery cart
emptying wastebaskets
raking
squeezing orange juice
grinding food (meat, cheese)

STORYTELLING

◆ Ghost Stories   *Ages 2 and up*

YOU WILL NEED:

flannel board (see page 28)
white felt or medium-weight pellon (not the iron-on variety)

(*Note:* Pellon is an interfacing material available at most fabric stores. It makes tracing, drawing, and cutting shapes for flannel board use simple and easy. It is perfect for ghosts.)
scissors

METHOD:
Ahead of time: Cut ghosts in different sizes and shapes. Place them next to the flannel board.
With the children: As the children play with the ghosts you will hear humor and imagination in original stories, fears shared in conversations, and even some math experimentation as they enjoy ghost counting and sequencing (biggest to smallest).

VARIATION for ages 4 and up:
Let the children create their own ghost shapes for the flannel board using pellon, pencils, and scissors.

TRIPS

◆ Visiting a Duck Pond or a Playground   *Ages 2 and up*

These two ideas make a pleasant playgroup morning on one of those last golden autumn days. Choose whichever is closer or better suited to your location, or combine both if it's easily done.

METHOD:
Duck Pond—Be sure the children have their own bags of breadcrumbs. Perhaps you could read Robert McCloskey's *Make Way for Ducklings* (New York: Viking Press, 1941) ahead of time. Do they know about kinds of ducks other than Mallards? Be sure they understand that it is not safe or kind to tease or scare the ducks.
Playground—It would be a good idea if you planned to have the children wear sneakers. Pack a picnic snack, making sure to include a large thermos of cider or juice.

WOODWORKING

◆ Hammering   *Ages 3 and up*

YOU WILL NEED:
work surface (child-height workbench, old table, packing crate, cellar floor)

lumber scraps
large nails with big heads, 1 to 1½ inches long
hammers (see page 29 for detailed information on equipment)

METHOD:

Set out materials, making sure to arrange them so there will be plenty of space between the working children. You may find it easier and safer to work with one or two children at a time while the others watch or play at something else. Demonstrate how to coordinate a nail and hammer, like this: "Hold the nail between your thumb and your pointer finger. See how a gentle 'tap, tap, tap' gets the nail started?"

Remind everyone that "bang, bang" begins when the nail is part way in and fingers are out of the way. Let the children practice. Move from child to child, helping each to hold the nail correctly, and checking that she is not holding the hammer too close to the hammer's head.

VARIATION:

Take the hammer and a few nails outside to the site of an old tree stump. Plant yourself by the stump and watch as the children take turns at a little nail driving practice and other outdoor pursuits.

◆ Screwing   *Ages 3 and up*

YOU WILL NEED:

lumber scraps, small pieces 1 to 2 inches thick
screws
screwdrivers (Phillips-head screws and screwdrivers are easiest)

METHOD:

Ahead of time: Nail a block or two of wood to the bench (or on a wall stud or door frame in an unimportant spot). Then hammer nails far enough into the blocks to make holes for the screws. Remove the nails.

With the children: Show the children how to screw in a screw. "Get the screw started with your fingers. Hold the bottom part of the screw-driver with the fingers of this hand [left] to keep it in the groove. Hold the handle with this hand [right] to turn it." Reverse the instructions for left-handed children. Let them practice with screws and screwdrivers. Give help as needed. You may find it easiest to work with only one or two of the children at a time.

This is a real challenge in coordination, but we have seen two-year-olds who could not manage scissors unscrew everything, including door hinges! The thrill of working with grownup tools helps to conquer difficulties.

NOVEMBER

NOVEMBER CONTENTS

◆

NOVEMBER GUIDEPOSTS

◆

THINGS YOU CAN COLLECT

Unless you live in one of the warmer climates, November can be a dreary month. A cursory glance outdoors may leave you feeling there is nothing left worth collecting. Take heart! This is the time of the dried arrangement, holiday greens, and preparations for special occasions.

Milkweed, Dried Grasses, and More

With or without your group in tow, bundle up and set out prepared with clippers and a bucket. Wherever you look—fields, woods, the backyard, even odd strips of ground near superhighways or big cities—there are the makings for future creativity. Snip anything that has an interesting look: milkweed pods, grasses, graceful dried twigs, and dozens of nature's offerings that you won't even know by name.

Now you are prepared to follow the suggestions for assembling the dried arrangements in the November activities art section. When the children are working, remember to have them tuck in a few of the flowers you dried in September.

No one is happier than a four-year-old helping you with a spray can. You will have enthusiastic helpers who would love to aid you in gilding some dried bits to save for creating decorations at Christmas time.

If you have pieces to spare, then collage making is forever fun. A new set of materials turns the project into a fresh challenge.

Evergreens and Pine Needles

Perhaps you are lucky enough to have a pine grove near you or an evergreen tree in your backyard. As the month draws to a close, you can begin to collect a variety of greens for holiday decorating. If you are able to provide precious little in the way of evergreens, use the slim supply for Contact paper designs. The children can arrange pine needles and tiny bits of greenery on the sticky side of a clear Contact paper strip. You press colored cellophane over it, and voilà! a unique holiday card or window hanging.

For the city dweller, the local variety store offers other options such as stickers, sequins, and artificial greenery.

If there are evergreens in sight, but not for the cutting, you have the perfect opening for a little chat about what makes evergreens different from deciduous trees.

Small Containers

Step up your indoor collecting in preparation for the holiday season. Set aside plastic and tin containers of various sizes. Ask friends with infants to remember you with a gift of empty baby food jars! The children will be whipping up nibble mix, cookies, relish, and the like in weeks to come. They will need something into which they can tuck their culinary endeavors. If time is short, fill decorated containers with purchased items such as birdseed, purchased instant cocoa, or easy-to-make snack mix (see page 69).

Old Christmas or Chanukah Cards

Have you saved any old Christmas or Chanukah cards? If not, one of your friends may supply you with some, or the children can find a few in their homes. In December your preschoolers can create a cut-and-paste paradise with these leftovers.

Old Toys, Games, Books

There is a certain sense of pride in taking something old and making it look like new. Create a feeling of Santa's workshop and have the children bring old dolls, trucks, games, and books they are willing to part with. Obviously at age three and four the children's skills are limited, but choose the items needing least repair and help them scrub, paint, and mend the toys. It would be wonderful if they could have a part in delivering them to a hospital or home. They will feel the reward of doing for others.

REMEMBER THE FAMILIAR

Thanksgiving

November brings the warmest of family holidays: Thanksgiving. There are dozens of ways to bring an awareness of our many blessings to your little group. Have a "Happiness is . . ." or "Love is . . ." session. Talk about it; draw about it; cut and paste about it.

Election Time

November is election time. Vote for something, such as what foods to have for lunch or what game to play outdoors.

Feeding the Birds

It is also time to begin to think about the creatures that have not migrated to warmer places. Discuss how the birds, squirrels, or rabbits are going to take care of themselves as the snows come. Make plans for feeding the birds.

Signs of Winter

Ask the little ones what makes them know that winter is on the way. Tammy may mention that the trees in the park have lost their leaves. Kenneth may point out his new snowsuit. Craig may bring up the fact that lots of the zoo animals are in their winter quarters now and decorations in the stores have changed. The preschoolers will come up with all sorts of ideas with just a gentle prod from you. You might even have an appealing poem or little story handy to enhance your discussion.

Nursery Rhymes

November days or any days are perfect times for the singing of a nursery rhyme or some other familiar song. Remember—your record or tape player can lead the group if you are faint of heart.

Modeling

As bad weather sets in you will be testing your ingenuity for ways to keep the group engrossed indoors. Modeling with playdough or clay tops the list as a most successful activity and one perfect for toning down a rambunctious group of youngsters. Let the children help mix and cook the playdough (see Best Ever Clay Recipe, page 24). They will love "squishing" and pummeling the results with their fingers and fists. One caution, however: If you want to end the day with some vestige of your sanity, add the food coloring yourself.

All of these "old familiars" are eternally fresh to preschoolers. You are sharing their first experiences with these ideas. Tune in, open your mind. The children are about to turn old ideas into new ones for you.

NOVEMBER ACTIVITIES

◆

ARTS AND CRAFTS

◆ Dried Arrangements in Holders   *Ages 3 and up*

YOU WILL NEED:
    conch, whelk, clam, or any other shells that would make good
       holders
    clay, plasticene, or playdough or, as a substitute, floral foam (used in
       flower arrangements, available at florist or variety stores)
    dried weeds, twigs, flowers, grasses of various textures and colors
    scissors

METHOD:

Each child presses the floral foam or substitute into a shell or other holder, then inserts the natural dried materials to make an arrangement.

VARIATION:

Small margarine tubs, cans, pintsize wooden baskets, or other containers can be used instead of shells.

◆ Styrofoam Turkey   *Ages 3 and up*

YOU WILL NEED:

1 set of the following materials for each person, including a
   demonstration set for yourself:
   2½-inch Styrofoam egg or ball
   7 regular pipe cleaners of various colors (2 should match to make
   legs)
   1 fuzzy red "bump chenille" pipe cleaner (if not available, use a
   regular red)
   1 3-to-4-inch circle of tag board or heavy construction paper
   scissors
   stapler

METHOD:

Ahead of time: Cut out circles of paper. Twist five pipe cleaners from each set into loops for the tail feathers. Bend the "bump chenille" cleaner to fashion the turkey's head. Shape two matching pipe cleaners into legs and feet. Trim excess length with scissors.

With the children: Demonstrate assembly. Stick the head into the narrow end of the Styrofoam egg. Line up the feathers along the back of the wide end of the egg. Staple the feet to the bottom circle. Children then do the same. You should refrain from making them place the pipe cleaners exactly as you have. The children will most likely place theirs slightly off-center. The result will be a delightful array of turkeys dancing, running, or pecking for food.

◆ Herb and Spice Design   *Ages 2 and up*

YOU WILL NEED:
   white construction paper, 9 by 12 inches
   glue and brushes
   herbs and spices in separate shakers or dishes

METHOD:
   Children spread glue in small amounts in designs on the paper, then sprinkle herbs and spices over the wet glue with shakers or their fingers. Next, everyone sniffs to notice differences in smell and appearance among the herbs and spices.

SUGGESTION:
   If you have an herb garden outside or growing on your windowsill, pick and dry some fresh herbs. Then let the children powder them between their fingers and smell.

◆ Playdough Bake   *Ages 2 and up*

YOU WILL NEED:
   cookie cutters
   rolling pins (borrow extras)
   implements for marking details on dough shapes, such as forks, spoon handles, hair curlers, Phillips-head screwdriver, cookie or butter design stamps
   cookie sheet
   bowl
   mixing spoon
   Recipe for dough:
    4 cups flour
    1 cup salt
    1½ cups hot water

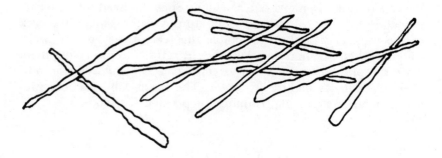

METHOD:

Ahead of time: Mix the salt and hot water in a large bowl. Add the flour and stir. Knead dough until smooth. Chill.

With the children: The children roll out the dough to about ¼ inch thick and use simple cookie cutters to make shapes. Help them transfer the shapes to a cookie sheet. Then the children decorate with small extra pieces of dough and use implements to imprint designs. You punch a hole at the top of each shape if it is to be hung later on.

Bake at 300° F for approximately 20 minutes. Watch closely and remove from the oven when shapes are light brown at the edges. The varying thicknesses created by the children make exact timing uncertain. Shapes will resemble sugar cookies, but don't bite in.

COOKING

◆ Hot Sippin' Cider   *Ages 2 and up*

YOU WILL NEED (for 4 children):
   3 cups apple cider or juice
   1 cup cranberry juice
   8-inch cinnamon stick, broken
   electric slow cooker or saucepan
   cup measure

METHOD:
   Ahead of time: Put all ingredients in the pot. Cook on high till mixture boils. Reduce to low and simmer 5 minutes. Serve warm or cold. Makes four 8-ounce servings.
   With the children: Talk about the fragrance. Does the smell make you hungry? What gives this a special smell? What other things do you like to smell cooking?

◆ Nacho Nibbles   *Ages 3 and up*

You can make this snack in a microwave or a conventional oven.

YOU WILL NEED:
   6 to 8 ounces cheddar cheese (will make 1½ to 2 cups when
      shredded)

optional: 2-to-4-ounce jar mild taco sauce
11-ounce package tortilla chips
grater (grinding type)
plastic knife
spoon
cup measure
large paper platter (or ovenproof pan)

METHOD:

Cut the cheese into chunks. Supervise closely as the children take turns grating cheese. Assign individual children separate steps in the recipe: Measure out 1½ cups of cheese. Pour the tortilla chips on the paper platter. Spoon sauce evenly over the chips, then sprinkle on cheese. Microwave on high 2 to 2½ minutes (with quarter turn halfway through) and cool, or place nachos in an ovenproof pan and bake in a conventional oven at 375° F for 3 to 5 minutes, until cheese bubbles. Allow to cool slightly before eating.

◆ Cranberry Relish   *Ages 3 and up*

Hear the cranberries pop!

YOU WILL NEED:

1 quart cranberries
2 oranges, quartered and seeded
½ cup crushed pineapple
2 cups sugar
food grinder
large baby food jars, 1 per child
extra jars or dish for leftover relish
spoons
optional: serrated plastic knives

METHOD:

One or two children take turns putting cranberries and oranges into the grinder. Some children may cut oranges into smaller pieces before grinding. Another child grinds. Someone else stirs in sugar, another the pineapple. A single child may be chosen to fill all the jars, or each child may fill his own.

DRAMATIC PLAY

◆ Leaf Pile Jump-up

Ages 2 and up

YOU WILL NEED:
pile of leaves

METHOD:
The children take turns leaping into the leaves. They huddle down in the leaves, think of an animal, person, or thing to be, then leap up and act it out. The others try to guess what it is. You may help by giving some ideas.

◆ Paper Bag Puppets

Ages 4 and up

YOU WILL NEED:
brown paper lunch bags
colorful construction paper
glue and cotton swabs
markers or crayons
yarn and trims
tape

METHOD:
Demonstrate to the group, then help individual children: Leave the paper bag folded the way it comes. A child slips her hand into the bag with her fingers over the inside fold. The bottom of the bag becomes the head. The fold will move as the child moves her fingers back and forth from fist to outstretched hand position. The moving fold will suggest a mouth.

Cut, paste, and draw with the materials listed above to make various characters and creatures. Eyes can be drawn or glued to the bottom of the bag (the head). Lips or a tongue can be created for the mouth area. Children might paste on yarn hair or paper hats. Someone might create a fiery dragon that shows the inside of its mouth when the fold is open. Someone else might draw a sleeping face that "wakes up" when the fold moves up.

Children will play and dramatize with these puppets as they work on them. Provide a special time for more pretend later on.

SUGGESTIONS:
1. Wine or liquor brown bags are narrow and are very good for making "creepy crawlies" or snake puppets. If the bottom does not come folded like a lunch bag, you will need to fold it.

2. Some older children may have reached a stage when they do not object to their faces being covered. Large grocery bags may be used to create over-the-head face masks.

GAMES

◆ Poor Kitty   *Ages 3 and up*

Children love and remember this simple game.

METHOD:

One child is chosen to be the kitty. The rest of the group sits on the floor in an informal circle. The kitty crawls on all fours and sadly stops by each person to say, "meow." That person must pat the kitty on the head saying, "Nice kitty," without a trace of a smile. The first person to smile, laugh, or giggle becomes the new kitty.

There is a little bit of dramatics in this game as each child's interpretation of kitty will be different. To vary the game you may want to have a foolish kitty or one that is angry or hungry.

◆ Egg Carton Shaker   *Ages 3 and up*

Count and compare for some math fun.

YOU WILL NEED:

ordinary egg carton with solid top, 1 per child
dried beans or buttons, 12 or more per child

METHOD:

The children drop one bean or button in the bottom of each egg cup and close the top. They hold the top and the bottom of both ends and shake to the right, shake to the left. They shake in a twisting motion, listening to the objects move around inside the carton. Then they open the carton to see what they get: two in one cup . . . three in another. The goal of the game is to see how many empty cups you have. The preschoolers love to compare the results of their shaking with one another.

MUSIC

◆ Marching Music
Ages 2 and up

Listen for the beat.

YOU WILL NEED:

record player or piano
marching music
  "MacNamara's Band"
  Marches by Sousa
  "Anchors Aweigh"
  "Seventy-six Trombones"
props appropriate for parades or soldiers

METHOD:

Have the children listen to a march. Marches have beats that are grouped into twos. You will hear a heavy beat which you call *one* and a lighter beat for *two* (if you are able to use a piano you can make this more pronounced). Let the children clap the beats and then have fun just marching as a parade, toy soldiers, or changing of the guard.

◆ Water Glass Musical
Ages 3 and up

This demonstrates the difference between high and low sounds.

YOU WILL NEED:

a glass
a small pitcher of water
a spoon

METHOD:

Leave the glass empty. Tap the spoon against the glass for the note to begin "Jingle Bells." Sing the whole song together but strike the glass each time you sing the words "jingle bells." Let each child try "playing" the glass in this manner. Talk about how they are making the same sound over and over.

Pour a little water into the glass. Tap the glass with the spoon. Ask the children what happened to the sound: "Did it go up higher?" "Did it go down lower?" Let a child pour a little more water into the glass. Let another child strike the glass. Ask again, "What happened to the sound?"

Let each person have a turn at pouring and tapping. Sing the song again while there is water in the glass, and have someone tap on the words "jingle bells."

Remind the children to *tap,* not *whack,* the glasses or you will have a flood and broken glass instead of music!

PHYSICAL EXERCISE

◆ Bean Bag Toss   *Ages 4 and up*

YOU WILL NEED:
bean bags, 1 per child
optional: markers, glue, googly eyes (available from craft stores)

METHOD:
If desired, have the children turn bean bags into flying creatures with googly eyes using the optional materials. Let glue dry. Then play a toss game, such as trying to get the bean bag into a wastebasket or a clothes basket. Or simply have the children play solitary toss by throwing the bag up into the air higher and higher and catching it themselves.

◆ Be a Rubber Man   *Ages 2½ and up*

METHOD:
Have the children pretend they are rubber people so they can stretch very far. They lie on the floor, arms up over head. They stretch, breathe deeply, and then relax, as they say the verse below, which you have repeated a few times.

VERSE:
Watch this funny, long Rubber Man,
See him stretch as far as he can.
Up go hands; down go feet.
Now relax and then repeat.

VARIATION:
For bending exercises this verse is fun:

"HINGE PEOPLE"
  I'm all made of hinges
  And everything bends
  From the top of my head
  To the tip of my ends.
  I've hinges in front
  And hinges in back
  If I didn't have hinges
  I think I would crack.

SCIENCE

◆ Magnet Experiment   *Ages 4 and up*

YOU WILL NEED:
  1 or more magnets
  different types of materials, such as:

plastic	fabric
cotton ball	safety pin
paper clip	foil
wood	tin can
nail	rubber band
pencil	thread

METHOD:
Allow the children to test one item. Ask, "What happens when you touch the magnet to it?" Test the other items one by one, asking the same question. The children will notice that nothing happens when the magnet touches wood, fabric, or rubber, but that certain metal objects "stick" to the magnet or that the magnet "picks up" the paper clip. Children should leave the experiment with this idea: Magnets attract *some* metals. (*Note:* aluminum and stainless steel are not magnetic.)

VARIATIONS:
1. Find two boxes. Mark one Yes; the other No. Children use magnets to pick up objects. Items the magnet can pick up go in the Yes box. Items that cannot be picked up go in the No box.
2. After doing these activities, see if the children can remember which objects go in the Yes and No boxes. This time, use the magnets to test the objects *after* the children have put them in the boxes where they think they belong.

◆ Pet Ball Walk   *Ages 2 and up*

Children observe animal behavior.

YOU WILL NEED:
   hamster or gerbil (borrowed if necessary)
   clear plastic animal exercise ball from local pet store

METHOD:
   Seat the children on the floor in a circle. Place the animal in the ball
   and leave it in the center of the circle. Ask questions in response to
   comments the children make as they watch the pet move the ball in
   different directions. Why do you think the animal is so active? (It
   likes to move, is having fun, is curious.) What happens when one of
   us speaks loudly or moves quickly? (The animal jumps, is startled,
   stops.) How long will it be content in the ball? (Various predictions.)
   Do not worry about the rightness or wrongness of the responses.
   The ball helps the pet survive the children's excitement and helps
   the children feel secure.

◆ Weather Bureau   *Ages 3 and up*

This activity involves on-going observation and recording.

YOU WILL NEED:
   wind indicator (a piece of yarn is fine)
   outdoor thermometer
   rain gauge: plastic tube (top end open) with inch marks painted on
      one side
   chart or notebook
   pencil
   compass

METHOD:
   Have the children choose a window in your house for regular
   weather checks. Post a compass near it. Tie yarn in view outside on a
   post, fence, or flagpole. Attach the rain gauge near the yarn. Put a
   thermometer outside the window so that it is visible from indoors.
   Check for wind direction, total rainfall, and temperature at regular
   times during the day. Record the results, especially noting changes.
   Empty the rain gauge each day so the daily reading is accurate without involving adding or subtracting. Talk about the observations
   with the children.

EXAMPLES:
   "Which way is the wind blowing? Let's feel it when we go outside."
   "The temperature says 40 degrees. Will it feel hot or chilly when we
   go out to play?"

STORYTELLING

◆ Flannel Board Sketch and Tell   *Ages 3 and up*

YOU WILL NEED:

pellon (see page 28), scraps of any shape, approximately 6 inches
   square per child
markers
scissors
flannel board (see page 28)

METHOD:

Read or tell a tried and true, easily illustrated story such as "Three
Billy Goats Gruff," "Caps for Sale," or "The Three Little Kittens
Who Lost Their Mittens." Or, discuss possibilities for creating origi-
nal stories.

Pass out art materials. The children draw on the pellon with
markers to retell the familiar favorite or to create their own imaginative stories. They will then cut excess pellon from around the
drawings. (Preschoolers do not cut precisely around details of figures but cut in a loose area around them. Younger children will
need help.) Older children may want to dictate words for you to
write with their pictures before they do their own cutting.

Using the flannel board, children can share their drawings and stories with the group or a partner or play alone.

TRIPS

◆ Nature in the City   *Ages 3 and up*

METHOD:

Allow the children to learn about nature through visits to a natural
history museum, zoo, or aquarium. Some cities offer game preserves
or sanctuaries. Watch your newspaper for special programs or films
that might appeal to preschoolers. Check to see if your public library
offers museum passes for groups. Taking the time to find this out is
well worth the savings! You will be more willing to tailor the length
of your stay to the interest of the children knowing you can return
any time at no cost.

WOODWORKING

◆ Wood-on-Wood Collage   *Ages 4 and up*

YOU WILL NEED:

  1 wood piece per child about ¾ inch thick, large enough to enable a
    child to nail on several smaller pieces (example, 12 by 10 inches)
  hammers
  nails (roofing nails work well)
  wood scraps from a lumberyard or building site—a large supply in
    interesting shapes (not too small or they will split)
  sandpaper
  optional: paint or marker
  glue (for pieces of wood accidentally split when hammering)

METHOD:

Let the children launch into hammering wood scraps to the larger
board. Some children may wish to smooth rough edges with sandpaper. If the smaller scraps split when nailed, produce glue to attach
them.

Some children may have interest in using paint or marker to
make their designs colorful. This will add to the three-dimensional
effect and can be done during free time at playgroup or later at
home.

DECEMBER

DECEMBER CONTENTS

◆

DECEMBER GUIDEPOSTS

◆

THINGS YOU CAN COLLECT

December is the month that generates the highest degree of excitement. The whole time, your preschoolers will remain perched on a plateau of enthusiasm, testing your resources and patience. Their sense of anticipation will sometimes result in swift degeneration of behavior. Fortunately there are ample activities to channel all their pent-up energy. Choose simple activities and try to avoid recognition of Christmas and Chanukah too early.

Evergreens

If you didn't have time to gather evergreen branches in November, wrap up everyone toasty warm and go out for a clipping session. If you do not have the resources for pine boughs, your florist or nursery may be willing to donate evergreen scraps for your nursery set. On returning, the children can create small arrangements in margarine containers, adding tiny Christmas balls and other frills for a holiday look. You might have them help you decorate your home with some of the larger greens, or send everyone home with sprays as a surprise for the family.

Ribbons and Wrapping Scraps

Maybe you are a ribbon and paper saver. If you are not, turn to the other children's parents or a thrifty friend. Surely there are scraps from current gift wrapping about. Collect some of the pieces that have been hoarded and have a gift-wrapping "party." You have probably set aside the results of some project for your preschoolers to give as Christmas or Chanukah gifts. Help the children wrap and decorate their gifts.

Little Boxes to Wrap

Even if there are no specific presents to be dressed up, keep in mind that children love the act of wrapping for itself alone. Assemble some cracker and cereal boxes to wrap just for fun or practice. If you do not have enough real wrapping paper (it *is* expensive these days), be original. Newspaper is a dandy substitute. Set the children loose with scissors, string, and tape. Put on a little holiday music to add to the atmosphere.

Gift Catalogs

Gift catalogs hold enchantment for little children. They enjoy leafing through them over and over. Gather some of these together. Supplied with paper, paste, and scissors, your group will become immersed in snipping and gluing favorite pictures.

To make it an especially seasonal activity, draw or glue bows onto big sheets of paper so that the paper suggests a gift box. Then ask the youngsters to "fill the box" with the things they would like to give or receive for Christmas or Chanukah.

Cookie Cutters

As you look through various shops and catalogs now and through the year, watch for interesting shape cookie cutters to add to your supply. Purchase ready-made cookie dough from the supermarket or premix your own so the children can help cut out cookies. Special tiny cutters or new animal shapes can add to the fun.

REMEMBER THE FAMILIAR

Doing for Others

The essence of this season is thinking of and doing for others. Of course the children are full of what they'd like and think they might get. Look beyond that. You will see that a sense of doing for others *does* pervade the atmosphere as the children perform the exciting familiar rituals of December.

Singing Holiday Songs

Learning a song is half of the fun. The other half is singing it for someone else. Perhaps you will take your little troop to sing for a person at a senior center or to entertain someone's grandparents. Sometimes it is hard to transport the group. If you are an apartment dweller and your building houses offices, share your holiday singing with some of the nearby workers. Suburbanites can walk to a neighbor's house.

Tree and House Trims

Old customs like "decking the halls" are the source of dozens of engaging projects. Make trims for trees. Decorate *your* tree. Create decorations for your home or for the preschoolers to take to their own homes.

The First Snow

If the weather cooperates, perhaps the first snowflakes will fall while you are engrossed in these seasonal pastimes. There is nothing so special as the very first snow of the year. Bundle up. Dash outdoors. Touch it. When it is deep enough and still unblemished, lie down and make snow angels. Come inside cold and breathless for a cup of cocoa and more holiday plans.

Shared in these simple, familiar ways with your starry-eyed preschoolers, this December will provide you with one of your warmest holidays ever.

DECEMBER ACTIVITIES

◆

ARTS AND CRAFTS

◆ Christmas Tree Bells

Ages 3 and up

YOU WILL NEED:
   Styrofoam coffee cups or waxed hot/cold paper cups
   scissors
   spoons (baby or demitasse spoons work well)
   glitter—red, green, gold—in separate dishes
   narrow gold braid or other ribbon or trim
   gold string
   glue and brushes

METHOD:
   Ahead of time: The inverted coffee cup is your bell. To make bells of
   different sizes, trim off some of the wide end of some cups. Invert
   the cup and loop string through for hanging. Cut pieces of braid to
   the proper length for gluing around the base of the bell.
   With the children: The children brush glue around the base of the
   "bell." You help them put on the pieces of trim. They brush glue
   over the remainder of the bell and sprinkle glitter on with spoons or
   roll the bells in the colors of their choice.

◆ Festive Wrap

Ages 2½ and up

With Stickers

YOU WILL NEED:
   roll of white shelf-lining paper   peel-and-stick stars
   holiday seals and stickers   scissors

METHOD:

Cut sheets of paper for the children to decorate with the stickers.

With Vegetable Printing

YOU WILL NEED:
shelf paper
poster paint
paintbrushes
vegetables (potatoes are best)
paring knife
holiday cookie cutters

METHOD:

Ahead of time: Press cookie cutters into the flat, cut surface of the vegetable and cut away outside the edges with a knife. Make several holiday stamps in this fashion.

With the children: Each child brushes paint on a relief shape and uses it to stamp his wrapping paper with designs.

◆ Gift Containers   *Ages 4 and up*

YOU WILL NEED:

1-pound coffee cans, 1 per child
precut felt (12¾ by 5⅛ inches)
white glue
scissors
fabric paint (plain or fluorescent colors *in tubes,* available in art supply store)
optional: marker art on white felt is fine if fabric paint is not easily available.

METHOD:

Ahead of time: Cut felt to fit around the outside of the coffee can. Set one color paint and one piece of felt at each child's place.

With the children: Let the children squeeze out paint designs and decorate one side of the felt piece. Encourage them to exchange paint tubes for a variety of colors. Once the paint is dry, they can spread glue on the other side of the felt and, with your help, press the covering onto the coffee can. If paints are not available, let the children draw designs on the felt with markers and cover the can in the same way.

◆ Glitter Pine Cones   *Ages 3 and up*

YOU WILL NEED:

pine cones (whatever kind is available)
glue glaze (white glue mixed with water to thickness of light cream)
containers
glue brushes or Popsicle sticks
glitter
wax paper

METHOD:

Ahead of time: Spread wax paper at each child's place. Set out a container of glue glaze with a brush, a pine cone, and a small amount of glitter.

With the children: Have the children spread glue glaze on the pine cone petals and then, with their fingers, sprinkle glitter on the sticky parts of the cone. This project is addictive for children and they will spend great lengths of time turning the cone, catching drips, and finding new hidden spots to glitter.

◆ Light the Candles on the Menorah   *Ages 2 and up*

Easy practice for cut-and-paste skill.

MATERIALS:
   paper menorahs, cut from 9- by 12-inch colored paper, 1 per child
   oaktag or cardboard, 9 by 12 inches, 1 per child
   yellow paper, quartered 9- by 12-inch sheets, 1 per child
   scissors
   paste and brushes
   optional:
      plastic wrap
      transparent tape
      string or ribbon

METHOD:
   Ahead of time: Draw a menorah on paper. Hold this over the other sheets of menorah paper so you can cut them all at one time. Glue these onto oaktag pieces.

Method: Give each child scissors, paste, a brush, yellow paper, and a menorah picture. Cut out a sample flame to show how. The children cut out their flames and glue them atop candles. (Children who cannot cut can tear flame shapes instead.) Try with small group as collaborative project: cut or tear flames for one large menorah picture. The flames cut by the children will be all sizes and shapes. Some will do only one or two flames. This project is aimed at practicing simple cutting and pasting. Any creativity lies in how different, not how much alike, the pictures look.

OPTIONAL:

You can help each child wrap the picture in plastic wrap, tape it securely, punch holes, and tie on string for hanging.

COOKING

◆ **Latkes** *Ages 3 and up*

These potato pancakes are a traditional Chanukah treat.

YOU WILL NEED (FOR 16 2- TO 3-INCH PANCAKES):
    ½ small onion, chopped
    1½ cups diced potatoes

1 egg
2 tablespoons flour
½ teaspoon salt
⅛ teaspoon baking soda
measuring cup and spoons
chopping board and knife
serrated plastic knives or french fry cutter (for children)
blender or processor
electric fry pan/griddle
margarine
spatula
applesauce and/or yogurt
paper plates and forks

METHOD:

Ahead of time: Chop the onion. Peel the potatoes and dice, or set aside for children to dice.

With the children: Finish dicing potatoes. Let each child measure and add an ingredient to the blender or processor. Blend 10 seconds or process till potato is finely chopped. Let each child spoon batter (1 tablespoon per pancake) into greased skillet and flip pancakes. Cook 1 to 2 minutes on each side. Serve with applesauce or yogurt.

◆ Rudolph the Red-Nosed Snack

Ages 3 and up

YOU WILL NEED:

pumpernickel bread (regular or cocktail size), slices as square as
  possible
peanut butter
pretzel sticks
maraschino or glacé cherries
raisins
plastic knives

METHOD:

Each child can cut a slice of bread diagonally in half. Spread triangle "heads" with peanut butter. Use a cherry on center point for a Rudolph nose. Press in two pretzels for each antler. Add raisin eyes.

SUGGESTION:

For a festive lunch, cut day-old bread with holiday cookie cutters. Spread with choices of sandwich fillings (soft cream cheese, peanut butter, tuna salad, deviled ham). Fill small dishes with trims (raisins, sliced olives, pickle pieces, chopped dates and nuts, cherries). Decorate the sandwich shapes. To simplify, skip shapes.

◆ Company for Tea   *Ages 3 and up*

A fun and simple way to show that the spirit of the season is doing for others.

YOU WILL NEED:
  holiday cookie cutters
  whole wheat toast, 2 slices per child
  red jelly or jam
  confectioners' sugar
  small strainer or shaker for sprinkling sugar
  small spreading knife
  tea things: pot of tea, juice for children, cups, sugar, lemon,
    napkins, tray, plate, spoons

METHOD:
  Invite an elderly person, someone who lives alone, or perhaps the driver of the day to come for morning tea. Have the children cut shapes from toast. Spoon a dab of jam in the center of each shape. Children spread over their shape and sprinkle confectioners' sugar on top like snow. Give each child a chance to pass something to the guest.

DRAMATIC PLAY

◆ Moving Day   *Ages 2½ and up*

This idea was created by children playing on their own. It's a great way to clean and reorganize as children play "movers."

YOU WILL NEED:
  cardboard cartons (a size manageable for preschoolers to carry or
    pull)
  optional: wagon

METHOD:
  Ahead of time: Choose a spot such as some toy shelves or the playroom corner where housekeeping toys (dishes, utensils, and so on) are kept. Place everything from this area into packing cartons. Stack together (on the wagon if you have one).
  With the children: Tell the children a new family has just arrived and needs to move all its belongings into its new home (the emptied spot). Announce that they are now workers in a moving company. Let them rearrange the contents of the boxes in the empty space in a new way. Preschoolers love being movers.

◆ Masking Tape "Roads" and "Rooms" *Ages 4 and up*

This is a kitchen floor or tabletop activity.

YOU WILL NEED:
    masking tape (different colors if possible)
    scissors
    toy cars, trucks, etc.
    doll house furniture

METHOD:
    The children make tape roads or outlines of rooms on the kitchen floor or table. They run the cars on the "roads," put furniture in "rooms," and so on. Some may just make tape designs or try letters and words.

GAMES

◆ Name Fingerplay *Ages 4 and up*

Practice coordination or one-to-one math correspondence.

VERSE:
    Tommy, Tommy, Tommy, Tommy [With right pointing finger,
        touch each finger on left hand, starting with pinky.]
    Whoops, Tommy! [Slide finger down to thumb.]
    Whoops, Tommy [Slide finger back to pointer] Tommy, Tommy,
        Tommy.

    Repeat, using left pointing finger, touching each finger on the right hand.
        Try again, substituting names of the playgroup children: "Whoops, Wendy" and so on.

◆ Dog and Bone *Ages 3 and up*

METHOD:
    One child is chosen to be the dog. She sits on a chair or stool at a distance in front of the other children. The dog closes her eyes. Her back is toward the other players. The dog's bone, which is an eraser, book, or any article of similar size, is placed behind her chair. Choose one child who tries to sneak up to the dog and touch her bone without being heard by the dog. If the dog hears someone

coming, she turns around and says, "Bow-wow!" Then the player goes back to the group and another child has a chance to outsmart the dog and touch her bone. If successful, she is the next dog.

Let everyone have a chance to be on both sides of the bone. Help the child playing the dog to turn and bark only when she really hears something.

◆ Dreidl   *Ages 4 and up*

YOU WILL NEED:
dreidls, 1 per child

METHOD:
Have the children spread out on the floor or around a table. Teach them how to spin the dreidl (top). While they practice they can chant this song:
Dreidl, dreidl, dreidl,
I made it out of clay,
And when it's dry and ready,
With dreidl I will play.

The four-sided wooden, plastic, or clay dreidl has a different Hebrew letter on each side. Children spin and chant, and when their dreidl stops they compare with others to see if they have a Hebrew letter match.

MUSIC

◆ Jingle Bell Mitts   *Ages 2 and up*

YOU WILL NEED:
old mittens, 1 per child
2 to 3 small bells per mitt
twist ties or yarn and darning needle
optional: tapes of holiday music

METHOD:
Ahead of time: Attach bells to each mitten with yarn or twist ties (slide through mitten, then through bell loop, and twist to hold). Yarn can be tied after needle threads it through the mitten.
With the children: Play holiday music and let the children jingle their mitts and move to the rhythm or sing "Jingle Bells" together. Let the children be horses prancing through the snow with bells on.

◆ Tape Recording Holiday Songs

Ages 3 and up

YOU WILL NEED:
tape recorder
seasonal songs
optional: musical instruments

METHOD:
Teach a seasonal song or two. Tape-record the children singing. Play the tape as background music during snack or project time—or let the children accompany their recording with bells and other instruments.

◆ The Toy Shop Dance

Ages 3 and up

POEM:
Did you ever see the toy shop late at night
When all the lights are out?
The toys wake up and start to dance
And move themselves about

Dolls and trucks and motor cars
And little wagons, too.
Horns and drums and rocket ships
For boys and girls like you.*

RECORD OR TAPE:
"Dance of the Sugarplum Fairy" (or any of the dances from the "Nutcracker Suite" by Tchaikovsky)

METHOD:
Read the poem.

Have each child tell which toy he wants to be. It is all right if they all decide to be the same thing. If they all decide to be dolls they may be different kinds of dolls—rag doll, baby doll, china doll. Each type will move differently. This is true of different types of cars, drums, etc. Let the children talk about the toy they choose—how it moves, how it looks. Play the record and encourage the children to pretend in rhythm to the music.

VARIATION:
You might do the same movement activity with the various sections of Saint-Saëns's "Carnival of the Animals," or Mussorgsky's "Pictures at an Exhibition." The children could move like different animals.

PHYSICAL EXERCISE

◆ Tumbling Mattress   *Ages 2 and up*

YOU WILL NEED:
discarded mattress or cushions

METHOD:
Let the children tumble under your watchful eye. You might help them begin to learn to somersault (one at a time).

◆ Musical Ball Game   *Ages 3½ and up*

YOU WILL NEED:
ball
record or tape (or you clap)
record or tape player

*Adapted from *Creative Movement for the Developing Child,* revised edn., Clare Cherry (Belmont, Calif.: Fearon Teacher Aids, Simon & Schuster Supplementary Education Group, 1971).

METHOD:

The children pass the ball to one another as they stand in a circle. The younger the group, the closer they stand. You stop the music at different points to "catch" someone with the ball. Keep on till everyone has had a chance to be caught.

SCIENCE

◆ Trees in Winter   *Ages 2 and up*

METHOD:

Have a walk outside or look out the window if the weather is inclement. Point out an evergreen tree and a tree with bare branches. "See those two trees? How are they different?" "Are they always this way?" Children may volunteer that in spring and summer most of the trees are green. Discuss the idea that some trees stay green throughout the year (evergreens such as pine or rhododendron), while others shed their leaves in winter.

◆ Snow Melt and Other Strainer Experiments   *Ages 3 and up*

YOU WILL NEED:
strainer
container (to fit underneath strainer)
coffee filter
1 cup snow

METHOD:

Line the strainer with a coffee filter and place it over a container. Put snow in the filter and allow it to melt. Check the filter; you should find dirt particles. Talk about what you find on the filter with your preschoolers. "Where do you think the dirt came from?" "How did it get into the snow?" As you hear the children's ideas, begin to use the word *pollution*. Discuss why we should not eat snow.

VARIATIONS:

1. *Larger/Smaller, Liquid/Solid:* Experiment to show that strainers can separate large from small or liquid from solid. Choose one or two items to strain, such as: pond water, defrosted frozen strawberries, vegetable soup, sand and pebbles, chocolate chip ice cream.
2. *Larger/Smaller, More/Less:* Use strainers and colanders with different sized holes to sift mixed birdseed or gravel. See how differently the same material can separate. Large holes let more of the seed or gravel sift through. Small holes let only the tiniest pieces pass.

STORYTELLING

◆ Gingerbread People   *Ages 3 and up*

Enjoy the spicy fragrance of holiday baking and the fun of cutting cookies to set the mood for an old favorite, "The Gingerbread Man," a folk tale retold by many authors.

YOU WILL NEED:
gingerbread people (bought or home-baked)

or

shapes pressed from pumpernickle bread slices with a cookie cutter
story, "The Gingerbread Man"
optional: tape recorder

METHOD:
Ahead of time: If you wish, cut the shapes with the children as a cooking project. Make sure the children know the story. Position the tape recorder inconspicuously. Children are less self-conscious when they do not feel pressured to perform.
With the children: Encourage each child to tell the story in her own way. Tammy's gingerbread girl may live in the city and is trying to run away from loud noises. Chrissy's gingerbread person may be running to look for a new friend. Ken's and Craig's gingerbread boys may be more like the one in the story, running away to tease or trick someone. Or perhaps their gingerbread boys eat people and become giants.

How will each child's story end? Maybe Phillip's gingerbread people will be eaten and Alan's will not. Encourage the children to create their own stories and not to make stories alike. Tape-record as the children talk.

SUGGESTION:
Milk and cookies or a sandwich snack can give a party finish to this story time. While the children munch, you can play some of the recording or read from the original story.

VARIATION:
Use a cookie cutter and a pencil to outline shapes on cardboard or brown construction paper. Cut out enough figures for your group. Children can glue on a variety of trimmings to dress up their figures. Attach to straws or Popsicle sticks to create puppets. Let the children tell their stories.

TRIPS

◆ Visiting a Nursing Home   *Ages 4 and up*

YOU WILL NEED:

individual gifts for each patient—decorated baby food jars filled
   with jam, cookies, or paintings the children have made
a few short nursery songs the children know well enough to sing

METHOD:

Nursing homes can be unsettling to someone unfamiliar with care
for the elderly. It is essential that you visit the home by yourself
before planning a trip with the children. Many homes are small,
friendly places where patients are primarily ambulatory. This makes
it possible to have the patients gather in the home's living room or
reception area. This would be a more natural arrangement from the
children's standpoint and makes the visit more of a party for the
patients. Consider carefully the children in your group. You may
feel they are too active to make a visit like this enjoyable. Perhaps
then you could do it with just your own family. If your group does
seem adaptable to this type of situation, check with the other parents
to see what experience, if any, each child has had with nursing
homes. If everyone feels comfortable about making such a visit and
you know of an appropriate home, then go ahead with plans.

Mention to the children in advance what they may see—older
people in bed or wheelchairs, some who are hard of hearing or have
difficulty seeing. Most children will not feel uncomfortable, and
their spontaneous enthusiasm will bring joy.

◆ A Nursery at Holiday Time   *Ages 3 and up*

This is a delightful outing for a frosty morning between Thanksgiving
and Christmas.

METHOD:

Check with the nursery to make sure it is all right for you and the
children to walk around looking at the different types of trees and
evergreens used in wreaths and swags. Although this is a busy season for a nursery, midweek does not tend to be as rushed and you
do not really need a tour. Nurseries often play Christmas music and
the children will come away filled with good spirits. Let them look at
the ribbons and other artificial materials sold individually. Perhaps
the children can buy a few clusters of berries or balls to mix with
pine cones they've collected to make a simple decoration at home.

WOODWORKING

◆ Nail Board
Ages 3 and up

YOU WILL NEED:

wood piece, about 9 by 12 inches, ¾ inch thick (*optional:* painted or
stained ahead of time), 1 per child
nails with large heads (roofing nails)
hammers
rubber bands, various colors and sizes

METHOD:

You may choose to work with just one or two children at a time.
Help each child hammer nails partway into his board at random.
Then let the children make designs—changeable ones—by stretch-
ing the colored rubber bands over the nails.

For permanent designs, use colored yarn or wire instead of rubber
bands to wrap in and around the nails.

The rubber band nail board makes a fun game and good travel companion for long car rides or a wonderful homemade gift from a
child to a friend.

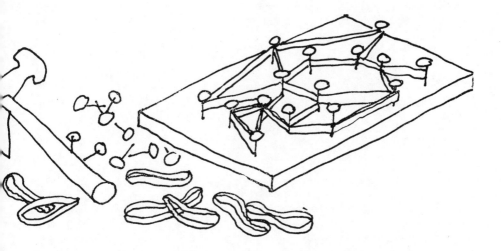

JANUARY

JANUARY CONTENTS

◆

JANUARY GUIDEPOSTS

◆

THINGS YOU CAN COLLECT

January can be a letdown after the exciting pace of the holiday season. It can also be a satisfying time. There is nothing comparable to the cozy feeling that comes when the weather is bitter outside, and you are protected and toasty inside.

For your collecting this month, you will turn primarily to indoor resources. Most of your activities also will be centered inside, with the exception of a few brisk adventures in the snow.

Calendars and Counting

Resist the temptation to toss out last year's calendars. They are ideal for cutting and pasting projects. To turn the activity into a game, you might suggest, "Snip out a pile of numbers. . . . Now, who can find a two? four? ten?" or "Does anyone see a five? Glue it onto your paper."

As you watch your group in action, you will notice how high each child can count and what numbers each recognizes. Confine yourself to numbers from one to twenty. The children will have received a large measure of exposure to these numbers on television.

Perhaps your group will be content to cut and paste the numerals in their own way without any direction from you.

Cards

With a view to Valentine's Day coming early in the next month, see if you can find any old valentines, lace, or artificial flowers. Turn to friends who are "savers" to add to your supply. Set the collection aside for activities in February.

Containers for Plants

Nothing can give winter quite the lift that flowers can. Gather a few containers for growing seeds and bulbs. Egg cartons are excellent for seeds, margarine containers for holding bulbs. Use your imagination.

If you send children home with narcissus bulbs set to grow or seeds nestled in a box of dirt, remember also to send directions on care. Bulbs require the least attention; take that into consideration when you are choosing what to do.

While you are collecting containers, look over the January science activity, New Plants from Old (page 156). There you will find other kinds of planting activities using different types of containers.

Snow

Snow? For collecting? If snow is falling, give everyone a piece of black construction paper. Capture snowflakes on it. Look at them outdoors under a magnifying glass.

Bring a handful of snow inside. See what happens when it melts in a dish. "Oh, dear! Look at all the dirty little bits left floating there." Take time for some talk about why we must not eat snow.

REMEMBER THE FAMILIAR

Show and Tell

The children will come to you full of tales about their holiday adventures. Let them take turns relating them. Chrissy may have brought her new markers. Let her demonstrate—or even share, if she wishes. Give everyone time to test out Tommy's new superspeed cars.

Fun in the Snow

Venture into a snowstorm to run and play. There is something thrilling about dashing about amid racing snowflakes. Riding on sleds and assembling snowmen are always popular. Be the first to make footprints on city streets.

Outside Toys Inside

In inclement weather, outside toys can become an indoor treat. Take the slide into the basement. If space allows, bring a tricycle or pedal car indoors. Set up a small sandbox in the laundry room.

In one household, the success of the winter was a big sandbox assembled on the screened porch. On the nastiest days the porch afforded some protection while the children burned off a little excess energy in the fresh air. Some sand was tracked inside, but few things are easier to vacuum up than a little loose sand.

Games with Winter Clothing

The biggest problem with taking preschoolers outdoors is the putting on and taking off of all that winter gear. In the interest of good sense, plan most outdoor activities when the children first arrive or just before they go home.

Turn the donning of snow clothes into a game: "Let's see who can get dressed first." Play "Who can show how" to zip a zipper, to button the buttons, to pull on the boots.

Playdough and Clay

It is time to pull out playdough or clay again, if you have not done so lately.

Familiar Songs

It is time, too, to sing some old favorites—new to the children, familiar to you.

Martin Luther King Day

Observe the day by thinking about how each of us is different, each of us is special. Share what-I-like-about-you ideas. Cheri likes Val's pretty copper hair. Scott likes the way Alan laughs.

Mount a few pictures of interesting-looking people that show differences in age, sex, dress, work, heritage. Share some time with the children looking for things they like or find appealing about these people—spiked hair, smile lines, skill. End by showing a picture of Martin Luther King, Jr.

Chinese New Year

It is time for the Chinese New Year. Share something special from Chinatown—a Chinese teacup, chopsticks, fans, or a picture of dragons on parade. At snack time, savor pineapple chunks and/or tangerines (the sign of good luck) while breaking open fortune cookies and listening to *The Story About Ping* by Marjorie Flack (New York: Viking, 1933).

Winter *can* be a wondrous time—a beautiful, white-crystal world outside, old favorites to do and new things to learn inside. Take advantage of the winter season before you must turn your attention to the special charms of coming spring days.

JANUARY ACTIVITIES

◆

ARTS AND CRAFTS

◆ Making "Lollipop" Traffic Lights   *Ages 3 and up*

This project provides early cutting practice. Use the "lollipops" to play
the Red and Green Light game, page 155.

YOU WILL NEED:
    green and red heavy construction paper, about 9 by 12 inches, 1 of
        each per child
    8-inch pie or cake tin
    pencil
    Popsicle sticks, straws, or other items to use as sticks for the
        "lollipops"
    scissors
    stapler, tape, or glue and brush

METHOD:
    Ahead of time: Make a large circle on each piece of paper by tracing
    around the edge of the pie tin with a pencil.
    With the children: The children cut out the circles. Some children may
    have difficulty and will need your assistance. Use stapler, tape, or
    glue to help attach the circles to the sticks lollipop-fashion.
    This is an excellent early cutting activity because the shape to be cut
    is very large and simple. Circles are one of the easiest shapes to cut.

◆ Snow Painting   *Ages 3 and up*

YOU WILL NEED:

red, blue, and yellow powdered tempera paint, premixed with water
to light-cream consistency in large, unbreakable containers
paintbrushes (large kindergarten size or small housepainting
brushes)

METHOD:

Go outside. Paint on snow!

The children will come up with their own ideas, but you might also
suggest dribbling or spattering paint, drawing abstract shapes, making letters, or drawing simple pictures. The children may decide to
experiment with one or two of the things they see you doing. Different effects will be achieved according to how wet or powdery the
frozen snow is.

◆ Paper Strip Sculpture   *Ages 3 and up*

Combines art and language skills.

YOU WILL NEED:

strips of construction paper, about 1 by 12 inches in a variety of
colors
cellophane tape (precut pieces or use from large dispenser)
9- by 12-inch construction paper for base, 1 per child, plus 1
demonstration sheet
scissors for everyone

METHOD:

Show the children how to do paper strip sculpture. They can begin
to work as you demonstrate. Tape the ends of a paper strip to the
construction paper base so you have a three-dimensional paper arch.
Arch another strip across the first strip. You can tape one end to the
first strip and attach the other end to the paper base. Explain that
ends of the paper strips can be taped anywhere on the paper base or
attached to other strips. Show how strips can be cut shorter, fringed,
folded, bent. Ask the children what different things they are finding
to do with the paper strips to make them "stand up" from the flat
paper base.

This is a great project for practicing language skills, too. The children like to explain the sequential steps they took to create the original art form: "First I did this. Then I did this." The work lends itself
to the use of prepositions like over, under, beside, and outside.

◆ "Scrap Pizza" Art   *Ages 3 and up*

Children consider this activity as much fun as eating pizza.

YOU WILL NEED:
 round base, made of cardboard or brown paper (6- to 8-inch
   diameter), 1 per child
 red tempera paint
 ½- or ¾-inch paintbrush, 1 per child (piece of sponge on end of
   spring clip clothespin also works well)
 construction paper scraps, generous supply
 scissors
 oregano in sprinkle container

METHOD:
 Have the children brush the "red paint tomato sauce" onto the circle
 base. While the paint is still wet, add paper scrap "toppings." Allow
 the children to create their toppings in any way they can devise. For
 meatballs, some will cut small circles from dark paper while others
 will prefer the three-dimensional look and crumble scraps into small
 balls. Other favorite ideas:
  cheese: yellow snips
  peppers: green strips
  pepperoni: medium red circles
  mushrooms, onions: white and brown snips
  tomatoes: red snips
   When the pizzas are finished, have the children sprinkle real
 oregano on top. The smell will stir up lots of food conversation. One
 playgroup mother got small pizza boxes from a local business and
 the children launched into pizza delivery role play.

◆ Car Tracks   *Ages 2 and up*

YOU WILL NEED:
 small toy cars and trucks, plastic, metal, or wooden, 1 per child
 pie tins, 1 per child
 tempera paint, 1 color
 large pieces of paper, 1 per child

METHOD:
 Pour *thin* layer of paint into each pie tin. Children run the car
 wheels through the paint and then over the paper to create a design.
 Another time, try the activity with a different color in each child's
 pie plate and let children trade paint and cars to make a multi-
 colored design.

VARIATION:

Group Project: Have the children run the paint-dipped cars over a large road map and then tell about their "trip."

COOKING

◆ Baked Bananas   *Ages 3 and up*

YOU WILL NEED (for 4 children):
  2 bananas
  2 tablespoons honey or 4 tablespoons orange juice
  2 teaspoons fresh lemon juice
  2 measuring spoons
  2 cups
  2 serrated plastic knives
  2 teaspoons
  1 glass baking dish
  paper plates

METHOD:
Ahead of time: Mix honey or orange juice and lemon juice in a cup.
With the children: Children work in teams of two. One peels the banana; the other cuts it in half crosswise, then lengthwise. (Any cutting system is fine.) Then one puts the pieces in the baking dish. The other spoons the lemon juice mixture over the fruit. Bake at 400° F for 10 to 15 minutes (or microwave on High 2½ to 3 minutes, quarter turn halfway) until fruit softens and sauce bubbles. Allow to cool slightly. Serves four.

◆ Egg Fu Yung   *Ages 3 and up*

Try eating this snack with chopsticks.

YOU WILL NEED (for 6 children):
  1 large carrot
  1 green onion
  3 eggs
  ⅓ cup bean sprouts (canned or fresh)
  soy sauce
  peeler
  serrated plastic knife
  grater (grinding type)

mixing bowl
fork or whisk
spatula
electric fry pan (nonstick)
large spoon
paper plates
forks or chopsticks

METHOD:

Ahead of time: Peel and cut the carrot into pieces sized to fit the grinding-type grater. Preheat the fry pan to 350° F.

With the children: One child can chop the onion into small pieces on a paper plate while one or two other children grate the carrot. You help someone else crack the eggs and beat them in the mixing bowl with a fork. Children take turns adding the prepared onion, carrot, and beansprouts to the beaten eggs. Choose one person to spoon mixture into the hot pan. Fry for 1 minute. Turn. Fry 1 minute more. Cut in wedges, sprinkle with soy sauce, and serve.

◆ Chinese New Year Cookies   *Ages 3 and up*

YOU WILL NEED (for 2 to 3 dozen cookies):
12-ounce package chocolate chips (milk chocolate works well)
5-ounce can chow mein noodles
double boiler or microwave-safe bowl
mixing spoon
2 teaspoons
tray or cookie sheet covered with wax paper

METHOD:

Melt chocolate chips in a double boiler or a microwave oven (1 to 3 minutes on Medium High). One child can add noodles to the melted chocolate; others can take turns mixing. Take turns making cookies: using a spoon in each hand, clasp a scoop of chocolate and noodle mixture and drop it onto the tray or cookie sheet. Let the chocolate set till firm (1 to 1½ hours at room temperature, or 20 minutes in the refrigerator).

DRAMATIC PLAY

◆ Rice or Oatmeal Sandbox   *Ages 2 and up*

A wonderful substitute for outdoor sandbox play.

YOU WILL NEED:
  rice or oatmeal, enough to fill pan halfway
  large cookie sheet with sides or jelly roll pan, 1 per child
  small toy cars (bulldozers, backhoes, bobcats, graders, dump trucks,
    and loaders are especially good)
  dustpan and brush, broom

METHOD:
  Ahead of time: If you need extra cars or pans, ask the children to
  bring some from home.
  With the children: Cover the bottom of each child's pan with rice or
  oatmeal. Give the children a good supply of the cars and encourage
  exchange with one another for variety. They will have a grand time
  making roads, transporting piles, and the like.

SUGGESTION:
  This is best done on the kitchen table or floor, or in the basement, as
  there is bound to be some spilling. Be sure you leave time for
  cleanup and have everyone help sweep up the floor.

◆ Animal Walk   *Ages 2 and up*

METHOD:
  Choose one child to be an animal (duck, turkey, goat, etc.). Let him
  lead the group in a parade around the room acting out the animal
  (hands on hips, knees bent, to waddle like ducks; strutting like turkeys, butting like a billy goat, etc.). When the leading child makes
  the noise of the animal (quack, gobble, and so on), everyone must
  turn around and move in the opposite direction. Every child will
  want a chance to be a special animal and lead the group.

SUGGESTION:
  Just Me by Marie Hall Ets (New York: Viking Press, 1965) is a perfect
  story to read before or after enjoying this dramatic play game.

GAMES

◆ **Following Snow Tracks** *Ages 3 and up*

Have an adventure in newly fallen snow.

YOU WILL NEED:
  any snack in plastic bags, 1 per child
  warm clothing

METHOD:
  Ahead of time: Prepare and wrap snacks.
  With the children: Bundle the children up well so they will stay warm
  and dry. Give each a snack bag. Have them each start from the same
  point and head in a different direction, carefully making a path with
  their footprints. Encourage them to go around trees, over sand-
  boxes, and so on to make their paths more interesting. When they
  find a good ending spot they bury their snack bag in the snow, turn
  around, and follow their own footprints back to the starting point.
  Then they exchange trails, each child following someone else's
  footprints until they each find a buried snack.

◆ **Snowballs for Summer** *Ages 3 and up*

YOU WILL NEED:
  newly fallen snow
  plastic bags or wrap

METHOD:
  Have the children make snowballs. Wrap them in plastic and place
  in your freezer to save for playing a target game (using good safety
  rules) with the children on a summer day (see page 153).

MUSIC

◆ **High and Low Sounds #1** *Ages 3 and up*

YOU WILL NEED:
  xylophone (or piano if you have one)

METHOD:
  Play the scale going from low to high on the xylophone. Sing the
  scale using "la-la-la" or "do-re-mi." Move your hand up as your voice

goes up. You and the children sing the scale as you play it. Then let each child play the scale while the others move their hands up as the sound goes up.

Do the same things going down the scale.

Now you are ready for a game. Play two notes. Let the children show with their hands whether the music went up or down. Let each child play two or three notes going up or going down the scale, followed by the others showing the up or down movement with their hands.

◆ Popcorn Dance   *Ages 3 and up*

SONGS:

"Popcorn in a Pot"*   (Tune: "I'm a Little Teapot")
    I'm a little popcorn in a pot,
    Heat me up and watch me pop,
    When I get all fat and white then I'm done,
    Popping corn is lots of fun.
"Pop, Pop, Pop, My Corn"   (Tune: "Row, Row, Row Your Boat")
    Pop, pop, pop, my corn,
    Pop it big and white.
    Popping, popping, popping, popping,
    'til it is just right.
Tune: "Jimmy Crack Corn"
Make up your own words with the children (four-year-olds and up).

METHOD:

Let the children pretend that they are popcorn. They may jump up and down or hop as they pretend to pop. Some may pretend to be little kernels that refuse to pop.

SUGGESTIONS:

1. Precede the activity with a snack that includes popping and eating popcorn.
2. Play a recording of "Pop Goes the Weasel." Have the children squat down on the floor. As they listen to the song they can jump up and clap hands over their heads each time it says, "pop."

---

*Adapted from *Creative Movement for the Developing Child,* revised edn., Clare Cherry (Belmont, Calif.: Fearon Teacher Aids, Simon & Schuster Supplementary Education Group, 1971).

PHYSICAL EXERCISE

◆ Block Bowling

Ages 3 and up

Good fun with a babysitter.

YOU WILL NEED:

large cardboard blocks are best, but the standard wooden blocks are
okay

METHOD:

This activity requires an appealing combination of block building
and ball rolling. Most of the children have never bowled, so the fun
of this is letting them set up the blocks in many original patterns.
Some may line them up while others group them or build towers to
knock down. Start rolling the ball not too far from the blocks. As the
children get better they can move farther back. Keeping score is not
necessary.

SUGGESTION:

Older children could have fun with this by establishing rules and
keeping score.

◆ Red and Green Light

Ages 3 and up

YOU WILL NEED:

large circles of construction paper—one red, one green—attached
to Popsicle sticks or straws lollipop-fashion (see page 147).

METHOD:

The children line up at one side of the room. You are at the other,
holding the sticks. Raise the green sign; the children move forward.
Raise the red sign; they STOP. Whoever reaches the other side first
wins, but this aspect should not be stressed. The real fun is that
everyone may take a turn being Director of Traffic. This game rein-
forces traffic safety sense, and presents an opportunity for physical
exercise.

SCIENCE

◆ New Plants from Old   *Ages 3 and up*

You can use carrots, potatoes, or sweet potatoes for this activity.

Project 1: CARROT

YOU WILL NEED:
   carrots, 1 per child
   small plastic container, 1 per child
   pebbles
   serrated plastic knife

METHOD:
   Help the children cut off leaves, if any, with the plastic knife. Then cut off 2-inch pieces from the thick sprouted end of carrot. The children put the 2-inch pieces in the containers, cut end down, and sprinkle pebbles to hold them in place. Send the plants home with directions to add water about halfway up the side of the carrot and to keep in a sunny place. Watch for signs of a lacy green plant growing from the top. When roots form at the bottom, the carrot can be transplanted into a pot with sandy soil, or left to grow in the water.

Project 2: POTATO

YOU WILL NEED:
   potato
   soil
   spoons
   plastic cups or flower pots, 1 per child
   knife

METHOD:
   Ahead of time: Punch holes in the bottom of the cups for drainage. Cut the potato into pieces so that each part has some eyes (the eyes are the buds of the plant).
   With the children: The children spoon soil into the containers and plant the potato pieces. Send the plantings home with directions to keep them in a sunny place and to water them daily. In a few days sprouts will begin to grow from the eyes.

Project 3: SWEET POTATO

YOU WILL NEED:
   fresh sweet potatoes (some are dried before marketing), 1 per child
   tall jars, 1 per child
   toothpicks
   serrated plastic knife

METHOD:

Help the children cut off the pointed end of the potatoes. They put toothpicks in opposite sides of the potato piece and hang it in a jar, pointed end up. Send the jars home with directions to keep them in indirect sun with water covering the tip of the potato. The sweet potato will sprout in about a week and leaves will appear soon after. As the vine grows, it can climb a stick or string.

◆ Feeling Box   *Ages 3 and up*

YOU WILL NEED:
 cardboard box
 scissors
 masking tape (or any sturdy cloth tape)
 cloth, enough to make a small sleeve
 objects interesting to touch (shell, stuffed animal, empty nest, spoon)

METHOD:

Ahead of time: Make a feeling box by cutting a hole in the box top that is large enough for a child's hand. Make a sleeve inside the hole by taping cloth around it. Put a familiar object inside the box.
With the children: The children take turns touching and reacting. Help them find "feeling" words like "slippery," "scratchy," "furry," "hard" that explain what helps them to identify the object.

VARIATION:

Instant Feeling Box: You can make a feeling box for small items by slipping a small margarine container into the bottom of a large sock. Every child can have her own. Try items like a paper clip, glue stick, or pine cone.

◆ A Tree for the Birds   *Ages 3 and up*

YOU WILL NEED:

discarded Christmas tree, set in a bucket of sand outdoors, or a live tree growing in the garden.
a selection from the bird-feeding recipes below

METHOD:

Follow your choice of recipes, then hang to decorate the outdoor tree. You can make several recipes over two or three playgroup days: store them in the freezer as you go along, then decorate the tree all at one time.

SUGGESTION:

Make just one recipe for the children to take home for outdoor hanging.

Recipes:

RECIPE 1: FEEDING CUPS

peanut butter	raisins
margarine	apple bits
paper cups or ½ orange rind,	bread crumbs
pulp removed	bird seed
cranberries	

Mix 1 part peanut butter with 1 part margarine. Trim the paper cups to shallow depth and attach string or wire for hanging. The children fill the cups with assorted mixtures of the ingredients.

RECIPE 2: BREAD SHAPES

stale bread slices
cookie cutters
wire pieces

The children cut the bread into shapes with the cutters. Help them insert wires through the shapes for hanging.

RECIPE 3: PEANUT BUTTER PINE CONES

peanut butter	wire or string
margarine	wax paper

pine cones   plastic picnic knives
birdseed

   Mix 1 part peanut butter with 1 part margarine. Twist wire onto
the pine cones for hanging. Use wax paper to work on. Each child
spreads some peanut butter mixture onto a cone with a knife and
rolls the cone in birdseed.

RECIPE 4: SUET BAG
   suet
   string
   onion bag or other mesh covering
   Help each child wrap some suet in a piece of mesh. Tie the mesh
to close.

RECIPE 5: FEEDING STRINGS
   Cheerios cereal
   string
   The children thread Cheerios onto string. Help them tie the ends
of the string together.

STORYTELLING

◆ Winter Mural   *Ages 3 and up*

Team artwork tells a story.

YOU WILL NEED:
   white shelf paper, 3 to 4 feet long
   scissors
   glue
   aluminum foil
   colorful paper and fabric scraps
   crayons or markers

METHOD:
   Ahead of time: Talk about what we see outside in winter. Help the
   children think about what they might put in a winter scene. Spread
   the shelf paper and other materials on the floor and encourage the
   children to create a cut-and-paste winter scene.
   Storytelling with the children: Display the finished mural so the children can study it closely. Ask the children to tell you where you
   might see this scene, when it is happening, who it is about, and what
   the people are doing.
      As they talk, you write the story in large print. The children will

ask you to read it aloud often and will love looking at their mural again and again.

The following is a description given by preschoolers two to five years old: "It's winter. It's cold but the sun is bright and hot. It's been snowing 6231 (a very long time). The story takes place in the snow, in the country near woods where it's dark. The story is about Jesus [church is in picture], cousins, snowmen, and a hunter. It is wet, cold, and fun."

TRIPS

◆ Trip to a Car Wash   *Ages 3 and up*

Let young imaginations make this into a fantasy trip!

METHOD:
Check to make sure the car wash you plan to visit is operating and that passengers and driver may remain in the car. Talk about how many of the children have been to one before and what their reaction was. Did they watch the brushes and sprays work? (To some this may have been very frightening, and perhaps then it would be unwise to go.) Ask "What does riding through a car wash make you think about?" The children may come up with ideas such as a jungle in a rain storm or a trip through outer space. Choose the one idea they seem to like best and take along any pretend props that will add to the fun and reality of their imaginary trip—rain hats for the jungle or space gear for the planet ride. Hop in the car. Bon voyage!

This trip can be a spur-of-the-moment adventure when the car needs washing and the playgroup has been confined to inside activities because of weather.

WOODWORKING

◆ Simple Clamping and Vise Use   *Ages 3 and up*

YOU WILL NEED:
C-clamp or bench vise attached to a child-height table or workbench
wood scraps, ⅛ to 2 inches in thickness, no more than 1 to 4 inches
  in width and approximately 6 to 12 inches in length

METHOD:

 Show the children how to make the vise or C-clamp open and close and how to put in a piece of wood. Let the children take turns experimenting, using one or more scraps of wood. Some will be entertained and gain a sense of accomplishment just by conquering the opening and closing of the vise or clamp. The coordination this activity requires makes it an appealing and age-appropriate challenge.

FEBRUARY

February Contents

♦

FEBRUARY GUIDEPOSTS

◆

THINGS YOU CAN COLLECT

Many of the items you collected and projects you did in the month of January will lend themselves equally well to February. In addition, you may need to plan a trip to pick up the special materials for some projects from the February activity section.

Lace and Old Jewelry

Rummage around for pretty frippery that will make appropriate trims on valentines—lace, bits of old costume jewelry, ribbons, and doilies.

Heart-Shaped Cutters

Dig out your heart-shaped cookie cutters. Different sized ones multiply the fun, so borrow or add to your own supply.

If the thought of more cookie baking leaves you quivering, have the children use the cutters for a playdough project. Your preschoolers might enjoy cutting out playdough hearts and pressing "jewels" into them. This is where cast-off bracelets and earrings will come in handy. Let the result dry, and present it as a unique valentine.

Stray Envelopes

It would be practical to collect a variety of envelopes. When the children are making cards you can precut colored paper to fit the envelopes. The youngsters do the decorating. Now cards and envelopes go together.

Plants as Valentine Gifts

Early in February you might take clippings from your indoor plants. Impatiens and begonia are especially fast at rooting. Root them in water, and they will be all set for the children to put in containers full of potting soil and take home as gifts.

REMEMBER THE FAMILIAR

Making Valentines

There are cards to be made for everyone—parents, grandparents, neighbors, friends. Prolific members of your group may turn out several cards, while others may labor over a single one or even lack enthusiasm for the whole procedure. That's okay, too!

Giving Gifts

Valentine's Day is a time for gifts. Look through each month's activities for a variety of gift-making ideas. If you are not too caught up in the activities, steal a moment to take a snapshot or two of your group. Surprise the other parents with them and use them to help you look back on these days with special fondness. Why not make duplicates of the best ones to share with all the children's families?

Valentine's Box and Party

February, too, can be a party time. With or without the children's help you can get creative with Valentine cupcakes, heart-shaped Jell-O molds, and sandwiches cut out with your heart-shaped cookie cutters.

Perhaps the children could adorn paper placemats with Valentine stickers or precut shapes to be pasted on—a good trick for any holiday party! The group can also be set to work decorating a box for their Valentine cards—individual shoebox ones to use at home or a larger one to use at *your* playgroup house. For a big box, let each person embellish one side in any medium of your choice. You will prearrange with parents for the children to bring Valentine cards to exchange. Keep it a happy occasion for every one by requiring that each person bring cards for everyone else. Each child should bring cards for everyone in the group so no feelings get hurt.

Patriotic Days

Remember those patriotic days—ideal for having some special marching activities. Who would like to carry the flag? Everyone! Take turns leading the march, flag in hand.

Poetry, Stories, and Music

You will not want to neglect poetry and stories that might be suitable for the month. For poetry, look into *Where the Sidewalk Ends,* by Shel Silverstein (New York: Harper & Row, 1974). For storybook suggestions use *The Read-Aloud Handbook,* by Jim Trelease (New York: Penguin, 1985). Turn to your local librarian for other samples of what to use for the nursery set.

Winter will fly by as an especially exciting season when you use even a few of these ideas for your group or family fun.

FEBRUARY ACTIVITIES

◆

ARTS AND CRAFTS

◆ **Cutting Snowflakes**   *Ages 3 and up*

YOU WILL NEED:
    white paper on which you have drawn large circles
    scissors, 1 per child

METHOD:
    The children cut out their circles, and then fold them in half twice. They snip pieces from the edges and unfold.

SUGGESTIONS:
    1. You can use large round doilies instead of the white paper for pretty results with a minimum of cutting.
    2. Squares can be used instead of circles.
    3. Take the snowflakes to an elderly or ill person and tape them on their door or window for cheer.

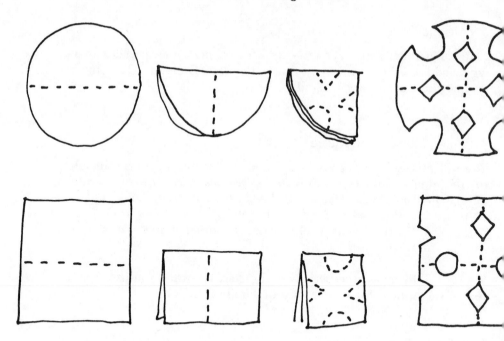

◆ Valentine Memories Tray

Ages 3 and up

YOU WILL NEED:
    small trays (solid color works best), 1 per child
    snapshots of group, or photos children have brought from home
    double-stick tape (sticky on both sides) or glue
    old paintings, drawings, cutouts, etc., done by the children on other
      occasions
    clear Contact paper

METHOD:
    Let each child arrange his snapshots on the tray, securing them with
tape or a dab of glue on the back side. Interesting shapes cut from
one of the child's paintings or other artwork add color. You cut the
clear Contact paper to fit the entire surface. Set it in place over the
tray for the child to press down. Smooth out the air bubbles.

VARIATIONS:
    Similar materials and technique can be used to decorate waste-
baskets, boxes, or canisters, or to make a hanging collage—a good
gift for any occasion.

◆ Whipping Snow
Ages 2 and up

A different experience in texture.

YOU WILL NEED:
1 cup water
¾ cup Ivory Snow
egg beater
mixing bowl
paper cups
dark colored construction paper, or brown paper cut from grocery
   bags, or pieces of sturdy colorful wrapping paper

METHOD:
While the children watch, pour just a small amount of water into the
Ivory Snow and beat, continuing to add water until the mixture has
the thick and creamy consistency of cake frosting. Give the children
paper cups of whipped "snow" and let them draw on the construction paper with their fingers. Some will "frost" the whole surface
with the whipped snow and then draw through it like finger paint.
Others will dab or smear smaller quantities.

VARIATION:
Have the children make a pretend birthday cake to celebrate someone's special day. Invert a one-pint cottage cheese container. Frost
with "snow." Sprinkle with sparkles. Stick in candles. Snow frosting
will gradually harden. Light candles and sing "Happy Birthday."

◆ Blot Mural
Ages 2½ and up

MATERIALS:
poster paint
paintbrushes
container of water (for rinsing brushes)
paper, preferably manila about 9 by 12 inches, 1 per child
strip of shelf paper or other large sheet, 3 to 4 feet long

METHOD:
Each child paints an abstract design in the color of her choice. While
it is wet, she blots it onto the mural paper, superimposing or slightly
overlapping it on other designs. Younger children may need your
help with the blotting.

◆ Foil Painting   *Ages 2 and up*

Hear the crackle as you paint.

YOU WILL NEED:
  aluminum foil strip, 14 inches long, 1 per child
  unprinted side of large brown grocery bag, 1 per child
  stapler
  tempera paint, 1 color for each child
  containers for paint, 1 per color
  brushes, 1 per color
  scissors

METHOD:
  Ahead of time: Cut the 14-inch lengths of foil. Cut unprinted sides
  from brown grocery bags. Staple each piece of foil onto a piece of
  brown paper. Pour paint into the containers.
  With the children: Let the children choose their color and paint on the
  foil, listening to the crackling sound as the brushes move back and
  forth. The children may trade paint containers and brushes to add
  another color to their work.

COOKING

◆ Antipasto   *Ages 3 and up*

Children will like this tasty gift from Italy.

YOU WILL NEED:
  Choice of:
    hard-boiled egg (wedges or slices)
    tomato (wedges or slices)
    green pepper, sliced
    radish (slash sides part way and drop in cold water to make a rose)
    ham or turkey slices
    canned tuna or salmon
    melon pieces
  paper platter
  paper plates
  serrated plastic knives
  serving spoon

METHOD:

Ahead of time: Prepare food up to the last step (cutting).

With the children: Talk about the word *antipasto*. It means "before the meal." It is something Italian people eat as an appetizer. Talk about how making food look pretty makes you want to eat it. Different colors and appealing arrangement make a difference. "Let's make our antipasto look pretty."

One child cuts egg, another tomato, another green pepper or melon, and so on. Someone can roll up cold cuts with or without melon inside. Pass the platter for each child to arrange his pieces in an attractive way. The children serve themselves on smaller plates.

◆ Soft Pretzels   *Ages 3 and up*

Too cold outside for a trip to the pretzel vendor? Make your own pretzels instead.

YOU WILL NEED (for 12 medium-sized pretzels):
  1½ cups lukewarm water (110 to 115° F)
  1 package yeast
  4 cups flour
  1 teaspoon salt
  1 tablespoon sugar
  1 egg, beaten
  coarse (kosher) salt or table salt
  large mixing bowl
  2 small bowls
  fork
  mixing spoon
  measuring cup and spoons
  foil or cookie sheet
  food brush
  margarine
  optional: candy thermometer for precise measurement of water
    temperature

METHOD:

Ahead of time: Preheat your oven to 450° F. (Child can fork-beat the egg in a small bowl and grease the foil pieces or cookie sheet.)

With the children: Child can measure water into a small bowl, and check temperature. Let someone sprinkle in the yeast and mix it until it is dissolved. Meanwhile, let others measure and mix the dry ingredients in a large bowl. Add the yeast mixture. You do the mixing. Let the dough rise for about 10 minutes.

Pull off about ¼ cup of dough for each person. Show the children how to knead and work their piece into a long snake (8 to 10 inches). On the cookie sheet or foil make a circle with the dough piece—let ends cross over each other. Then let the children make their own fat snakes, skinny snakes, and different-shaped pretzels. Paint pretzels with beaten egg and sprinkle with salt. Bake 20 minutes or until brown.

HINTS:
Flouring hands keeps stickiness under control. Younger children can enjoy this activity if dough is premixed and ready to shape.

◆ Aggression Cookies   *Ages 2 and up*

Pounding, squeezing, and mashing help work out winter blahs.

YOU WILL NEED (for 4 to 6 dozen cookies):
1½ cups brown sugar
1½ cups margarine
3 cups oatmeal
½ teaspoon baking soda
1½ cups flour
large bowl
measuring spoons and cup
mixing spoon or mixer
2 cookie sheets, ungreased
small glass
sugar, in dish
margarine

METHOD:
Ahead of time: Measure brown sugar, margarine, oatmeal, baking soda, and flour into a bowl and mix. Grease the bottom of a glass with margarine and dip it in sugar. Preheat the oven to 350° F.
With the children: Make sure all hands are washed thoroughly. Give each child a portion of dough. Children squeeze, beat, mash, knead. The more they do, the better the cookie will turn out. Form small balls (aim for ¾ to 1 inch—preschoolers' sizes vary). Place them on the cookie sheet and take turns pressing each cookie with the bottom of the glass. You may need to regrease and sugar the glass bottom. Bake about 10 minutes, depending on size. Cookies are done before browning.

DRAMATIC PLAY

◆ Phone Fun

Ages 3 and up

YOU WILL NEED:
Choice of:
toy phones
real phones (disconnected current models or discarded older ones)
soup cans attached to either end of long string
optional: tape recorder

METHOD:

Let the children show how they answer the telephone. Guide the activity by encouraging them to use appropriate language such as "Hello," "Who is calling?," "Just a minute please." Children may continue to talk on the phone. After each child has had a turn, tape and play back conversations.

Depending on how the parents of your group feel about it, you may choose to talk about emergencies. Show how to dial 0 or 911. Be sure to say "nine, one, one," *not* "nine, eleven" (in real emergencies children have wasted precious time searching for a nonexistent eleven on the telephone). Practice telling the family name and address on the phone.

◆ Hike in the House

Ages 2 and up

YOU WILL NEED:
sack lunch for each child

METHOD:

The children go for a "hike" through the house pretending that they are outside. Example: up the side of a mountain (up the steps), past a forest (the dining room chairs), and so on. Help children decide on a good spot for their picnic (by the workbench? in a bedroom?). Everyone sits in a circle to eat. After lunch, everyone cleans up scraps and papers, stuffs them into his bag, and hikes to a trash barrel for disposal. Promote some discussion of how a good camper leaves the site the way he found it and does not pollute picnic areas by leaving trash behind.

GAMES

◆ Buzzing Bees Fingerplay   *Ages 2 and up*

METHOD:

Repeat the verse below with the gestures two or three times by your-self, then repeat them with the children a few times.

VERSE:

"Here is a beehive. Where are the bees? [Make a fist.]
Hidden away where nobody sees.
Soon they come, creeping out of the hive.
One, two, three, four, five." [Release fingers one at a time.]

◆ Fishing with Magnets   *Ages 4 and up*

This activity is good practice for coordination.

YOU WILL NEED:

sticks (pencils will do), 1 per child
string
magnet(s) (strong horseshoe shape or with hole in center)
paper
scissors
paper clips
bucket or other large container

METHOD:

Ahead of time: Make one or more fishing rods by tying a stick to one end of a piece of string and a magnet to the other. Cut several fish shapes 2 to 3 inches long. Attach a paper clip to each fish.
With the children: Put the fish into the container. Children take turns seeing how many fish they can catch with the magnet.

VARIATION:

Fishing for Apples: Screw large cup hooks into the apples and tie an-other hook to the end of a line. Try to hook apples as they float in a tub of water.

◆ Huckle Buckle Beanstalk   *Ages 3 and up*

YOU WILL NEED:

Choose a small object to hide. Start the game by having the children cover their eyes while you put the object in a spot that is visible but not conspicuous. The children search around the room with their hands behind their backs, looking for a glimpse of the object. The minute they see it they look away and say "Huckle Buckle Beanstalk." The game continues until everyone has seen the object. The first to see the object is "it" next and rehides the object.

This is a quick game that can be done easily when there is a gap in time. For variety, you can change the object or room where you're playing.

MUSIC

◆ **Teapot Song and Dance**   *Ages 2 and up*

VERSE:

I'm a little teapot short and stout, [Point to self.]
Here is my handle, [Put one hand on hip.]
Here is my spout. [Direct one hand away from you with arm
   crooked at elbow.]
When I get all steamed up,
Here me shout,
Tip me over and pour me out. [Lean in direction of spout.]

SUGGESTION:

Sing the song until the children know it well, then practice the motions. Hum or play the song a second time and let the little teapots do a creative dance to just the music. For additional verse, see Appendix 2 (page 311).

◆ **Thumbkin**   *Ages 2 and up*

A musical fingerplay.

TUNE:

"Are You Sleeping?" ("Frère Jacques")

VERSE:

Where is Thumbkin? [Keep both hands behind back.]
Where is Thumbkin? [Keep both hands behind back.]
Here I am. [One hand appears with thumb up.]
Here I am. [Other hand appears with thumb up.]
How are you today, sir? [Wiggle right thumb.]
Very well I thank you. [Wiggle left thumb.]
Run away. [Put one hand behind back.]
Run away. [Put other hand behind back.]

Use other fingers: Pointer, tall one, ring man, pinky.

PHYSICAL EXERCISE

◆ Paper Punching Bag   *Ages 4 and up*

YOU WILL NEED:
medium-sized bags (paper or plastic)
old newspapers
string
scissors

METHOD:
Children "scrunch up" pieces of newspaper and stuff the bags. Tie
each bag securely shut with a piece of string long enough to hang
the bag within punching reach of the children. One or more bags
are hung and the children punch them until the bags break apart or
the children tire of the activity. Bags can be hung from a clothesline,
basement pipe, screw eye, or cup hook, or they can be secured to a
smooth ceiling with heavy tape.

This idea came from four-year-old Craig, who has done it several
times with friends. It has a surprising fascination and works off a lot
of energy.

◆ Shadow Partners   *Ages 2 and up*

Large muscle movement is the focus of this exercise game.

YOU WILL NEED:
favorite music

METHOD:
Each child picks a partner and moves to an area that has space for
movement. One child in the pair assumes the role of leader and the
other follows as shadow. The shadow children mimic their leading
partners as they bend, stretch, and twirl to the beat of the music.
The children take turns leading as they think up new ideas for
movement.

After doing this many times with the group, turn it into a performance by giving each pair of children a chance on "center stage."
Everyone enjoys watching as much as participating.

◆ Musical Friends*   *Ages 2 and up*

Share music in a happy, friendly way.

YOU WILL NEED:
  music

METHOD:
  Choose music to accompany the children as they move around the room in a variety of ways (dance, gallop, tiptoe, skip). Stop the music. When it stops, the preschoolers must greet the friend nearest them with a smile, "hello," hug, handshake, or giggle. Continue the music and begin the game again. Since both the greeting and movement are left up to the child, you will find the preschoolers observing others, imitating, inventing, and expanding the possibilities for happy greetings.

SCIENCE

◆ Salt Water Magic   *Ages 3 and up*

Observe the differences between salt water and fresh water.

YOU WILL NEED:
  2 quart jars
  2 drinking glasses
  water
  marker and 2 labels
  1 cup salt
  2 whole eggs (may be hard-boiled)
  2 ice cubes
  long-handled spoon

METHOD:
  First, experiment with the eggs. While the children watch, fill the jars with plain, fresh water. Have someone pour about ½ cup of regular salt into one of the jars. Someone can stir until the salt dissolves. Label the jar Salt. Say, "Let's put an egg in the jar of salt water. What does it do?" (It floats.) Then ask, "What happens when we put an egg in the fresh water?" (It sinks.) Talk with the children about the differences between salt water and fresh water. Perhaps someone will mention how it is easier to stay afloat in salt water at the seashore than in fresh lake water.

*From *Before the Basics*, Bev Bos (Turn-the-Page Press, Inc., 203 Baldwin Avenue, Roseville, CA 95678, 1983). Used with permission.

Using the drinking glasses, go through the same process, putting an ice cube instead of an egg in each glass. Have the children check from time to time to see that the ice really melts faster in the salt water. Talk about how salt is used in some places to melt ice on roads and sidewalks. (You might also mention that some places do not do this because of damage to the environment.)

◆ Birdseed Pictures in the Snow   *Ages 2 and up*

Walk in the park or your own backyard.

YOU WILL NEED:
    birdseed in plastic bag, 1 per each child

METHOD:
    Encourage the children to make designs in the snow by sprinkling birdseed—circles, letters, numbers, abstractions, faces. Later, birds and squirrels can dine on the designs.

◆ Magnifying Magic   *Ages 2 and up*

YOU WILL NEED:
    magnifying glasses, 1 per child (borrow extras if necessary)
    variety of objects to look at (examples: sandpaper, coins, tweed
        fabric, toothbrush, sugar)

METHOD:
    Give each child plenty of time to examine objects with the magnifying glass. Talk about the difference the glass makes and which objects they felt changed the most when magnified.

SUGGESTIONS:
    Another time, have the children explore other objects around the room. Go outside and investigate objects—bark, bricks, even insects.

STORYTELLING

◆ Tube Talk   *Ages 4 and up*

This is an old game played a new way.

YOU WILL NEED:
    cardboard tubes (from rolls of toilet paper, paper towels, or
        wrapping paper), 1 per child

METHOD:

Sit on the floor in a circle. Give each child a tube of equal length. Choose a child to start the game. She speaks through her tube into her neighbor's ear. The second child whispers what he heard through his own tube into the next child's ear. This continues until every child has had a turn and the message comes back to the first child. The fun is seeing if the message is the same or different. Give each child a chance to begin the circle secret. Experiment with different lengths of tubing.

TRIPS

◆ Visiting a Florist *Ages 3 and up*

A nearby florist will welcome little visitors during the quiet season between Christmas and Easter. A midwinter breath of spring!

METHOD:

Call ahead and plan with the florist for a visiting day. The children will love seeing and smelling flowers when it's still very much winter outside. They will also want to watch the florist make an arrangement and hear how the flowers travel to the shop and what kind of refrigerators help keep them fresh. You can also find elaborate floral displays in many supermarkets.

SUGGESTIONS:

If it is the right time, perhaps you could buy some white stones and narcissus bulbs to plant in paper cups when you get home (see page 95).

WOODWORKING

◆ Sawing Cardboard *Ages 3 and up*

This is a very good early sawing experience!

YOU WILL NEED:

cardboard pieces from corrugated cardboard boxes or Styrofoam
    packaging
hacksaw or coping saw
vise
masking or cellophane tape

METHOD:

Help the children put cardboard or Styrofoam into the vise. Let the children saw the cardboard or Styrofoam into pieces. They may then enjoy taping the pieces together to make abstract shapes.

SUGGESTIONS:

1. More sophisticated four-year-olds may enjoy sawing "windows" and "doors" from a cardboard box "house," using tape for hinges. (Boxes that major appliances come in are good for this.)

2. An exceptionally well-coordinated child may hold a cardboard or Styrofoam piece on a low table with a hand and knee, sawing with the other hand and forgetting the vise altogether.

MARCH

March Contents

◆

MARCH GUIDEPOSTS

◆

THINGS YOU CAN COLLECT

It is March! You and the children experience a growing sense of excitement. The sun is warmer, melting the snow more quickly after each new storm. Nature gives dozens of other reminders that there are warmer days to come. This month offers its own special set of collectibles.

Treasures under the Snow

For the sake of sheer whimsy, plan a trek with the children to find "treasures" under the melting snow. You will see fresh green things beginning to peep up. Unforeseen surprises will add spice to the hunt. Sharon may find an old mitten. Eric may emerge from behind a bush with a long lost Frisbee. A penny may appear in the gutter. This can be an exciting game for a playgroup collecting session.

Pussy Willow

Now is the time for you to cut a few pussy willow branches. Perhaps the "pussies" are already visible on the stalks. Have them ready so each child can take at least one sprig home to put in water and enjoy indoors.

Buds to Force

This is the month, too, to force some early blooms or greenery. A favorite, of course, is forsythia, because of its brilliant yellow blossoms.

Quince works well also. For that matter, almost any branch you see that has leaf buds can be snipped and encouraged to produce foliage in a glass of water. Explicit directions are in the March science section (page 197).

Bugs

Are you a biologist deep down? Pop a few early insects into a jar with holes punched in lid. Save for later examination indoors. Maybe you are equipped with an identification book. Children love to see the real thing and compare it with a picture. As spring nears, a variety of bugs can often be found in swarms jumping about on the snow in woodland areas.

Eggshells

Indoors, you can begin setting aside eggshells. Save whole ones, with the yolk painstakingly blown out (page 190), for egg painting and other decoration. For gift eggs that will last, try the Hand-Painted Eggs activity (page 190) as a seasonal project.

Easter or St. Patrick's Day Cookie Cutters

If the kitchen remains your favorite workshop for family and playgroup projects, it can be cookie time again. Find cutters in bunny and other Easter shapes, shamrocks for St. Patrick's day, flowers for spring. Keep in mind that the cutters are excellent for clay or playdough projects. What about dough tinted green for cutting out and drying a shamrock to take home to Dad?

REMEMBER THE FAMILIAR

Signs of Spring

The neighbor couple on their daily stroll, members of many classrooms, the reporter for the local paper—everyone is looking for signs of spring! See what your preschoolers notice: crocus blooms, a robin, leaf buds, a great big worm. On your return from a walk you could let the children review their finds as you print their words on a piece of paper. Read their "story" out loud to them. Print small copies so each child has a story to take home.

Mixed Puzzles

Looking for a new quiet time idea? Scramble a few of your often used preschool puzzles. Some of the children will love the challenge of sorting out the jumble and assembling the pieces.

Outside Play Equipment

It is not too soon to put up the outside play equipment. The first days of climbing and swinging after the long winter are especially exciting. Have you been to the local playground lately to test the slides or tunnels?

March Winds

After an invigorating outdoor playtime you might read a poem or two about windy March days. Talk about what the wind is like. It is . . . "cold," "loud," "strong," "fast." It makes . . . "the trees bend," "dry leaves rustle," "cheeks pink."

St. Patrick's Day

Mid-March brings St. Patrick's Day, when everyone is Irish! Remind the parents to let the children wear something green. *You* wear something green. Have green snacks—green canned drink, green spread on crackers. Do projects in green. Make green hats. Decorate green placemats. Leaf through each month's activities for others that can be "turned green."

Seasonal Music and Other Songs

Put on a few records of sprightly Irish music to dance to or as background music for snacks and projects. Then wind up singing a nursery rhyme just for fun.

Early Easter

If this is a year when Easter and Passover are celebrated early, turn to April's activities for special ideas, or try the Hand-Painted Eggs project in this chapter (page 190).

March *does* have a great deal to offer. Pick your favorites and enjoy them with your family or preschoolers.

MARCH ACTIVITIES

◆

ARTS AND CRAFTS

◆ **Follow-the-Dot Sewing**   *Ages 3 and up*

Forerunner of following numbered dots to make pictures.

YOU WILL NEED:
    hole punch
    oaktag or posterboard, one 4½- by 6-inch piece per child
    long shoelaces, 1 lace per child

METHOD:
    Ahead of time: Prepunch a number of holes in each card.
    With the children: The children "sew" from hole to hole with shoe-
    laces, making abstract designs. You can unlace the cards and let the
    children exchange them for more "sewing," or pass out crayons for
    drawing dot to dot.

◆ **Painted Burlap Gifts**   *Ages 4 and up*

Burlap-covered wastebaskets, pencil holders, and mail holders are
useful gifts that showcase the child's art.

YOU WILL NEED:
    orange juice cans for pencil holders
    inexpensive mail holders or wastepaper baskets
    enough burlap or burlap Contact paper to cover the items you are
        using
    glue and brush
    scissors

single-edge razor
damp cloth
brightly colored braid, enough to finish around the top and bottom
   of the items
poster paint, mixed to consistency of thick cream
paintbrushes

METHOD:

Ahead of time: Cut burlap piece a little larger than you think you
need for covering an item. Cover the surface of the item with glue
and press the burlap on. It is difficult to cut the burlap to exact size,
but once glued to the object it can be trimmed easily with a single-
edge razor. Use a damp cloth to wipe away excess glue. Complete
one container for each child.

With the children: Let the children paint free-hand designs on the covered containers with several bright colors. Encourage children to keep paint colors separate to avoid a muddy effect. When the paint dries, help them measure and glue the braid around the tops and bottoms of the objects.

◆ Resist Painting

Ages 3 and up

YOU WILL NEED:

white paper, 9 by 12 inches, 1 per child
crayons
poster paint (black or other dark color is most effective)
paintbrushes

METHOD:

The children draw with crayons, making marks by pressing very hard, then paint over all marks and bare area. The crayon will resist the paint, giving an interesting effect. Four-year-olds bear down with crayons more successfully than younger children, with more eye-catching results.

SUGGESTIONS:

1. Use bright-colored crayons to make autumn leaves, then paint with blue or black to get effect of cold autumn day.
2. Use white crayons to make snowflakes, snowmen, and so on, then use black paint for wintry night effect.
3. Create underwater scenes with bright-colored crayons for fish and plants, and blue or green paint.

◆ Shaving Cream Painting

Ages 2 and up

YOU WILL NEED:

spray can of shaving cream
tabletop covered with plastic cloth (A dark-colored cloth makes a
    particularly good contrast for the white cream.)

METHOD:

Help children spray cream on the table. The children draw pictures in the cream with their fingers and hands.

VARIATION:

If you have a plastic laminate tabletop, children can work directly on the table surface. You can also have each child work on a plastic tray.

◆ Hand-Painted Eggs   *Ages 3 and up*

These sturdy gift eggs will last a lifetime.

YOU WILL NEED:
   white eggs, 1 per child
   scissors (small with pointed tip)
   needle
   quick-drying plaster
   teaspoon
   paintbrushes
   tempera or acrylic paints
   containers (margarine or deli tubs work well)
   optional: clear acrylic spray paint

METHOD:
   Several days ahead of time: Using the scissor point, poke a ⅛-inch hole in one end of the egg. Turn the egg over and make a slightly larger hole in the opposite end. Insert a needle to break the yolk and stir the contents. Hold finger and thumb over the holes and shake. Place your mouth over the smaller hole and blow the egg contents into a bowl.

   With scissors, carefully cut an oval piece, about 1½ inches long, from the side of each blown egg. Mix plaster, enough to fill all the eggs, according to package directions. Spoon plaster into the eggs. Allow several days for drying.

   Fill containers with tempera or acrylic paints.
   With the children: Sit eggs plaster side down. Children will then be able to paint the eggs without rolling and cracking problems. After the paint has dried you can seal the surface with acrylic spray. This is a preschool gift to parents that will last. To make the presentation even more special, put the eggs in a small basket with a little shredded paper grass.

COOKING

◆ Bread Shapes   *Ages 2½ and up*

YOU WILL NEED:
   bread dough (fresh from a bakery or frozen from the supermarket)
   large bowl
   paper plates
   greased cookie sheet
   plastic bag, food storage size

METHOD:

Ahead of time: Defrost dough if it is frozen. Let it rise in a bowl. Preheat oven to 400° F.

With the children: Give each child a chunk of dough the size of a snowball. On plate knead and create shapes—bunnies, baskets to suit the season, or whatever strikes the whim. Place on cookie sheet and bake until brown, about 20 minutes (smaller shapes will take less time, fatter objects more). When cool, bag to take home.

◆ Shaking and Baking Chicken

Ages 2 and up

YOU WILL NEED:

1 package of coating for baking chicken by the shaker-bag method
chicken drumsticks, enough for the group
baking pan

METHOD:

Allow each child to shake one or two drumsticks of her own and to place them in the baking pan. Bake at 400° F for 40 to 50 minutes and serve as part of the children's lunch.

VARIATION:

Dip skinned, boned chicken breasts in Italian salad dressing. Shake them in a bag containing plain or seasoned bread crumbs. Bake as directed above.

◆ Dip 'n' Munch Veggies

Ages 2 and up

YOU WILL NEED:

½ cup small-curd cottage cheese
4 tablespoons grated cheese
½ teaspoon dill
1 teaspoon Worcestershire sauce
optional: ½ teaspoon salt
cup-up vegetables of your choice, for example:

zucchini	cherry tomatoes
cucumber	green or red bell peppers
broccoli	cauliflower

small mixing bowl and spoon
measuring spoons
serrated plastic knives or french fry cutters
cutting board
paper plates

METHOD:

Ahead of time: In a small bowl, mix and mash cheeses, dill, and Worcestershire sauce. Prepare vegetables: wash, peel, and cut partially where necessary.

With the children: The children cut the veggies into bite-size pieces and put them on plates. Everyone dips them into the cheese mixture and munches.

DRAMATIC PLAY

◆ Midwinter Day at the Beach   *Ages 2 and up*

This is an indoor, down-in-the basement pursuit. Apartments dwellers, clear the decks.

YOU WILL NEED:

Any or all of these:
  beach bags
  towels
  sack lunches
  pails with shells or stones
  tub or plastic paddling pool filled with sand, containers and
    digging equipment (shovels, scoops, spoons)
  painter's plastic drop cloth (to put under sand tub)
  inflatable boat or cardboard carton(s) with broomstick mast and
    pillowcase sail

METHOD:

Ahead of time: Ask the children to bring some of the supplies listed above and to wear summer attire. Prepare the props and anything else you can think of to add to the atmosphere. Tape a big, cheery cutout of the sun to your front door.

METHOD:

Play-act "A Summer Day at the Beach." Include a picnic in the boat or on beach towels.

◆ Space Travel Play   *Ages 2 and up*

A big hit with preschoolers.

YOU WILL NEED:

space record (A good one is *Storytelling, Sing and Learn Macmillan Program,* New York: Macmillan Book Clubs Inc., 1989.)

or

blank tape and tape recorder (Create your own space drama.)
optional: 1 or more space capsules (box, baby bathtub, large animal carrier)

METHOD:

Ahead of time: To make your own tape, record a series of space directives and comments such as:
"Enter space capsule."
"Fasten seat belt."
"Check controls."
"Count down. (Nine . . . eight . . . seven . . . etc.) Takeoff."
"Look out the window at the [planets, earth etc.]"
"Get ready for moon landing."
"Open the capsule door."
"Walk in space."
"Duck a shooting star."
"Collect moon rocks."
"Return to your spaceship."
"Buckle up for return trip."
"Hurry, a burning comet is headed straight for us."
"Steer clear. Another spaceship is in the way."
With the children: Children can lie on the floor pretending to be in a capsule or use the space capsules you have provided. Play the record or tape which will determine the beginning and end to the make-believe.

SUGGESTION:

Leave the tape or record available for further play when the spirit moves someone. If you used the record, maybe the children will enjoy creating their own original space drama on tape with your help. Imagination may take them to a new planet to visit space creatures or might include activities at the space center, photographers, and spectators. Add props as children extend the fantasy.

GAMES

◆ Beach Stone Games

Ages 3 and up

YOU WILL NEED:
stones

METHOD:

Beach stones are fun to play with, touch, and sort. In water their colors become more brilliant. They are a pleasant reminder of summer and can be the start of many simple and effective games. Be sure you have an ample and varied supply for each child.

SUGGEST:

counting games	sorting by color
big, bigger, biggest	small, smaller, smallest
big, little	hiding games
designs with stones	guessing games (Which one is missing?, and so on)

Let the children see if they can work out a simple game pattern from any one of these ideas. They may want to include others or play by themselves. Have a pan of water available. Preschoolers will have a good time just putting the stones in and playing. No throwing games, please. Make it clear to the group that throwing stones is against all rules, for obvious reasons.

◆ Table Hockey   *Ages 4 and up*

This game is a rainy-day invention of two seven-year-old boys.

YOU WILL NEED:
cardboard tubes from paper toweling, 1 per child
1 plastic lid
a large table

METHOD:
Two players position themselves at opposite ends of the table and begin shooting the plastic lid back and forth, using the tubes as "hockey sticks." For preschoolers the object of the game is to see how long the children can keep the lid from going off the table. If there is room at the table more children can join in at one time.

◆ Clothespin Drop   *Ages 4 and up*

Teaches eye-hand coordination.

YOU WILL NEED:
clothespins, pencils, crayons, or other slender objects
large plastic peanut butter jar, empty oatmeal container, or any
    similar container

METHOD:
Children take turns standing over the container and trying to drop the clothespins or other objects in.

MUSIC

◆ Music Boxes—Play and Listen *Ages 2 and up*

YOU WILL NEED:
any variety of music boxes or musical gadgets:
musical stuffed toy
musical teapot
baby's pull-cord music box
musical Christmas tree
small boxes with revolving figures on top
jewel box
old-fashioned, crank-type music box

METHOD:
Let the children wind, turn or pull to make the music boxes play . . .
one box and one child at a time.

SUGGESTIONS:
1. This is especially fun if you do it while having cocoa together out
of a musical tea- or coffee-pot.
2. You may request ahead of time that each child bring a musical
object or toy if he has one.

◆ Hot Cross Buns *Ages 3 and up*

Teaches rhythm—long and short values.

METHOD:
Have the children rhythmically chant the poem "Hot Cross Buns." It
should have the following long and short values.

Hot cross buns	= short, short, long	= ♩♩♩
Hot cross buns	= short, short, long	= ♩♩♩
One-a-penny, two-a-penny	= very quickly	= ♪♪♪♪ ♪♪♪♪
Hot cross buns.	= short, short, long	= ♩♩♩

After they've practiced chanting, have the children chant and clap
simultaneously.

PHYSICAL EXERCISE

◆ Circle Game   *Ages 3 and up*

YOU WILL NEED:
string or masking tape

METHOD:
Make a circle on the floor with string or tape. Tape works well even on carpeting. Everyone gathers around the circle. Children take turns saying what to do—"Run around the circle," "hop," "jump," "crawl around." Everyone follows the directions until you call on another child for a new idea of what to do.

VARIATIONS:
The circle game lends itself to music activities. For example: marching music, hopping music, music that makes you think of something special can be used as children move around the circle.

◆ Aerobics   *Ages 2 and up*

YOU WILL NEED:
brisk exercise music

METHOD:
Children warm up, exercise rapidly, and slowly wind down during a 5 to 10 minute exercise session while you play the part of your favorite exercise coach. Cheer your preschoolers on as they move. Make them aware of their heartbeats by helping them find and feel their pulse. Talk about how rapid the beat is as they exercise faster. Explain how they are pumping blood through their bodies and that this is important to their good health. Show them how to exercise and at the same time breathe in and let out air.
Routines appropriate for preschoolers include
   warm-up:
      stretch arms in punching, boxing motion (upward and
        forward)
      body bends
      windmill toe touching
   rapid exercise:
      jogging in place
      jumping jacks
   wind-down:
      slow down jogging pace

bend and stretch
rotate head in a circle
relax limbs

SCIENCE

◆ Forcing Buds

Ages 2 and up

YOU WILL NEED:

any bush or tree that has buds on its branches (pussy willow,
forsythia, rhododendron)

METHOD:

Take a walk with the children to look for buds. Clip enough for each
child to have a sprig or two to take home. Place in a container with
water until the children are ready to leave. Send sprigs home with
instructions for care—"Put in container of water in sunny spot.
Watch buds open."

◆ Sound Matching

Ages 2 and up

Listen carefully.

YOU WILL NEED:

A selection of noise-making objects such as:
squeak toy
bell

    stove timer
    alarm clock
    toys with sirens or clickers (push and pull toys, cars)
    musical instruments with no mouth piece (cymbals, triangle, drum,
      xylophone, piano, guitar)
    tape recorder and tape

METHOD:

Ahead of time: Collect enough noisemakers for each child to have
one. Tape their sounds, leaving a few seconds of silence between
each new sound.

With the children: Spread the noise-making objects in front of the
children. Play the tape. Let each child take a turn matching an object
to a sound on the tape. Each child will want to handle her noise-
maker and create the sound to check whether it matches the sound
on tape. Ask the children to suggest other objects that make sounds
so you can do more collecting, recording, and game playing.

STORYTELLING

◆ **Stamp Pad Story Books**   *Ages 3 and up*

YOU WILL NEED:

    rubber stamps in a variety of shapes (roller stamps are fun)
    water-base ink pads in assorted colors
    paper (computer paper works well)
    fine-point markers
    stapler

METHOD:

Encourage the children to experiment as they stamp out picture stories. Some discover that repeating and overlapping the same stamp
gives an appearance of motion. Markers can be used to fill in detail.
For example, a spider stamp and a marker can create a spider and
its web. Some children will produce one or two pages; others may do
more. If some children seem interested, let them dictate a story for
you to print on their pages. Staple pages of the "book" together.

SUGGESTION:

Use a copy machine, if available, to reproduce enough copies so
every child has a complete set of the groups' books.

VARIATIONS:

Easy Substitute Ink Pad: Place folded paper toweling or sponge in a
pie tin and soak with tempera paint.

Homemade Stamps: Cut shapes in relief from a halved potato by pressing a small cookie cutter into the flat cut surface of the potato and cutting away the outside edges with a knife.

TRIPS

◆ Ride on a Train (Bus, Subway, Streetcar)   *Ages 2 and up*

METHOD:
Choose a point of departure, a destination, and a point of return that fit into your time schedule. At the destination, you might stop for an ice cream treat, but the real point is the ride itself.

DISCUSS AS YOU GO:
1. Schedules: the idea that the bus or train comes and goes at a special time.
2. Fare: a ticket must be purchased or money put in a slot (children can do this).
3. Conductor (or driver): collects the fare, helps passengers with any problem that might arise.
4. Station (or stop): where passengers get on and off; may be marked by a building, a shelter, or simply a sign, as in the case of many bus stops.

WOODWORKING

◆ Filing   *Ages 3 and up*

This activity generates all sorts of excitement. "Look at the pile of sawdust!" "See the wood getting smaller and smaller!"

MATERIALS:
file, fairly coarse (10-inch combination shoe rasp is very good)
scrap wood
vise or C-clamp

METHOD:
Demonstrate the use of the file by moving it back and forth on an edge of the wood. Let the children take turns experimenting.

APRIL

April Contents

◆

APRIL GUIDEPOSTS

◆

THINGS YOU CAN COLLECT

Perhaps this month is bringing more showers than flowers when you had anticipated that first taste of true spring weather. Springlike activities can be planned for both indoors and out. Rain need not dampen anyone's enthusiasm. Put on your happy face! Think spring and collect for spring.

White-Shelled Eggs

Maybe March slipped by without your collecting a single eggshell. When you use eggs in cooking, save the blown-out or cracked shells. Hard-boil a batch of white eggs in vinegared water and tuck them in the refrigerator for later dyeing projects.

If you are both ambitious and artistic, use your imagination for painting or further embellishing fragile hollow shells to hang on bare branches for an egg tree. Use your handiwork as a centerpiece for a special playgroup Easter party and for your own family's enjoyment.

April offers other opportunities for dipping into March egg projects (pages 184–190). Take time this month to let the children crush broken eggshells and glue them to various surfaces for primitive mosaics. Shells can be colored by you or the children either before or after the gluing, for varying effects. Markers, watercolors, and crayons all offer means of ornamentation. Do you envision results to rival intricate Roman design? A few pieces affixed to a surface with a dash of bright color represents work ambitious enough for the preschool set.

Simply dyeing hard-boiled eggs is a perennial favorite. Use the kits available at the grocer's or the food coloring already handy in your kitchen cupboard. One trick is to crayon a name or design before spoon-dipping the egg in food coloring and water. The result is very effective. Maybe one of the small fry would like to see what happens if you mix different dye colors together. What a perfect time to learn more about colors with a little controlled experimentation.

Stickers

If dyeing seems too messy an undertaking, whip out crayons (Cray Pas are most colorful) or stickers for a tidier means of achieving colorful results. The stickers will lend a pretty decoupage effect. Some youngsters may enjoy seeing their very own name or initial on an egg. Alphabet stickers or crayons can turn that trick most successfully.

You will want to include the seasonal holiday theme in your sticker supply. Have an assortment of bunnies, chicks, and the like for making cards, putting on packages, or dressing up plain napkins and paper cups for a special holiday party.

One helpful hint to remember is that preschoolers find the peel-and-stick variety of sticker easier to use. Licking a sticker without removing the glue can be tricky business for some children.

Cotton Balls

Set aside some cotton balls for this season's projects, too. The fuzzy round tufts can make a bunny appear on almost anything! Your preschoolers will take delight in creating a picture of bunnies hiding in the grass—an effect easily achieved on drawing paper with a few quick strokes of green crayon for grass and several dots of glue atop which the youngsters pop their cotton balls. "See, the bunnies couldn't hide their tails, so we can count how many are hiding in each picture!"

Tuna Cans

If you save enough tuna cans and cover them with felt, you can help the children make three-dimensional bunnies. Lay the cans flat. A cotton ball placed on one side of a can makes a bunny tail. On the opposite side, across from the cotton tail, face and whiskers can be added with paper, felt, markers or any combination of materials. Above the face place paper ears and presto! You have a bunny that can double as a jellybean container.

Baby Leaves

If that spring fever weather you had hoped for does come along, you can have a breath of fresh air with your group as you go out to inspect the green mist wrapping the trees and discover tiny, fragile leaves, which will grow into the sturdy leaves of summer. Talk about how they will mature. Point out how you all saw leaf buds on these very same trees during your midwinter walks. Let everyone take a sprig to show Mom or Dad. Make a collection to press in a heavy book when you return from your walk. Miniature oak, maple, and other leaves, and a few tiny pressed flowers can be put under Contact paper to make bookmarks, cards, a small hanging, or other projects for now or later.

REMEMBER THE FAMILIAR

April Showers

What child doesn't love raindrops and puddles? Bundle up in weatherproof clothing, pull out gaily colored umbrellas—giant sized black ones, too—and set out in small groups for some puddle jumping and maybe even a little tricycle riding in the rain.

As you are enjoying your wet weather spree, someone may notice how the once-dead winter ground is now covered with a haze of green. Take a minute to talk about how rain helps things grow, and how warmer weather continues to bring more things to life.

Somehow certain children lose all sense of perspective when confronted with a puddle. Your outing could well turn into an impromptu splash party. Be prepared with some extra dry clothing for the children. In spite of rain gear someone will have managed to get thoroughly soaked! Be ready, too, with cups of soup or cocoa to warm the memory of good fun.

The rainy day is the perfect one for drawing rain pictures or making "drip" pictures. Some children might have stories they would like to tell about their rain pictures. If someone does several papers, staple them together and show the resulting "rain book" to the others. The colorful pictures may even lead to making a poem together about colored rain. You can be the secretary and write it down. This would be the time to play a little "rain" music as a background while you do your projects. Learn a rain song together or read the group a selection of rain poetry.

Easter Egg Hunt

Everyone loves an Easter egg hunt. Supply your preschooler with a bag for collecting. Quart vegetable and fruit baskets or even small pails made from thoroughly cleaned liquid bleach bottles (see May collecting ideas) are equally useful. Fill each with paper grass. The same containers will double for carrying the results of the egg dyeing or a nature hunt.

Have your little ones seek colored hard-boiled eggs that you have concealed. For extra appeal, send them on a quest for jellybeans tucked in the grass or treat-filled plastic eggs that you have buried in the sandbox. Remember to hide the eggs in a partially visible way if they are spread over a wide area.

Before the hunt begins, state a few simple rules. Set limits so all the children will end up with an equal quantity of booty. You do not want to be confronted by one triumphant preschooler determinedly guarding his own vast hoard while the others wail that they did not get their share. One solution is to tell them what their quota will be. When a child finds his allotment, he proceeds to help someone else who is having difficulty.

If the weather is not balmy or dry enough for an outdoor hunt, simply switch operations to the confines of the house.

Playdough and Clay at Passover and Easter

If you lacked time to prepare something as elaborate as an egg hunt, the old standbys, playdough or clay, can lend themselves to seasonal activities. What about making "eggs" from the colored materials to put in Easter baskets, or readying for a pretend Passover feast by shaping matzos.

Earth Day

Celebrate the wonders of our Earth and its preservation. Play "America the Beautiful." Pull out Pete Seeger's rendition of the "Russian Lullaby." Sing "This Land is Your Land."

Turn to Bill Peet's books *Farewell to Shady Glade, Wump World,* and *Knats of Knotty Pine,* (Boston: Houghton Mifflin, 1966, 1970, 1975 respectively) that speak to the protection of this planet in gentle and amusing ways. *The Little House* by Virginia Lee Burton (Boston: Houghton Mifflin, 1942) is an old favorite that delivers similar messages simply.

Enjoy these first warm sunny days. April suggests myriad exciting possibilities for fun with your preschoolers. Turn rainy days into indoor and outdoor adventures as you bid goodbye to winter's final remnants and welcome spring's first signs.

APRIL ACTIVITIES

◆

ARTS AND CRAFTS

◆ **Drawing from Life**   *Ages 4 and up*

Increase powers of observation.

YOU WILL NEED:
  crayons
  paper, 9 by 12 inches
  a familiar object with basic shape and color. For a first experience
    choose something round, such as:
      apple   orange
      ball   balloon
  (If everyone has one object of her own to keep touching the activity
  will be more successful.)

METHOD:
  Let everyone hold their object. Talk together about its roundness or
  straightness. Talk about its color. Put the object in the center of the
  table. Give out art materials and let the children draw it. Let them
  make more than one drawing on the paper. Encourage them to
  make their drawings big.
  After the discussion, let your artists "do their own thing." A child
  may simply have an orange-colored scribble for her orange, but at
  least she understands the "orangeness" of the fruit, if not its shape.
  Lend importance to the finished product by printing a title
  ("Oranges") and artist's name on it. Mount on a larger colored sheet.

◆ May Day Baskets

YOU WILL NEED:

  paper plates, 1 per child
  ribbon, about 9 inches per child
  scissors
  real or artificial flowers and choice of lollipops, sticks of gum,
     messages
  stapler or tape

METHOD:

  The children fold the plates in half. You put a slit in each plate and
  tape or staple the basket shut above the slit. The children put ribbon
  through the slit to make a handle. You tie bows for the children
  while they insert flowers into the edges of the basket. If necessary,
  use the stapler to make the flowers more secure.

◆ Torn Paper Rainbow

Ages 2 and up

This April Showers activity involves teamwork: tearing, sorting, and sticking.

YOU WILL NEED:

   construction paper in six or more different colors (Scraps are fine.
      You need the equivalent of about twelve 8½- by 12-inch sheets.)
   paste
   pencil
   posterboard or paper, large poster size
   sorting containers, 1 per color (shoeboxes, pie tins, etc.)

METHOD:

   Have the children tear the paper into smaller pieces of random size
   and sort them into the containers according to color. Then put the
   poster board on the table. You lightly pencil in a series of large rainbow arcs. Help the children decide which color to use first and have
   them fill in one of the arcs by pasting paper pieces. They will tear
   the paper into smaller pieces when necessary. Choose the next color
   and complete the next arc the same way. Children can leave and
   return to this project throughout their playgroup day and finish another day if time runs out. Some will do a lot, others only a little.
   The rainbow results delight everyone and add a bright spot on gray
   April days.

◆ Glossy Pastels

Ages 2 and up

Soft colors dry to a smooth and shiny glaze.

YOU WILL NEED:

   can of condensed milk
   food coloring
   small paintbrushes, 1 per child
   white construction paper, 1 sheet per child
   small containers for paint, 1 per child

METHOD:

   Ahead of time: Mix different colors using 3 tablespoons of condensed
   milk to 1 to 2 drops of food coloring. Give each child a container
   with one color. Replenish children's containers as they work.
   With the children: As the children paint their designs on the white
   paper, encourage them to exchange colors and brushes for variety.
   Some will notice that as they move their brushes from paint to paper
   paint drizzles and pools, making the design even more interesting.
   The results give a feeling of springtime, perfect as the Easter and
   Passover seasons near.

◆ Tissue Paper Flowers   *Ages 3 and up*

A festive decoration and a thoughtful gift.

YOU WILL NEED:
  pipe cleaners, generous supply
  pile of colored tissue paper (can be bought at craft stores in precut
    squares)
  florists' tape
  optional: doilies or May Day Basket (page 209)

METHOD:
  Ahead of time: Cut tissue paper into 6-inch squares or circles. Precut
  florists' tape to the length of the pipe cleaners.
  With the children: Show the children how to poke a pipe cleaner
  through the center of a piece of tissue paper and gather or squeeze
  the paper to the center. Help them start the florists' tape at the base
  of the flower and twist it along most of the length of the pipe cleaner
  to hold the flower in place and create the look of a stem. Children
  who make several flowers may stick them through a doily or May
  Day basket to create a bouquet. Green tissue paper leaves can also be
  added to complete the flower arrangement.

COOKING

◆ Orange Julian   *Ages 2 and up*

YOU WILL NEED (for three 8-ounce or six 4-ounce servings):
  ¼ cup honey
  ½ cup milk
  ½ cup water
  ⅓ cup orange juice concentrate
  ½ teaspoon vanilla
  1 tray ice cubes
  blender
  measuring cups and spoons
  small paper cups

METHOD:
  Ahead of time: Premeasure ingredients. Keep in separate containers.
  With the children: Take turns putting ingredients into the blender
  starting with ice. Blend. Everyone loves to push the button. Serve
  and sip.

◆ Peanut Butter Roll-Around

Ages 2 and up

Big balls, small balls, crooked balls.

YOU WILL NEED:
  1 cup peanut butter
  1 tablespoon butter or margarine
  ¾ cup nonfat dry milk
  mixing bowl and spoon (or mixer)
  1 cup graham cracker crumbs
  plastic or paper bowls

METHOD:
  Ahead of time: Mix peanut butter, butter, and dry milk. Arrange separate bowls of dough and crumbs for each child.
  With the children: Roll the dough into small balls. Roll the balls in cracker crumbs. Place them in a bowl for serving. Refrigerate leftovers in a sealed container.

◆ What's Shakin' Butter

Ages 2 and up

YOU WILL NEED:
  ⅓ cup heavy cream
  large baby food jar with lid
  bowl of cold water
  crackers
  plastic knives

METHOD:
  Pour the cream into the jar and screw the lid on tight. The children sit in a circle and take turns shaking until a butter ball separates from the liquid. Rinse the butter in water. Spread it on crackers. Delicious!

SUGGESTIONS:
  1. Add your choice of herbs or sprouts.
  2. You may want to keep two or three jars in action at once.

DRAMATIC PLAY

◆ Let's Play Veterinarian

Ages 2 and up

This is very popular with the preschoolers.

YOU WILL NEED:
  table and chair

signs (VET, OPEN, CLOSED)
stuffed animals
doctor's supplies (white coat, rubber gloves, mask, stethoscope,
    gauze, scissors)
optional: pen and pencil for appointments, telephone, doctor's bag
    equipped for house calls

METHOD:

Ahead of time: Ask each child to bring an injured or sick stuffed animal from home. Choose the best area for a vet's office. Place the
table, chair, and doctor's supplies in this space. Hang the signs.
With the children: Children take turns role-playing vet or owner of an
animal. They will come up with all sorts of imaginative ideas for
more vet play.

◆ Shadow Play   *Ages 4 and up*

YOU WILL NEED:

lamp with 100- or 150-watt clear light bulb
                or
slide projector without slides
clear wall space or screen
stick puppets (greeting card or storybook pictures stapled to straws)

shelf paper
masking tape
markers or crayons

METHOD:

Ahead of time: Make simple stick puppets: Staple straws to figures cut
from cards or dismantled old story books. Choose shapes that will
make good silhouettes. Set up the light or projector so there is an
area for shadow play between the light and a clear wall.

With the children: Let the children experiment with the puppets, casting shadows on the wall. Tape paper to the wall. Have the children
use markers to create a very simple mural that shows a few roads,
houses, trees, and other scenery. They will enjoy taking their
shadow friends for walks down the roads, into woods, and for visits
to the different houses.

GAMES

◆ Water Play   *Ages 2 and up*

YOU WILL NEED:

large container (plastic dishpan, large cooking pot, baby's bathtub,
old tire cut in half horizontally)
water
water toys such as:

toy boats	plastic containers
funnel	baster
paper or plastic cups	sponge

optional: plastic aprons (also excellent for painting activities)

METHOD:

Fill the container with water. Place it where spills won't matter—for
example, near a drain hole in the cellar floor or even in the bathtub
where children can play two at a time. Let the children play! This is
a great activity after a messy art project. Put a little soap in the water
and children get clean while playing.

◆ Back in Order   *Ages 3 and up*

Children find this memory game appealing.

YOU WILL NEED:

3 to 4 interesting objects.
(toy car, dice, crayon, animal figure, game piece)

METHOD:

Line up three or four objects on the floor. Choose one child to leave the room while you or another child rearrange the objects. Ask the first child to return and put the objects in their original order. Play until each child has had a turn.

SUGGESTIONS:

It is good to begin this with familiar large objects. Start with just three and work up to more as the group seems ready. Sometimes it might be appropriate to choose seasonal objects to play the game with: pumpkins, pine cones, and so on.

MUSIC

◆ Colorful Dancing   *Ages 2 and up*

YOU WILL NEED:

colorful scarves, 1 per child
          or
crepe paper streamers (3-foot pieces of several colors, stapled
    together), 1 set per child
music (tape, piano, your choice)
stapler
optional: small plates (Paper streamers stapled to a plate are a little
    easier to hold.)

METHOD:

Before playing the music, give each child a scarf or paper streamers and let them try out body movements that make their colors dance. Once the music begins you will find that with something in their hands preschoolers become less self-conscious and move freely with an amazing degree of imagination. The result is colorful, fun, and good exercise on an indoor day. Take the scarves or streamers outside on a windy day. No music is really needed, but if you wish you can take a tape player along.

◆ Familiar Tunes with New Words   *Ages 3 and up*

Improvising words for familiar tunes captures children's spontaneity and allows them to make a song their very own.

METHOD:

Have the children sing a familiar song, replacing the words with their own creations. For example, "Row, Row, Row Your Boat" was quickly changed by Laurie to:

"Catch, catch, catch a frog.
Chase him round the yard.
Under leaves and hidden streams,
Catching frogs is hard."

Improvising with music can be used to describe, give directions, be silly, share thoughts, and express feelings. Children really enjoy it.

PHYSICAL EXERCISE

◆ Ball Toss Game   *Ages 4 and up*

This fun activity will encourage eye-hand coordination.

YOU WILL NEED:
 rubber ball, preferably large
 1 or more cartons, laundry baskets, or other containers

METHOD:
 Line the boxes up varying distances from a point where the children have been told to stand. Children take turns throwing the ball, trying to get it into a container. It is "extra special" to get the ball into the box that is farthest away. You can move the point where the children stand farther and farther back to test and increase their skill.

◆ Preschooler's Hopscotch   *Ages 3 and up*

Use up lots of energy in a controlled way.

YOU WILL NEED:
 masking tape
 chalk
 playing piece (coin, bottle cap, or chip)
 note: Hopscotch sets with vinyl playing surfaces are available in toy
  stores.

METHOD:
 Ahead of time: Use masking tape indoors or chalk outdoors to draw a playing grid about 8 feet by 4 feet, divided into eight squares 2 feet by 2 feet.
 With the children: Have the children line up at the end of the grid. When it is his turn, a child will throw the playing piece into a box. He will hop, skip, or jump into the box, lean over and pick up the

piece, and throw it into another box. His turn will last until he has been in all the boxes.

Preschoolers love going through the motions of this game on a very simple level. Rules for scoring and winning are not part of the game for them. They focus on the toss of the playing piece and on having a chance to hop, jump, or skip into all the boxes. Each child works on improving his gross motor skills with each new turn.

◆ Who Changed the Motion?   *Ages 3 and up*

Any number of children can play this guessing game.

METHOD:

Everyone sits on the floor. You explain the rules: "One of you will be 'IT' and leave the room. Someone else will be chosen to lead the group doing some motions. Here are some ideas for motions: clap hands, rub stomach, slap knees, touch head. Maybe you have some other ideas. When the leader has begun her choice of motions, 'it' will come back in the room and watch carefully. The leader will suddenly add a new motion for everyone to copy. 'It' will try to figure out who the leader is. The leader will keep changing motions when she thinks 'it' is not looking, until 'it' guesses correctly. If the leader is guessed she is next to leave the room while a new leader is chosen."

Play until everyone has had a turn as both leader and "it." You will find some children guessing names without really looking around. Tell the children, "Wait, watch, *see* who the first person is to change the motion. *Then* say the name."

SCIENCE

◆ Signs of Spring   *Ages 2 and up*

Encourage the children's observation skills.

YOU WILL NEED:

nice day for a walk

optional: rope long enough for each child to clasp (helps on city streets to keep children together)

optional: bags for collecting

METHOD:

Tell the children they are going on a walk, a special look-and-see hunt, to see what is going on now that winter is over. You might ask,

"What happens outside when spring comes?" Responses might be, "It is warmer." "Snow has melted." "Plants grow." "People wear different clothes." You might add a few more ideas. "There are more birds. Bugs appear."

As you walk, the children will notice what people are wearing, planted windowboxes, store windows decorated for spring, leaves on park trees, vendors selling ice cream, other children playing outdoor games, and so on.

If you are walking in a suburban or rural area the children can use bags to collect stones, twigs, and other treasures. Encourage respect for living things by leaving most things as you find them.

◆ Sink or Float with Vegetables and Fruits   *Ages 2 and up*

Sink or float? See what happens in this observation game.

YOU WILL NEED:
dishpan, ⅔ full of water
colander
jelly roll pan (to catch drips)
cutting board
knife
a variety of produce samples:

squash	potato
eggplant	carrot
banana	pineapple
beets	turnip

METHOD:
Ahead of time: Fill the dishpan with water. Set the colander filled with your vegetable selection on the jelly roll pan.
With the children: The children observe differences as they move vegetables from the colander to the water and back. Some will notice that certain vegetables float (on top of the water or slightly submerged). Some note "sinkers" that hit bottom and stay. Listen as the children explain to one another why the vegetables behave differently. You can help by asking questions like, "Where is the vegetable sitting? Why do you think some sink and some float?" Have the children make two piles—one of "floaters," one of "sinkers."

STORYTELLING

◆ Collaborative Biographies*   *Ages 2 and up*

YOU WILL NEED:
pencil
paper

METHOD:
During a quiet time announce the special story child for the day. Have each member of the group make observations about the chosen child. Encourage them to talk about this child's family, friends, or favorites (colors, books, play area). Write the comments in the form of a story. Read the biography aloud. On other days choose other children until a biography has been written for everyone.

SAMPLE (as told by four- and five-year-olds):
"Benjamin Cohen is four years old. He likes to play with different people. Ben plays two guitars. He can play different tunes. Sometimes he dances and shakes to the music. He has a great smile. He has big brown eyes. Ben likes to build with the wooden blocks. He comes to nursery school with Leah."

TRIPS

◆ Visiting a Neighborhood Artist   *Ages 3 and up*

Be aware of different crafts and hobbies that people in the neighborhood enjoy—ceramics, photography and developing, gardening, stained glass, painting, weaving.

METHOD:
Ask a neighbor if he would be willing to let the group watch him work some morning for a short while. Emphasize that you do not expect them to understand the technique of the skill, but rather to gain an appreciation of what others can do.
A nice way to say thank you would be to bake a simple cookie recipe before you go and share a snack with the person you're visiting. This allows for an informal time to ask questions.

*From *Before the Basics,* Bev Bos (Turn-the-Page Press, Inc., 203 Baldwin Avenue, Roseville, CA 95678, 1983). Used with permission.

WOODWORKING

✦ Hook Boards

The children can make a key hanging board, potholder hanger, or multihooked board for sorting washers of different sizes to develop math skills. Take your pick.

YOU WILL NEED:

piece of wood, ¾ inch thick, convenient size for the purpose you have in mind (For example: 6- by 10-inch key hanger or 10- by 12-inch sorting board), 1 per child

cup hooks (Number will depend on the board size. Plan so hooks will be far enough apart for easy removal of keys, holders, or washers.)

hammer

nails

Deft or other quick-drying varnish (available at hardware stores)

white glue

paste brushes

picture hangers on tape, 1 per child

colorful pictures or stickers (You can use pictures or parts of pictures from the children's work, brought from home, or pictures precut from calendars or greeting cards. Nature pictures are favorites.)

damp cloth

large supply of different-size washers if you are making a sorting
board

optional: stain or paint

optional: paintbrush

METHOD:

Ahead of time: Stain or paint the pieces of wood if you choose. Place
nail holes in the boards where the hooks are to be screwed in.

With the children: Help the children glue their pictures to their
boards. Use glue sparingly. Wipe excess away with a damp cloth.
Allow time for the glue to dry. Have the children brush varnish over
the whole piece of wood. Help them attach the picture hanger to the
back side, then screw the hooks into the holes.

MAY

May Contents

◆

MAY GUIDEPOSTS

◆

THINGS YOU CAN COLLECT

No doubt about it—spring is finally here. Wherever you live, in northern climes or southern, sunshine and comfortable temperatures prevail. You may want to begin collecting a few items in further preparation for the many warm days to come.

Bleach Bottles

Pails and scoops will be in demand for sandbox or mud pie play. They will also be needed for the summer collecting of shells, stones, tadpoles, and minnows. Pails and scoops are frequently lost or left behind, so why not plan to accumulate some bleach or detergent bottles for making a few? Alert your friends so they will set aside some plastic bottles for you.

To make pails, slice off the upper part of the bottle, including the handle. Make a pail handle by tying a cord through holes punched on opposite sides of the container.

For scoops, leave the existing handle on the bottle. Holding the bottle on its side, cut a piece diagonally from the bottom, leaving a generous opening for scooping.

Plan a pail and scoop decorating project. Supply markers, crayons, Contact paper, glue, and felt, or any combination of materials that strikes your fancy. Ornamenting the toys can be as much fun as using them. Some children may be eager to scamper off and dig right away. That's all right—later they will remember what materials you suggested for decorating and may try it by themselves. Others will find the art project more absorbing than the digging.

Perhaps someone will even have an original decorating scheme. One artistic child gathered an assortment of leaves and flowers and taped them to her pail for a whimsical springlike touch. Of course, it did not last, but it was completely original and creative.

Seeds or Seedlings

Get ready for some earnest gardening projects. Maybe you can save a few seeds from the fruits and vegetables in your kitchen. If a store visit is easier, choose seed packets there. Check the germination time. Early sprouters such as beans, corn, squash, marigolds, or zinnias are most encouraging to watch. Once children plant something, they want near-instant results!

While you are seed shopping, pick up some potting soil. If you have a green thumb, you might enjoy making your own. Dig earth from under trees in the woods; find soil from gardens or vacant lots; gather sand from a creek (seashore sand is too salty). Mix the lot and toss in peat moss for good measure. This combination, with the help of a little fertilizer, will give the children's plants a good start.

When your preschoolers appear on the scene, equip them with whatever containers you have handy. Egg cartons, paper cups, tin cans, microwave pans, Styrofoam cups, or milk cartons are all good. Punch a few holes in the bottom for drainage or simply line bottom with a few stones or packing foam. The children can spoon soil into the pots and be all ready for planting their seeds or transplanting seedlings (page 239).

Take a minute to talk about the care of the plants—why they need water, enough sunlight, and proper planting. Make it a point to brief the parents if they are not familiar with simple gardening techniques.

Shovelful of Woods

Woods may be at your doorstep. Troop out with your preschoolers, bucket and shovel in tow, and scoop up a clump of soil and flora. Choose carefully to be sure there is plenty of life within. Bring it home to watch for a few days. Keep the clump moist. What do you see? What plants? What creatures? Watch for bugs, new sprouts.

REMEMBER THE FAMILIAR

Plants Popping Up

You may not have time for a full-fledged springtime gardening project with your preschoolers, but if you do have a garden, let the children troop out to search for fresh sprouts. Show them how to walk around the garden's edge and how to gently push aside the leaves to reveal the new shoots of old plants beginning to pop up.

Stories and Snack Outside

Another way to enjoy the warm lovely days together is to plan normal indoor activities for outside. For example, you can spare yourself kitchen crumbs: help your youngsters fill thermoses and sandwich bags with snacks or lunchtime goodies. Hunt for an appealing picnic site by a pond, in a nearby park, or under a tree in your own backyard. Make sure you have tucked a storybook or small volume of spring poems into your bag, so you all can share storytelling time while everyone munches the picnic treats.

Later you might continue the outing with a trek to look for window boxes in early bloom, watch a sweeper clean the streets, or drink in any exciting "happening" along the way. City streets, suburban roads, or country lanes will offer equally absorbing surprises.

Paper Bag Kites

Ready for an outdoor art-and-run project? Supply each child with a brown grocery bag to embellish with markers or paint. Provide some crepe paper streamers to be affixed to the bag bottom with tape. Punch a hole or two in the middle bottom of the bag so you can tie a long, long string to come up through the open bag ready for grasping by a running preschooler. Air will catch in the paper bag as it trails behind the child with streamers flying.

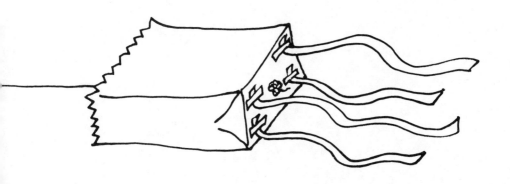

Mother's Day

Do not forget that May is the month for Mother's Day. Children take pleasure in creating surprises to show their love. If you think you will not have time for a special project, you can set aside some of the children's work from April—provided, of course, that you planned ahead. Perhaps you were particularly pleased with their April biographies (page 219). These would make delightful Mother's Day cards. Maybe you can tuck away the May Day Baskets (page 209) to send home closer to Mother's Day.

Parents always enjoy photographs of their offspring. You may have taken pictures of the group singly and together. Have one reproduced for each child. Let the youngsters personalize a picture placemat with pretty decorations as a frame.

Make special stationery for Mom using photocopies of children's photos or artwork.

If your preschoolers are about ready for another cut-and-paste activity, let them cut and paste "the reasons why I love my mother." Snip pictures from magazine pages and glue onto a big heart or placemat for a Mother's Day collage. Cover with clear Contact paper to preserve.

The world outside is coming alive. The additional time you spend in the fresh air will give everything you do an added excitement and fresh perspective. You will notice that it is not just the plants that are growing—the children are, too! They are taller, but more importantly they are more mature, have a longer attention span, and are *so* much easier to manage! Whether you are tackling a bleach bottle project or searching for sprouts, you will find yourself relaxing more when you are in their presence and looking forward to sharing summer days with them.

MAY ACTIVITIES

◆

ARTS AND CRAFTS

◆ Fence Artists   *Ages 3 and up*

Artists collaborate in a special art celebration.

YOU WILL NEED:
    fence
    mural paper, long enough for everyone in your group to have room
        to work (brown wrapping paper cut from a roll is fine)
    clip clothespins (chain fence) or tacks (for wood fence)*
    tempera paint (variety of colors) in quart-size plastic containers
    paintbrushes, easel size

METHOD:
    Ahead of time: Clip or tack mural paper to fence at an appropriate
    height for your small artists. Fill the paint containers and place them
    with brushes on the ground at regular intervals along the length of
    the mural paper.
    With the children: Let the children come and go to add brush strokes
    to the mural. Some children will use wide arm sweeps with the brush
    while others will focus on tiny details in a small area. Some will add
    large splashes of paint, others will put in dots or a single line. The
    result can be a remarkably stunning piece of artwork.

*Less tearing occurs with clothespins

◆ Carbon Copies   *Ages 3 and up*

YOU WILL NEED:
   carbon paper
   paper, light enough for use with carbon paper
   pencils
   paper clips

METHOD:
   Clip two pieces of paper with carbon between for each child. The
   children experiment with drawing and lifting the paper to see the
   identical impression beneath.

◆ Egg Carton Monsters   *Ages 3 and up*

YOU WILL NEED:
   egg cartons
   tempera paint and brushes, or colored markers
   pipe cleaners, 2 per child
   construction paper
   cellophane tape or stapler
   scissors

METHOD:
   Ahead of time: Cut egg cartons so each child will have one set of
   carton compartments to work with (examples: a block of four, a strip
   of six, a strip of four). Cut two wings for each child from construction paper. Mix paints and store in jars.
   With the children: Let the children paint or draw designs on their egg
   carton monsters. When the work is dry, help them attach wings and
   pipe cleaner feelers with tape or stapler.
   Egg Carton Animals: For caterpillars, use half an egg carton with pipe
   cleaner feelers; for ladybugs, one carton section with pipe cleaner
   feelers; for turtles, one carton section with construction paper head,
   legs, tail.

◆ Writing Whimsy   *Ages 3 and up*

A preschooler's version of office time.

YOU WILL NEED:
   table and chairs
   assortment of office supplies such as:
      used envelopes (the "window" type is especially appealing to
      children)

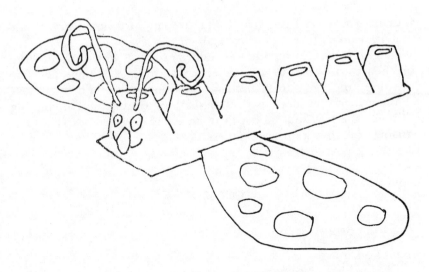

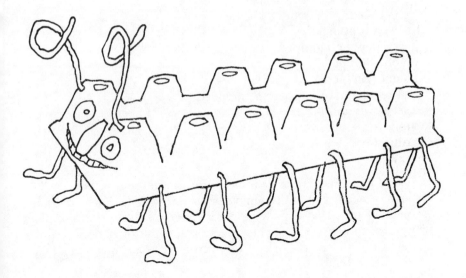

assorted paper (letterhead, lined, unlined, graph, discarded form
  letters)
pencils, highliters
paper clips
stapler
ruler
boxes for organizing supplies

METHOD:
  Ahead of time: Place table and chairs in a quiet space and call it "The
  Office." Organize supplies so they are accessible at the table. Offer

four or five items from your office supplies at a time, varying the
materials on different playgroup days.

With the children: Encourage the children to draw, doodle, and write
on their own. Watch as they experiment with letter shapes and line
drawings and work to manipulate desk equipment. They will love
stapling their "business" papers, highliting printing, and attempting
to make their writing visible through envelope windows. The possibilities for invention are limitless.

COOKING

◆ Syrian Bread Pizza   *Ages 3 and up*

YOU WILL NEED:
  Syrian bread, 1 piece per child
  12-ounce jar thick pizza sauce
  8-ounce package shredded cheese
  choice of toppings:
    green pepper, chopped
    onion, chopped
    hamburger, cooked
    chicken, ham, or pepperoni, chopped
  paper bowls and plates
  spoons
  baking sheet

METHOD:
  Ahead of time: Prepare the toppings and place them in bowls.
  With the children: Set out the ingredients buffet style. Each child puts
  a piece of bread on a plate, spreads sauce on the bread, sprinkles
  toppings, ending with the cheese, and places the pizza on the cookie
  sheet. Broil the pizzas briefly or microwave them on paper plates
  until cheese bubbles.

◆ Yogurt and Fruit Sundaes   *Ages 2 and up*

YOU WILL NEED (for 4 to 6 children):
  ½ cup fresh or canned peaches
  ½ cup fresh or canned pineapple
  1 banana
  1 cup yogurt
  ¼ cup unroasted sunflower seeds

¼ cup chopped walnuts, peanuts, or pecans
½ cup fresh or frozen strawberries
plastic knives
paper plates
paper bowls (1 to serve each kind of fruit and topping, and 1 for
  each child to use for eating)
spoons (for serving and eating)

METHOD:
Ahead of time: Wash, peel, chop, and partially cut fruits and nuts
where necessary. Put yogurt, nuts, and seeds in separate bowls.
With the children: Each child cuts up a fruit on a paper plate. Place
fruits in separate bowls. Line them up and serve buffet style with
yogurt, seeds, nuts, and strawberry toppings.

◆ **Apple Juice Shake**   *Ages 2 and up*

YOU WILL NEED:
1 cup apple juice
½ teaspoon cinnamon
1 pint vanilla ice milk
measuring cup and spoons
blender
large spoon
paper cups

METHOD:
You pour the apple juice into the cup measure. The children take
turns adding juice, cinnamon, and scoops of ice milk to the blender.
Whirl till smooth. Serve and sip. Coooool.

DRAMATIC PLAY

◆ **Styrofoam Puppet**   *Ages 3 and up*

YOU WILL NEED:
Styrofoam balls of various sizes, 1 per child
Popsicle sticks, 1 per child
straight pins
glue, brushes, and cotton swabs
11-inch fabric square for covering stick and hand, 1 per child
small fabric scraps for details

yarn, ribbon, or string
scissors, 1 per child
cupcake papers (good for collars or hats)
markers

METHOD:

Ahead of time: Select fabric scraps that are interesting in design and texture. Cut out the squares of fabric. Sort and spread out the other materials.

With the children: Decorate the ball (head) of the puppet first. Cut or loop yarn, string, or ribbon for hair. Attach with pins. Make the face with markers or with fabric scraps and glue. Next, put the fabric square over the Popsicle stick and push both up into the ball. (If this is done before decorating the head, the stick hole will become too large and loose).

SUGGESTIONS:

1. This type of puppet is durable and can be kept simple. Some four-year-olds are interested in detail. They can be encouraged to add accessories—hats, pockets, and trim glued onto the main square, yarn eyebrows and beards, and so on.

2. If pins prove too hazardous to keep in the puppets, let the children glue features to the puppets, then insert pins to hold them while they dry. When they are dry, pull out the pins.

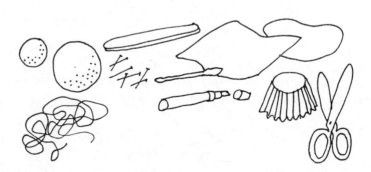

♦ Acting Out Stories and Songs   *Ages 2 and up*

YOU WILL NEED:

Choice of a story or song
    Stories:
    "Goldilocks and The Three Bears"
    "Three Billy Goats Gruff"
    "The Tortoise and the Hare"

Songs (see pages 313–315 for words):
"I'm a Little Teapot"
"Old MacDonald"
"London Bridge"
"Sing a Song of Sixpence"
"Little Jack Horner"

METHOD:
Enjoy reading the story or singing the song until it is very familiar to everyone. Let the children choose the part or parts they would like to act out and keep rotating until everyone has had a turn to try his choices. Let the children use their imaginations for simple props, facial expressions, and body motions. The more often you repeat this activity the more creative it becomes.

SUGGESTIONS:
At first the children may do just the motions while you read or sing the accompaniment. Later, let them try to express the story ideas in their own words.

GAMES

◆ Ring the Bell   *Ages 3 and up*

Try this eye-hand coordination game.

YOU WILL NEED:
   bell (The larger the size, the easier for young children to hit. A
      bunch of small bells will do.)
   3 soft plastic foam balls in different sizes
   rope or string long enough to hang the bell at a good target height

METHOD:
   Attach the bell to one end of the string. Hang from a tree branch,
   ceiling pipe, or other convenient height. The children take turns
   throwing the ball to ring the bell. Encourage them to see how far
   away they can stand and still hit the ball.

VARIATION:
   Through the Hoop: Hang a plastic hoop instead. The wide opening
   gives greater space for success.

◆ Match It Board Game   *Ages 3 and up*

YOU WILL NEED:
   posterboard or piece of paper
   colored pencils
   container of small objects, such as:

key	clothespin
toys	safety pin
block	notebook rings
comb	colored rubber band

METHOD:
   Ahead of time: Trace the objects on the poster using colored pencils.
   With the children: The children take objects out of the container one
   at a time. They try to place each object on its outline in only one try.
   Older children with tracing skills may have fun making their own
   outline answer boards.
      Follow up this matching activity with questions that help the chil-
   dren categorize. "How many objects are rectangular? Which objects
   are used to hold things together?"

MUSIC

◆ Musical Chairs

Everyone will enjoy this old favorite.

YOU WILL NEED:
chairs
music (use a record or tape player or clap your hands)

METHOD:
Line up chairs—always one less than the number of children play-ing. Children move around the chairs, sit down when the music stops, and the one left sits to the side. Remove a chair, then another and yet another until only one child is left.

◆ Mood Music

Ages 3 and up

YOU WILL NEED:
record or tape player
a story record or tape with mood music accompaniment ("Red Riding Hood," "The Three Little Pigs")

METHOD:
Listen to the record. Then talk about the way music was used for the trip through the woods, the wind, the wolf, and other descriptive themes. Ask questions like: "Does this sound happy?" "Is this a sad sound?" "How does this part make you feel?"

PHYSICAL EXERCISE

◆ Copycat

Ages 2 and up

METHOD:
Choose a child from the group to be the leader. This child acts something out in front of the other children. Everyone follows the dramatics of the leader while saying the following verse together. Each child will want many turns.

VERSE:
Let's play copycat, just for fun!
Let's copy [name]. She's/He's the one.
Whatever she/he does, we'll do the same,
That's how we play the copycat game.

◆ The Trick of Touching the Line   *Ages 2 and up*

This is a fun way to practice large-muscle coordination.

YOU WILL NEED:
   string or masking tape

METHOD:
   You make a big circle with string or tape (tape works well even on carpeting). Everyone stands around the circle and each person takes a turn telling the group a part of the body to touch the line.

EXAMPLE:
   touch your nose to the line;
   touch your elbow to the line;
   knees, knuckles, and so on
   Real coordination is involved as the children learn parts of the body.

SCIENCE

◆ Testing Our Senses   *Ages 2 and up*

What do we see, hear, feel, smell?

METHOD:
   The place is *anywhere!* Lie on your tummies. Close your eyes. Talk about these one at a time:
   What can we hear?
   What can we feel?
   What can we smell?
   Open your eyes.
   What can we see?

◆ Scientific Questioning   *Ages 2 and up*

Children do this quite naturally.

YOU WILL NEED:
   opportunities for observation (indoors, outdoors, on trips)

METHOD:
   Develop the children's awareness of different plants and animals. Logical questioning will help them to see similarities, differences, and dependencies. The children may repeat the same questions but eventually each child sees relationships and acquires new under-

standings. Listen as they respond to your questions and ask new ones of their own about living plants and animals.

EXAMPLES:

"What does it eat and drink?"

"How is it fed?"

"Does it react to temperature changes?" (A plant wilts, a dog pants.)

"When does it sleep?"

"Does it live a long time?" (*Lifetimes* by Bryan Mellonie [New York: Bantam Books, 1983] is an excellent resource for explaining death.)

"How can it protect itself?"

"What are the changes as it grows?"

◆ Transplanting Fun   *Ages 3 and up*

This makes a great Mother's Day gift.

YOU WILL NEED:

disposable plastic cups (with holes punched in bottom for drainage)

or

small plant pots, 1 per child

spoons

trowel

plants from your garden (something that needs thinning, such as phlox, bleeding heart, or calendula)

or

a flat of annuals from a nursery or produce market

pebbles (can be purchased at a garden center)

soil (can be purchased at a garden center)

optional: fertilizer

METHOD:

Let the children put a few pebbles in the bottom of their cups or pots. Then they spoon in a little soil. Help them each dig up a small plant, troweling wide around the plant and deep enough to get all the roots. Plants from a flat can be used instead. Explain that the plant drinks water and takes food from the soil through the roots. Each child will put her plant in the cup and spoon in extra soil to fill the cup. Show how to pat down the dirt to prevent large air pockets. Water the plants and add fertilizer, if desired. Send the plants home with directions for care: "Keep in a sunny window or transplant to the garden. Water."

SUGGESTION:

All ecologists! Rescue endangered plants from a prospective construction site or other threatened habitat. Transplant to your yard or window box.

STORYTELLING

◆ **Sign Language Stories** *Ages 3 and up*

Seeing symbols helps preschoolers to understand story sequence and to follow from left to right as they will when they learn to read.

YOU WILL NEED:

paper

marker

easel or other means for holding paper upright

METHOD:

As you tell a simple story to the children, draw symbols to represent key words. For example, as you say, "It was a bright, sunny day. A fish wiggled through the water. It swam under a big bridge," you would draw a sun, a fish, water, and a bridge, from the left side to the right. Let the children take turns making up a story using the same set of symbols placed in different order.

VARIATIONS:

Later, children can use pencil and paper to create their own original stories with symbols. They might make three to four picture cards to tell a sign language story. They can use these on their own or share stories with a friend.

Seasonal symbols are great for sign language stories. For example: moon, cat, bat, and jack-o'-lantern for Halloween.

TRIPS

◆ Visiting a Carnival or Circus   *ages 2 and up*

Plan a trip to watch the circus train unload or go to a nearby neighborhood carnival site and watch the setting-up.

METHOD:

Plan transportation so that everyone can go in one car. Circus train arrivals are usually very early in the morning—thrilling to see, but maybe difficult to organize for a group at that hour. Neighborhood carnivals are usually set up during the day preceding the opening. Park at a distance so you will not be in the way.

LOOK FOR:

Circus	*Carnival*
different animals	equipment and how it is
how they traveled	assembled
what they eat	carnival games
unusual performers and	how carnival workers traveled
costumes	where food is cooked
where they live between	
performances	
where they get dressed	

Some children will be more interested than others in the mechanics of setting up. If the day is nice, take along a picnic blanket and snack.

WOODWORKING

◆ Sawing

Ages 3 and up

Children will be ready to saw wood scraps after practicing on cardboard first (see page 179).

YOU WILL NEED:

hacksaw or coping saw

vise or C-clamp attached to workbench or table

thin, narrow wood scraps, ½ inch thick, 2 inch wide (scraps of molding are excellent)

METHOD:

The children take individual turns to enable your close supervision. Help each carpenter tighten his choice of scrap in the vise with enough length to saw. Demonstrate how to hold and move the saw. You saw first, chanting rhythmically, "Slow and easy. Slow and easy," in time with your sawing. Let the child try to hold the saw and chant the rhythm. You may need to guide his hand at first. Then he will be able to do it independently. For younger children, cardboard and styrofoam are easier to work with than wood.

Help the children to understand that tools are not toys. If there is some flagrant misuse of a tool, put the tools away. When you bring them out again, remind everyone how to use them properly.

Do not expect the children to saw a great deal. The going is slow. It is the experience that is important. Each child will enjoy taking home the piece he has worked on.

JUNE

JUNE CONTENTS

◆

JUNE GUIDEPOSTS

◆

THINGS YOU CAN COLLECT

Summer brings a new dimension to your playgroup arrangements. You will be planning around the vacation schedules and trips of your preschoolers' families. You may continue to have playgroup regularly, or perhaps you will decide to have a few get-togethers with parents and children instead. Either way, time and location can be more flexible and the day less structured. The wealth of outdoor activities possible in the summertime will add a fresh spirit of fun. You may notice that the children have developed a comfortable camaraderie over the months they've spent getting to know one another well.

If your group does not meet during the summer months, try some of the suggested activities with your own family. Outdoor walks and "treasure" hunts are fun at any age. Whatever form your outings take, accumulate a few items along the way and get a headstart on materials and ideas for your next playgroup year. Why not save postcards received or purchased during summer travel? A September storytelling activity about vacations could feature a postcard movie about summer trips. The children can make the movie by taping together the postcards and then view it by running the "film" through slits in a box.

Bubble Wands

The best bubble-blowing weather is right now. Begin a collection of bubble wands. This can be everybody's project. The children and parents can come up with contributions—anything from utilitarian items culled from home clutter to whimsical gems spied during holiday jaunts. Plastic berry baskets with crisscross openings, toilet tissue tubes, funnels, or plastic strips from six-packs are great for bubble blowing and can all be found at someone's home. The novelty counter at a turnpike stop or the children's gift section of a historical landmark might turn up giant wands or little ones with special shapes for the group's collection. Everyone can have fun looking. As the collection grows, share periodic bubble-blowing sessions (page 257).

Pictures—Moving and Still

Summertime is picture-taking time. Think of ways you can capture your playgroup's summer fun. Take pictures to share instantly and then save for later, when summer is just a memory. Perhaps you have an instant camera and can treat your preschoolers to the fun of watching their own pictures develop. Over a span of time you might assemble a collaborative album using an assortment of photos the preschoolers bring from home. Children love to gaze at their friends and themselves over and over.

Catch scenes of outdoor play on videotape to show at once, then review at leisure on a cold winter day months later.

REMEMBER THE FAMILIAR

Repeating favorite warm-weather pastimes from year to year is part of what makes summer such fun. Your family may look forward to long car trips complete with maps and restaurant stops. Maybe fishing and mountain climbing constitute your summer magic. The ocean, a mud hole at Grandpa's farm, the ice cream truck's nightly neighborhood stop, regular trips to a nearby frog pond—any or all may make summer an adventure for you. Remember some of your old favorites, then share one or two with your group. You may be introducing the youngsters to a completely new experience.

Safety

Whatever your plans are, make safety a part of them. Spend time with the children going over rules for safe fun in the water, on a bicycle, and hiking. You might play "pretend" and help the children act out some summer problem situations—what to do if you are lost in the woods or in a crowd, or how to seek help quickly if a friend is having trouble in the water. It would not hurt for you to review some simple first aid procedures so you will be better prepared should an emergency arise.

Father's Day

One of the first celebrations of the summer months is Father's Day. Gifts made with love mean so much. Let the children have a real part in deciding what gift to give. Thinking of something to please their dads will teach them that part of the fun of giving is the planning and anticipating.

The present can be something as simple as a painting mounted on construction paper or a pencil holder (page 126) made especially with Father's office or workshop in mind.

All parents enjoy photographs. Perhaps you could use some of those pictures your group collected as part of a Memory Tray gift (page 167), or let each child create a decorative border on a piece of construction paper and mount a single photograph on it.

The preschoolers could plan a special culinary treat for Dad—cookies, Bag a Snack (page 69), or Peanut Butter Popcorn (page 277) are a few simple tasty ideas from which you can choose. How about writing special invitations for a walk or bike ride with Dad? Hook it to or print it right on the bagged goodies. Daddy and his little one can enjoy the snack while they are off on their special outing together.

Cookouts

Everyone loves the special summer edibles offered at cookouts, picnics, and other outdoor feasts. When you are planning a cookout, let your preschoolers shape their own hamburgers for the grill. Odd meatball shapes of all sorts add to the free spirit of the summer event.

Skewering chunks of vegetables and meats for shish kabob barbecues is a task older preschoolers take on with enthusiasm. With extracareful supervision, this can work out quite happily.

Sun Tea

Also fun to make is Sun Tea: three to four tea bags to one quart of water, refrigerated or iced after a day in the sun. Have members of your group help set it out in a sunny spot to brew at the beginning of the playgroup day. Everyone can check the deepening amber color as the day progresses. Preschoolers enjoy the exercise in observation and parents will savor the warm-weather beverage.

Ice Cream "Cake"

What is summer without ice cream? Embellish the Father's Day or Fourth of July cookout with a fanciful ice cream cake created by preschoolers. Bring out the cinnamon red-hots, colored sugar sprinkles, and squeeze-tube frosting. Set out a quart brick of ice cream or frozen yogurt and let each child add a decorating touch. Freeze until celebration time.

Planting Annuals

Whether you live in the city or the country, June is planting time. Apartment-dwelling preschoolers will love to tuck annuals into window boxes or pot gardens. Their country cousins will dig right into the ground. Think of other planting projects.

Sunflower Seeds

The planting of raw sunflower seeds is a satisfying undertaking. Pressed into soil a foot apart in a very sunny spot, later thinned and kept watered, these seeds will pop up and grow 6 to 12 feet like Jack's beanstalk. They are fun to check as the summer progresses. By late summer they will yield gigantic, bright blossoms loaded with more seeds. Harvest the seeds around Labor Day, then hike to a pet store with the bounty, or bring to a friend's gerbil. Watch a creature feast as if the kernels are the nectar of the gods. Simplest of all is hanging a sunflower upside down for birds to enjoy. You can also harvest the seeds for yourself; they make a delicious snack. Dry 2 cups of seeds on a baking sheet in a 200° F oven for 30 minutes. Stir in 2 tablespoons of melted butter or margarine with 1 tablespoon of Worcestershire sauce. Sprinkle with salt and return to the oven until the seeds are crisp and brown (about 1 hour).

Bird Watching

The preschoolers' fascination with live animals never ceases, and you can spy some birds just about anywhere, even if they're only pigeons parading on nearby roofs. Arm yourself with a bird book and marker and set off with your troop of playgroupers—to the park, streets, fields, or woods. When you see a bird, put a mark by the picture you find in the book. Who can spot the next bird first? See how many marks can be made during the walk.

To lend an air of importance to the event, have actual or toy binoculars for everybody. Two toilet tissue tubes taped side by side with string or ribbon attached for draping over the neck do just fine. Plan this craft project a day or two before your outing.

Performances in City Streets

Look around. In warm weather, all sorts of folks pop up with the flowers. Vendors tempt you with their wares. Actors and students of music take to streets and parks to entertain the crowds. Ahead of time, scout lively spots and then share them with the children. Jugglers, magicians, singers may all be a part of the scene.

Many shopping plazas or malls have scheduled performances that are announced in your local paper. Add a sack lunch to your carry-along list. Munch and watch what the lunch-hour business crowd is doing. You can venture farther than you did in winter, unencumbered by heavy clothing and cold.

Everything you do in June is just a preview of things to come. This is the very beginning of summer—warm days stretch ahead with the promise of time to repeat a favorite hot weather outing or activity. Enjoy.

JUNE ACTIVITIES

◆

ARTS AND CRAFTS

◆ Decorated Seashells or Stones

Ages 3 and up

YOU WILL NEED:

medium-sized clam, scallop, or other shells to use as base

assorted tiny shells, starfish, or stones

other tiny ornaments that would look good with shells (colored crushed glass, small pearls, tiny plastic sea horses)

glue and brushes

Note: Most of these materials are available at hobby shops if you do not have access to a beach.

METHOD:

The children decorate the medium-sized shells or stones by gluing on smaller ornaments and shells.

VARIATION:

If you do not have access to tiny items for gluing onto the shells, let the children paint them using a small watercolor set with brush.

◆ Clothesline Art Show

Ages 2 and up

YOU WILL NEED:

clothesline (hung low)

clothespins (spring clip type)

variety of artwork done by children (save during the year or have children bring a few samples from home.)

METHOD:

Have any four-year-olds in the group help you clip the art to the clothesline. Invite willing neighbors, the driver of the day, and other available parents and guests to view the artwork. Serve some goody the children have made to share with guests at snack time.

For an added art gallery flourish ask the children what they wish to name their works. Put the titles on the pictures with markers. Make sure the artists' names are on them too!

◆ Ziplock Finger Painting   *Ages 2 and up*

This project provides a solution for the child who hates messy hands.

YOU WILL NEED:

ziplock bags, largest size, 1 per child
tablespoon measure
finger paint, 2 colors (tempera *will not* work)
optional: self-adhesive labels with children's names to stick on each
    bag

METHOD:

Ahead of time: Choose two colors of finger paint that will mix to make a new color (see Mixing Colors, page 68). Measure 1 tablespoon of each color into each ziplock bag. Flatten bag to remove air and close the ziplock firmly. Add name labels, if desired.

With the children: Let them move their fingers over the bag finger-paint fashion to create a changeable paint design inside. Paint will stay moist for a long time, so children can rework their designs even a few days later. The bags look beautiful hanging in a window as light shines through the color. If the bags are sent home, busy parents can whip them out to occupy demanding preschoolers during phone calls or other distractions.

◆ Hinged Abstractions   *Ages 3 and up*

YOU WILL NEED:

brass paper fasteners
scraps of colored construction paper
optional: one-hole paper punch (for adult's use)

METHOD:

Ahead of time: Punch holes in some of the paper scraps, if desired.
With the children: Show the children how to poke a hole through one

scrap with a paper fastener and then through another scrap. Then demonstrate how to spread the two ends of the fastener to connect the two pieces of paper. The fun of hooking together pieces of paper will be contagious as the children's imaginations take over. The results will be abstract designs with a number of moving parts. Some children just like to put fasteners in and take them out again. Others like lining up one fastener with a number of holes.

SUGGESTIONS:

1. Leave containers of fasteners with punched and unpunched paper pieces in a spot for more fastener play at a later time. Preschoolers will tear paper pieces to the sizes and shapes they desire.

2. Ahead of time, draw and cut arms, legs, bodies, and heads of people, or animals. Punch holes for fastening. The children fasten pieces together so the creation has moving parts. You might also provide crayons for adding features.

COOKING

◆ Taste of Tropics Soda   *Ages 2 and up*

YOU WILL NEED (for 4 to 6 servings):
   1 cup unsweetened pineapple juice
   ⅓ cup orange juice
   1¼ cups (10 ounces) carbonated water
   orange sherbet, slightly softened
   measuring cup
   spoon
   paper cups
   pitcher

METHOD:

Taking turns, the children measure the juices into the pitcher, *slowly* add carbonated water, then spoon a scoop of sherbet into each cup. You *slowly* pour the juice mixture into their cups.

◆ Cheesy Wheats   *Ages 2 and up*

YOU WILL NEED:
   1 stick margarine
   8-ounce package shredded cheese

4 cups spoon-size shredded wheat
optional: choice of seasonings (garlic, onion, celery salt, etc.)
measuring cup
stirring spoon
frying pan
sandwich bags or paper plates for serving

METHOD:
Melt the margarine and the cheese in the frying pan. The children take turns measuring cups of shredded wheat into the mixture, stirring, and sprinkling with seasonings. Serve. Refrigerate leftovers.

◆ Sunshine Salad

Ages 2 and up

Eat the sunshine!

YOU WILL NEED (for up to 8 servings):
½ cup plain yogurt
1 teaspoon honey
1 slice pineapple per serving
measuring cup and spoons
small bowl
paper plates
forks

METHOD:
Assign each child a task: measuring yogurt and honey into the bowl, mixing, putting pineapple slices on the plates, spooning 1 tablespoon of yogurt mixture in the center of each fruit slice.

DRAMATIC PLAY

◆ Prop Box

Ages 3 and up

Children enjoy a chance to "make believe."

YOU WILL NEED:
large box containing props and dress-up clothing that suggest one
   or more roles, such as:
   gypsy (scarf, jewelry)
   pirate (patch, gold earring, kerchief)
   cowboy (cowboy hat, vest)
   doctor or nurse (operating room hat, gowns, mask)

car mechanic or gas station attendant (play tools, "engine" made of
   Styrofoam block and electrical wires*, cap)
ballet dancer (tutu, headband)
mother or father (variety of grown-up clothes and accessories)
police officer (hat, badge)
firefighter (hat, piece of hose)
bride or bridesmaid (curtains as veil, artificial flower bouquet)
bus driver (hat, tickets, money)

METHOD:

Spend time going over the contents of the box with the children and
hearing their ideas on how to use them. Then it is time to dress up
and pretend. Encourage both boys and girls to be astronauts, nurses,
and so on.

SUGGESTIONS:

Change the box contents from time to time. Read a story and have
appropriate props in the box to dramatize it. For example, nurse
and doctor props can follow a story about a trip to the hospital, or
you can read a cowboy story before pulling out a box full of western
cowboy props.

◆ Poetry Pantomimes   *Ages 2 and up*

This activity requires few props and lots of imagination.

YOU WILL NEED:

A familiar, short action poem or nursery rhyme that has a limited
   number of characters and would require only a few props if acted
   out [*Poems to Read the Very Young*, by Josette Frank (New York:
   Random House, 1961, revised 1977) is a good source. "Humpty
   Dumpty," "Little Boy Blue," and "Little Miss Muffet" are excellent
   nursery rhyme choices.]
necessary props

METHOD:

Choose children to take the part of each character in the poem. Assign whatever props are needed. Read or recite the rhyme with all
the children joining in while the performers act out the story. Rotate
parts to give others a chance.

EXAMPLE:

"Little Miss Muffet": The person playing Miss Muffet sits on a small
chair using a plastic dish and spoon for eating her curds and whey.

*Cut off sharp metal strands, leaving colored plastic pieces.

The one chosen to be the spider eagerly creeps from behind to frighten Miss Muffet. Miss Muffet throws down the dish and spoon and runs back to her place in the group.*

After all the children have had a turn at the different parts, try an interpretation popular in a Roseville, California, nursery school. As a surprise, *you* sit in Miss Muffet's chair. Begin reciting the rhyme. The children will know that *they* are spiders and will creep up to scare Miss Muffet. If they don't, then give a hint. Scaring the adult is always great fun and a great ego-building activity for preschoolers.

GAMES

◆ Blowing Bubbles

Ages 3 and up

YOU WILL NEED:
   assortment of bubble wands and pipes (plastic berry baskets and
      toilet paper tubes also work well)
   liquid dishwashing soap (Joy brand works best)
   water
   plastic containers or pans

*From *Before the Basics,* Bev Bos (Turn-the-Page Press, Inc., 203 Baldwin Avenue, Roseville, CA 95678, 1983).

METHOD:

Ahead of time: Mix one part soap and one part water in plastic containers for a good bubble-blowing consistency.

With the children: Blow bubbles! It's best to do this outdoors for fewer cleanup problems. *Caution:* Straws for blowing bubbles *do* work, but very young children may forget and suck in instead of blowing out, gagging and sputtering in the process. Using pipe and wands solves this problem.

◆ Shadow Tag   *Ages 3 and up*

Enjoy this game on a sunny day.

METHOD:

Two or more players are needed. One child is "it." She gives the signal for everyone else to start running around the designated area (backyard, playground). "It" chases the others until she is able to step on or touch a running child's shadow. The player whose shadow is caught becomes "it."

MUSIC

◆ A Kitchen Orchestra   *Ages 3 and up*

A homestyle rhythm band—children learn to listen to musical patterns made from melodies that are the same or different.

YOU WILL NEED:

pans, pots
wooden and metal spoons (to use as drumsticks)
cardboard containers
plastic containers

SONG:

Hot cross buns,
Hot cross buns,
One-a-penny, two-a-penny,
Hot cross buns.

METHOD:

Sing or say the familiar "Hot Cross Buns." Have the children raise their hands on the line where the melody and words change (one-a-penny). Repeat, letting the children sing or chant with you and raise their hands again at "one-a-penny."

Let everyone choose an "instrument" from the kitchen supply. Divide the group. Part will accompany the "hot cross buns" lines in the melody. The other group will play during "one-a-penny, two-a-penny."

SUGGESTION:
Records with one melody repeated frequently would be pleasant background music and good listening practice during some other activity.

◆ Musical Art   *Ages 3 and up*

YOU WILL NEED:
large sheets of newspaper
markers
record or tape—perhaps a lively collection of short nursery rhymes
record or tape player

METHOD:
Spread out newspaper on the kitchen floor. Give each child one crayon. Play the record or tape, changing the song at one- or two-minute intervals. Every time the song changes, have the children exchange colors with one another. The children draw in rhythm to the music.

PHYSICAL EXERCISE

◆ Ball Kicking Practice   *Ages 3 and up*

YOU WILL NEED:
large ball—more than one if available

METHOD:
The children choose partners. One partner faces the other. They kick the ball back and forth. Gradually widen the distance between the partners as the game goes on.

VARIATION:
Teams can face one another and do the same.

◆ Balloon Volleyball   *Ages 4 and up*

YOU WILL NEED:
  string (tie taut at child level to make a "pretend" net)
  balloon

METHOD:
  Half the group on either side of the "net" bats or throws the balloon
  across to the other side. Remove string when game ends to prevent
  children from running into it unexpectedly.

SCIENCE

◆ Shadows   *Ages 3 and up*

Exercise the children's observation skills.

YOU WILL NEED:
  chalk
  bright, sunny day

METHOD:
  The children use their hands or objects that happen to be nearby
  (sandbox shovel, ball) to see how shadows can change. You can ask
  such questions as, "How does the shadow change as you move close
  to it?" "What happens to how it looks as you move your hand away?"
  "When does the shadow completely disappear?" The children will
  discover that if they hold something near a surface the shadow will
  look crisp, dark, and small. Held farther from the surface the object's shadow becomes larger, pale, and fuzzy. The shadow disap-
  pears if they try to put the object right on top of it. As the children
  play with their changing shadows, they will have fun experimenting
  with shaking shadow hands or connecting by touching shadow toes.
  Older children (four and up) may enjoy using chalk to trace one
  another's shadows on a hardtop area. First tries are difficult and
  incomplete but great fun.

◆ Making Nature Collections   *Ages 3 and up*

YOU WILL NEED:
  box bottoms or lids, 1 per child
  glue and brushes
  tape

variety of stones, shells, feathers, empty bird's egg, twigs from bird's nest, or other small items

METHOD:

After a "treasure-hunt" walk in the place of your choice, children glue or tape their treasures onto the box bottom or lid. Cover the box with clear wrap and tape to make a "glass" front for viewing. Some children may put in only one or two items.

VARIATION:

Let the children paint and decorate empty cigar boxes to use for collecting summer treasures. That way they are free to handle, sort, and periodically inspect or swap their findings.

STORYTELLING

◆ Teddy Bear Picnic   *Ages 2 and up*

Children enjoy this get-to-know-you-better activity.

YOU WILL NEED:

teddy bears
picnic snack in a basket
large blanket

METHOD:

Ahead of time: Invite the children to bring their teddy bears (or another favorite stuffed animal) to the next group sessions. Pack a snack in a basket. Have extra teddies to be adopted by children who forget their own.
With the children: Allow free play with the teddies when the children first arrive. Gather the children together and ask each child to tell about his bear. What is its name? What friends does it have at home? What does "Teddy" like about playgroup? Spread a blanket outdoors (or indoors, depending on the weather) and enjoy a teddy bear picnic.

TRIPS

◆ Visiting a Marsh, Pond, or Stream   *Ages 4 and up*

YOU WILL NEED:

pails or plastic bottles, 1 per child
strainers and/or a net

magnifying glass

optional: a well-illustrated paperback book on marsh, pond, or stream life

a knife or scissors for snipping samples

METHOD:

Supply each child with a container. Ask the children to see what discoveries they can make.

Look for:	*Where to look:*
plants	the water's surface
animals	under the water
stones	at the water's edge
	under rocks
	amid waterside growth
	some yards away from the water
	in bushes and trees

What you might find:	
algae	salamanders
waterbugs	insects
tadpoles	water plants
frogs	birds
turtles	water lilies
fish	irises
newts	cattails

Look at small discoveries under the magnifying glass. Let the children collect some of their finds to take home. Use the strainers for scooping creatures and plants from the water. Help the children identify what they have found. Let them tell what they already know about it. You may add a fact or two.

SUGGESTIONS:

1. Remember that you are not giving a college course in biology. The experience of looking closely at the surroundings is the important thing. A deluge of facts is unnecessary.

2. Help the children learn to respect the environment. Avoid littering. Obey rules that may be in effect regarding the picking of plants. It is forbidden in some areas. If you take a creature such as a frog or turtle home, let the children know it is happier in its own environment and that you plan to return it to the pond. Supervise the children closely when near the water.

WOODWORKING

◆ Drilling

Ages 4 and up

YOU WILL NEED:

eggbeater-type drill

scrap wood—thin pieces requiring minimum drilling before
   breakthrough

vise or C-clamp

METHOD:

Put the wood in the vise and show the children how to drill. Super-vise closely as each child takes turns experimenting. Encourage them not to turn the handle too quickly and to bear down slightly, putting pressure on the drill.

The drill is somewhat unwieldy. Well-coordinated four-year-olds will manage very well. Others may enjoy just a few tries.

SUGGESTION:

1. By now the children have had experience with several woodwork-ing skills. Each can operate a different tool while awaiting a turn at the latest addition.

2. Have a supply of cord handy for the drilling activity. Children love to put cord through the holes they make in one piece of wood. They also enjoy stringing and tying pieces together.

JULY

JULY CONTENTS

◆

JULY GUIDEPOSTS

◆

THINGS YOU CAN COLLECT

July is the month of retreat to the mountains or beach and of flam-
boyant celebration of Independence Day. Warm-weather collecting
reaches its peak as summer provides an explosion of possibilities for
you and your playgroup.

Beach Treasures

Children greet the prospect of hunting for sea treasures with a fever of
excitement no matter how frequently they have done it before. Even
on the last beach trip of the season, they will bring back a full pail with
the same enthusiasm for the favorite lucky stone, sand dollar, egg case,
seagull feather, or sand-smoothed beach glass.

If the children are familiar enough with the names of beach objects,
your hunt may take the form of a game with a specific list of items to
find. This project is perfect for a summer birthday party at the beach,
too.

The collection may be the inspiration for any number of creative
projects. Someone may want to use dried specimens to decorate a block
of wood, can, or box cover. An accumulation of small smooth stones
and a little glue may inspire the creation of whimsical stone animals. A
mobile may be the result of discovering a perfect-sized piece of drift-
wood and several particularly lovely shells.

Extra scallop and clam shells could serve as appealing dishes for
holding glue. Set aside some surplus to add a summer feeling to winter
cut-and-paste projects. Making Sandcastings (page 290) is well worth
the effort if you have a variety of dried and "descented" sea creatures
and shells. Sand dollars, baby horseshoe crabs, starfish, and snail shells
make interesting designs.

You and the children might enjoy remembering a cousin or friend who does not live near a beach. Special prizes culled from the shore, then cleaned and coated with a little shellac or clear plastic spray for shine, can be prettily wrapped and mailed as surprise gifts.

Temper your enthusiasm for gathering nature's gifts with an honest respect for the environment, and leave the land undamaged by your visit. Help your preschoolers become aware of what it means to be good ecologists and to respect local rules regarding what can be taken and what must be left.

If you live in a landlocked part of the country, don't despair. Beach collecting with the group may be impossible, but one or more of the children may travel with their families to the seaside. They will feel especially important if they are assigned the task of bringing back treasures to share with everyone for scientific inspection or art projects. Nearby lakes and rivers also offer a wonderful source of stones. Some other hard-to-find nature treasures may be available at a local hobby shop. Explore the possibilities convenient to you.

Bugs and Other Wigglies

Wherever you are, small creatures abound in warm weather. Ask your preschoolers to clap some fireflies into a jar on a hot summer night to enjoy with everyone the next day. Have an inchworm collection spree. Capture grasshoppers. Be tomato plant detectives—can anyone spot the chubby, brilliant green tomato caterpillar hidden in the leafy camouflage of the plant? Inspect colorful moths close up. Pluck locust shells from tree trunks. How many can you find? Who knows what you will discover.

Make inspection of your findings easy by supplying your eager biologists with clear plastic jars. Punch holes in the lids or slit plastic wrap covers for air. Have each person pop a leaf or two in her jar for insect food and shelter. Keep a magnifying glass handy.

Popsicle Sticks and Empty Ice Cream Cups

Put manufactured collectibles on your list. For example, there are few places where the ice cream vendor is not a part of the summer scene. The Popsicles become worth the price (almost) if you save the sticks. If you need more sticks than you can collect by eating Popsicles, turn to your local craft store for supplements. Let the children stain, paint, or crayon them and use in any of a hundred ways. Glue them around the sides of juice cans for pencil holders; attach to old greeting cards for puppets; wind with yarn to make shade pulls or window decorations; glue crisscross in a square and decorate for hot pads. You can even use them for making your *own* ices.

Paper cups are another ice cream vendor bonus. They are versatile enough to use for mixing paint, planting seeds, or storing paper clips and fasteners.

REMEMBER THE FAMILIAR

Fourth of July

The Fourth of July is the most exciting of summer celebrations. The children will eagerly anticipate parades, picnics, and fireworks displays, so plan to talk about the occasion before the actual day.

Let the children make their own "fireworks" with marble painting (page 273). Many children love to make loud, explosive noises as they bang several marbles together.

For a holiday craft project, make "firecrackers" from toilet-tissue tubes or other cardboard tubes cut to 5 or 6 inches. Seal one end of tube by taping on a piece of construction paper. The children then cover the tubes with red paper (precut to size by you) and decorate with gold stars and flag stickers. You precut circles of construction paper with the same circumference as that of the tube. Put a hole in the center of each circle. Insert a few inches of string through the hole and tape firmly on one side of the circle to make a firecracker "wick." Use tape to hook the circle hinge fashion to the open end of the tube. What a delightful firecracker, and it can double as a snack holder, too!

The children may have a spontaneous or planned parade complete with rhythm band instruments, flags, and wagons or tricycles decorated in red, white, and blue ribbons and streamers. Choose a route down the street or around the block to show off your parade.

If weather permits, have a cookout on the grill at lunchtime. You can make the party as elaborate or simple as you please. Include a game or two. Four-year-olds love to try potato-sack racing—noncompetitively, of course. Old pillowcases can substitute for sacks, and the activity can be done indoors with equal success.

Trips Close By

Don't overlook the wealth of July events listed in the newspaper or on other summer calendars. If a craft fair is in the neighborhood, it may offer an opportunity to watch artisans at work and to see their wares.

Maybe a nearby street offers a farmers' market on one of your play-group days. Plan a stroll in that direction. Someone's mom or dad may work in an office or other spot not far away. Businesses sometimes have a slower summer pace and would welcome a brief visit from enthusiastic preschoolers who love showing off what mommy or daddy does.

Whatever kind of trip you choose, be sure your destination is easy to reach and plan your stay to suit the energy and attention limitations of your group.

Flexibility is a top priority. Maybe your little ones are in a fever pitch over the outdoor plan for the day when the rumble of thunder and rush of summer rain spoils the plan. Shift gears. Find a happy substitute for that trip to the farmers' market, fair, or park. For instance, go to the local mall instead, and carry your sack lunches and storybook to a spot beside a fountain or potted plant. Any place can give birth to adventure.

Pretend Trips

When real trips aren't part of the plans, it is time for "Let's Pretend." Brief the other parents ahead of time, and coach your playgroupers. On a given day they are to come with an old handbag or small duffle stuffed with anything they would want to carry if they were going on a real trip. Chat about possible contents: dark glasses, map, small mirror, old tickets, perfume, pad and pencils, change purse or wallet.

Who wants a set of keys? Everyone. The local hardware store will often set aside discarded keys from the key-making counter. String them together in bunches for preschool play. Cull extras from your own household collection of obsolete keys.

Other additions to the travel bags might be small toys or games. For instance, dice to be used for a Dice Decide game: Who rolled the biggest number? The smallest? Or use an incomplete deck of cards for playing impromptu red and black match games: First turn the deck face down. The first player must guess "black" or "red," then pick up a card. If his guess is wrong, he must put it back into the deck. If it is right, he keeps the card. Let everyone take turns until the pile is gone. See how many cards each child can "win."

On the assigned day everyone can divulge what they have concealed in their bags. Allow lots of time to share and pretend.

Such simple things are the real stuff of summer.

Outdoor Jobs

With the lazy drone of nearby bees or distant lawnmowers, summer sets the mood for all sorts of uncomplicated activities. Sponges, a hose, a bucket, a little plain dishwashing liquid, and one dirty car can provide a barrel of fun. Both car and children will end up damp and scrubbed.

A broom is better than any new toy: Hand out a couple and the playgroup brigade will whisk your steps or driveway clean. Preschoolers *love* to sweep.

Fill a watering can part way. Your group will sprinkle flowers and anything else that they spy, including themselves.

Think up other jobs—even cleaning up the wading pool and scattered toys can end up feeling like a game.

Indoor Things Done Outdoors

In winter you did outdoor things inside. Now it is time to turn the tables. An art project feels totally different done on a picnic table. A story read in a tent or beside a tree takes on a different dimension. Thumb through the activities in this book. Any one of them becomes brand new when it's done outdoors.

Bare Feet

Take off your shoes. Wiggle your toes. The sun-warmed hardtops of the driveway or sidewalk will toast your bare feet. Let cool velvety moss or rain-sprinkled grass stroke the skin. Test the feel of black soil. Gingerly step on gravel. Simple sensations belonging to summer—to be savored with the children.

Savor the height of the season. Choose favorite projects from June or last summer to repeat before the warm weather is over.

JULY ACTIVITIES

◆

ARTS AND CRAFTS

◆ Fourth of July Marble Roll   *Ages 3 and up*

Make a fireworks display on paper.

YOU WILL NEED:
   box lids with sides 1 to 2 inches high, or sturdy cake pans, 1 per
      child
   paper cut to fit inside box lids or pans
   margarine tubs, 2 per child
   plastic spoons, 2 per child
   tempera paint, 2 colors
   marbles, 2 per child

METHOD:
   Ahead of time: Cut paper to proper size and put inside each pan or
   box lid. Partially fill tubs with paint, one of each color for each child.
   Put a spoon and a marble in each tub.
   With the children: Give each child a box lid and two tubs of paint with
   marbles and spoons. Show the children how to spoon a marble out
   of the paint into the paper lined lid or pan. Tell the children to tilt
   the box carefully, making the marble roll in different directions,
   trailing the paint across the paper to create an interesting design of
   intersecting lines. Then have them use the second color and marble.
   The older children in the group will like to work at this a long time
   to see how much of the paper they can "cover up."

VARIATION:
   Coffee Can Roll: Line coffee can sides with paper cut to size. Place
   paint-covered marbles in bottoms of cans. Put lids on tightly. Chil-

dren hold top and bottom of cans and shake so marbles hop and skip in the cans to make surprise designs along the side that you see only when the marbles and paper are removed.

◆ Shadow Box Designs

Ages 4 and up

YOU WILL NEED:

boxes or box lids, ¾ to 1 inch deep [note-card boxes with see-through lids work well], 1 per child
shells
scissors
tape
clear plastic wrap or see-through box lid
glue and brushes
markers
optional: colored paper

METHOD:

Ahead of time: Glue colored paper to the bottom of the boxes for background, if desired.

With the children: The children glue shells inside to make butterflies, birds, flowers, and so on. [Clam or mussel shells side by side make good butterflies. Tiny clam, scallop, or jingle shells make good flower petals or leaves.] Use markers for details [antennae, wing designs, stems]. You put on the clear lid or stretch clear wrap around box to make a "glass" front, and tape it securely in place.

VARIATION:

Instead of shells, use varieties of seeds (different color beans, popping corn, lentils, split peas, barley, sunflower seed) or different kinds of dry pasta.

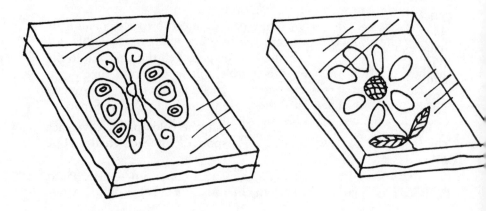

◆ A Child's American Flag

Ages 2 and up

This activity is perfect for children who find cutting difficult.

YOU WILL NEED:

1 piece each of red, white, and blue paper, at least 5 by 7 inches, 1
set per child
gold star stickers or a smaller piece of white paper for making stars
paste or glue and brushes
picture of an American flag, or a sample one made by you

METHOD:

Show the children the American flag and ask what shapes and colors
they see in it (blue rectangle, red lines, stripes). Distribute the paper
and encourage children to *tear* red stripes and a blue piece to paste
onto the larger white piece. For stars, some children may wish to
tear a few pieces of white to glue onto the blue, others will use star
stickers. Numbers of stripes or stars and accuracy do not matter.

◆ Sponge Painting

Ages 3 and up

Preschool impressionism!

YOU WILL NEED:

sponges cut into pieces, about 1 to 2 inches square (can be different
thicknesses and shapes), 1 piece per child
scissors
paper, any size, 1 sheet per child
tempera paint, 1 color
paint containers (margarine tubs work well), 1 per child
optional: spring clip-type clothespins to attach to sponge pieces as
handles (Some preschoolers are distressed by messy hands.)

METHOD:

Ahead of time: Cut the sponges into various sizes. Attach clothespin
handles if desired. Pour paint into containers.
With the children: Have the children dip the sponges into the paint
and then dab, twist, and sweep over the paper for different effects.
You can demonstrate some of the possibilities. If the sponge shapes
are different, children can exchange them to vary results.

On another occasion, mix more than one color paint. Give each
child a set of paint containers with sponges for each shade. Have
them do multicolor sponge art.

COOKING

◆ Turtles

YOU WILL NEED (for 12 snacks):
12 wheat crackers
3-ounce package cream cheese
1 cup raisins
6 pitted prunes
knife
4 small bowls
small paper plates

METHOD:

Ahead of time: Cut each prune in half. Cut cheese into 12 equal parts. Arrange ingredients in separate bowls.

With the children: Place a cheese chunk on each wheat cracker. Press a prune half, cut side down, on the cheese to make the turtle's back. Add raisins for head, legs, and tail. (You can substitute whipped cream cheese or peanut butter for cheese chunks).

◆ Fruit Dip

YOU WILL NEED:
honey
Grape-Nuts cereal
sesame seeds
chopped nuts
choice of sliced bananas, apples, strawberries, melon, or other fruits
serrated plastic knives
paper bowls, plates

METHOD:

Ahead of time: Put the honey, cereal, seeds, and nuts in separate bowls. Prepare the fruit so that the children can easily slice it.

With the children: Slice the fruit. Arrange it in bowls in the center of the table with a bowl of honey for dipping fruit. Each child serves herself a plate of fruit. Sit and dip. Enjoy the party.

◆ Peanut Butter Popcorn
Ages 3 and up

YOU WILL NEED:
1 bag microwave popcorn (or 4 cups conventionally popped corn)
3 tablespoons butter
3 tablespoons chunky peanut butter
tablespoon measure
small saucepan
large mixing bowl
mixing spoon
paper cups or sandwich bags

METHOD:
If using microwave popcorn, one child can put the popcorn in the microwave oven and push the necessary buttons, with your help. You melt the butter in a saucepan. Another child can measure in the peanut butter with the melted butter and stir until smooth. When you check that the popcorn bag is cool enough, someone else can pour the popcorn into a bowl. The others can take turns spooning the butter and peanut butter mixture over the popcorn and stirring. Cool. Fill cups or bags. Enjoy indoors or out.

DRAMATIC PLAY

◆ Superhero Clay Play
Ages 3 and up

Have some powerful play in a quiet space.

YOU WILL NEED:
superhero activity books
Popsicle sticks
scissors
glue
clay (see recipe on page 24)

METHOD:
Ahead of time: Cut out a selection of the children's favorite super-heroes. Glue the figures to the Popsicle sticks to create superhero puppets. (If these are good silhouettes, you can use them for Shadow Plays, page 00). Make or buy a batch of colorful clay.
With the children: Let the children choose their puppets. They will manipulate them, using the clay to hold the figures upright and to make small props for the action play. The children's conversations may reveal feelings about power and control.

◆ **Crocodile Crossing***   *Ages 3 and up*

Act out a preschool melodrama!

METHOD:

You narrate and act this out with the children. Tell your preschoolers to lie on their tummies, because they are now the
crocodiles in your story. Then say:

"I'm lost in a faraway jungle. I know I need to cross the river to find
my way home, but I see a crocodile in the water. Maybe I can cross
over the river here, and he won't see me. [Start to wade slowly into
the "water" toward the children.] Oh, no! I see another crocodile . . .
and another . . . and another. I can't make it! HELP! HELP! [Start
dodging the swimming crocodiles headed toward you. Jump up on a
chair to get away as the crocodiles move closer.]

Let one of the preschoolers act the part of the lost hero as you
narrate. The children love moving on their stomachs as crocodiles
and solving the imaginary crisis as the hero. As they act they will
offer such rescue suggestions as, "Make a bridge" (with cardboard
blocks, balance beam). Soon the children will be able to narrate by
themselves. What starts out as a drama directed by you will become a
game of pretending, filled with the children's own improvisation.

GAMES

◆ **Hot Potato**   *Ages 3 and up*

YOU WILL NEED:
small ball
signal (whistle or music and music player)

METHOD:

Have your group sit on the floor in a circle. The children roll the
ball around the circle from one child to the next as fast as possible so
they won't be the one to get caught when you give the signal to stop.

---

*Adapted from *Creative Movement for the Developing Child*, revised edn., Clare Cherry
(Belmont, Calif.: Teacher Aids, Simon & Schuster Supplementary Education Group,
1971).

◆ Duck, Duck, Goose   *Ages 3 and up*

This old favorite is a great impromptu game for restless children.

METHOD:

Sit in a circle. One person is the goose. The goose goes around the outside of the circle and taps each person on the head while saying "duck," "duck," "duck,"—then taps someone saying "goose." The new goose runs around the circle after the old goose. If the new goose does not catch the old goose before the old goose sits in the space left by the new goose, then the new goose becomes "it" and begins tapping people. If the new goose catches the old goose, then the old goose is "it" again! Make sure that the same child is not "it" three or four times in a row.

MUSIC

◆ Musical Imaginations   *Ages 2 and up*

YOU WILL NEED:

instruments such as:
  piano
  finger cymbals or bells
  drum

METHOD:

Divide your group into kittens and big bears (or ask the children to choose small and large animals). When you play high piano notes, finger cymbals, or bells, the kittens move to the music. Bass piano notes or drum beats accompany the bears' rhythmic movement. Accentuate the difference by making the kitten music soft and the bear music loud and heavy. Another time divide the group into elves and giants. You can adapt other instruments that you have available.

◆ Spice Tin Shakers   *Ages 3 and up*

YOU WILL NEED:

large empty spice tins, 2 per child
containers of noise-making materials such as:
  rice   small dry pasta
  dried beans   sand

barley   coffee beans
plastic spoons
optional: small funnel (may make filling easier)

METHOD:

Encourage the children to spoon some noise-making materials into the spice tins, using all of one kind or creating a mix. See if they are able to give each shaker a different sound. Make them aware of the difference in sound as they put more items in the tin. Encourage them to fill a little and test-shake a lot before adding more.

PHYSICAL EXERCISE

◆ Cat and Mice   *Ages 3 and up*

METHOD:

One child is the cat and hides. The rest of the children are mice and sneak up to the cat's hiding place and scratch. This is the signal for the cat to chase the mice and try to catch one. Then choose another child to be the cat. The game continues until everyone has had a turn to be cat. Background music adds to the fun of this game.

◆ Outward Bound Obstacle Course   *Ages 3 and up*

YOU WILL NEED:
   obstacles—Choose what is already in place in your rooms and add
      what is needed to vary the challenge:

table	paper
chairs	marker
Hula Hoop	traffic cones (cardboard blocks)
balance beam	tunnel (box with ends cut out)
(tape on floor or	climbing set
ladder laid flat on ground)	

METHOD:
   Ahead of time: Set up your obstacle course appropriate to the space
   available. It could span two connecting rooms. Make signs that read
   "over . . . under . . . around . . . between . . . through," using arrows
   to show the path the children are to take. Number each sign so they
   can follow the course in sequence.
   With the children: Explain how the numbers and arrows will help
   them complete the course. Have the children go through the course,
   allowing ample time for each child to have a good head start before
   the next child begins. For example:
   under the table
   around the Hula Hoop
   between the cones (blocks)
   across the balance beam
   through the tunnel
   over the climbing set
   Another time, take this activity outdoors (around the tree, over the
   sandbox).

SCIENCE

◆ Ice Cube Melt   *Ages 2 and up*

Children discover what makes ice last longer in this cool-off game of
observation.

YOU WILL NEED:
   warm day
   thermal container holding ice cubes (at least 1 cube for each child)

METHOD:
   Choose an area for outdoor play (backyard, sandbox area, grassy
   area at park) that offers some good alternatives for the following

game: Give the children one ice cube each. Tell them to find a special place where they think their ice cubes will last a long time. One
person may choose a rock for a resting spot, another a mound of
dirt, a shaded patch of soft moss, a sunny piece of pavement, or a
hole covered with leaves. Your preschoolers will enjoy checking their
ice cubes from time to time as they play.

When enough time has passed for some melting to occur, have the
group check on all the cubes. Which one is lasting the longest? Why
is this a better place to put the ice cubes? The children may use
words like "cooler," "darker," "softer" (more insulated), "covered
up," and so on.

VARIATION:

Do the project indoors using ice cubes in paper cups.

♦ Flashlight Fix-It   *Ages 3 and up*

Helps teach problem solving.

YOU WILL NEED:

flashlights (type that can be taken apart), 1 per child
batteries for flashlights

METHOD:

Let the children experiment with turning the flashlight on and off.
Have them unscrew the flashlight and take out the batteries. Re-
screw. Test without batteries—no light. Put in batteries. Unscrew everything including the light bulb cover and light bulb. Count the
parts. Try different ways to make the flashlight work again. The
problem solving will encourage amazing preschool technical conversation, logic, and abilities.

SUGGESTION:

Have a flashlight adventure. Let the children take their flashlights
on a walk with you. Investigate places where a hand should not go
but the light can shine, such as an animal hole in a tree trunk. Look
into storm drains, alleyways, and other mysterious places.

STORYTELLING

◆ Sharing Summer Fun   *Ages 2 and up*

YOU WILL NEED:

treasures collected by children on summer outings:

captured insect	new book from library
travel brochures	blueberries picked to eat
rocks or stones	shells

METHOD:

Share each treasure in an appropriate way: reading the storybook, tasting or cooking the blueberries, learning more about the insect, or starting a collection of brochures, rocks, and so on. Children are usually excited about their treasures and have lots to say about them.

SUGGESTION:

Items with a distinct shape or feel, such as stones, can later be used with the feeling box game (page 157).

TRIPS

◆ Visiting the Post Office or Mailbox   *Ages 3 and up*

Writing Whimsy in May (page 230) introduced the children to the idea of office time, writing letters, making cards, and doodling secret notes. What fun to connect that experience with the actual mailing of something to someone special. With a little advance notice, most post offices will be glad to take you and your group behind the scenes to watch the sorting of mail. Preschoolers are impressed with the volume of mail as compared to what arrives in their home mailbox each day. If the post office is too far away or not available to little visitors, pick a nice day and plan a walk to the nearest mailbox.

METHOD:

Ahead of time: Plan a special art and writing activity with matching-size envelopes for the children to do in advance. Get the address of the recipient of each child's card.

With the children: Talk about the upcoming trip to the post office or mailbox. Let the children seal and and stamp the envelopes to be mailed. On arrival at the post office or box, have them deposit their mail in the right slot. Then enjoy the post office visit or the return walk from the mailbox.

WOODWORKING

◆ Building Floating Barges and Boats   *Ages 4 and up*

This activity assumes previous experience with hammering, and works well indoors or outdoors.

YOU WILL NEED:
   scrap lumber
   hammers
   nail assortment
   wire pieces
   glue
   tub of water (a plastic baby tub or dishpan is fine)
   sheet or newspaper to catch water splashes

METHOD:
   Suggest that the children create some kind of boat. Distribute the materials and let them use gluing, hammering, and other skills they have practiced during other activities. Then let them play with their results in the water. Some children may go as far as partitioning off sections of a "ferry boat" and lining up small cars for the crossing. Small plastic figures make good boat passengers. All sorts of interesting ideas will emerge.

AUGUST

AUGUST CONTENTS

◆

AUGUST GUIDEPOSTS

◆

THINGS YOU CAN COLLECT

Hot as it is, the days are shortening. It is time to try to fit in all the summer things you have meant to do—and it is time to ease into the transition of summer to autumn.

Vegetables

Harvesting is at full tilt. Now is the perfect time to collect vegetables for sculpture projects. Home gardens, supermarkets, roadside stands, or farmers' markets are all sources. Choose a nearby spot and have your preschoolers help you pick out a handsome supply of colorful vegetables.

Later, set out toothpicks, plastic knives, and produce to create edible art. Oversized zucchini with radish eyes and clothespin legs may be one child's creation. Perhaps eggplant is the working base for someone else's sculpture. A stegosaurus may suddenly appear as a zucchini creature with summer squash scallops on the back. People with string bean hair or various abstractions might emerge.

Flowers to Press

Harvest time won't mean vegetables to everyone. For some groups selections may center around a profusion of wildflowers in a nearby field or vacant lot. Treasures in this case may be armfuls of Black Eyed Susans or other blossoms to be transported home in paper drinking cups or juice cans. A selection of blooms might be saved and pressed in an extrathick book to use later in craft projects. They also may be used to adorn note paper or placemats, covered with clear Contact paper for permanent preservation.

Pods

Have a pod hunt. How many pods do you see? See how many kinds of pods you can collect—milkweed, bean, pea—or at the beach, beach peas (just look, don't pick). Maybe you will find some that you can't identify.

REMEMBER THE FAMILIAR

Going Fishing

Summertime and fishing just go together. Keep it simple—a line wound around a piece of wood or a stick, a hook, and local bait. Think of your own ways for easy fishing. See what you can catch at a nearby pond—maybe nothing. Preschoolers won't want to wait long. You won't need or want a line for everyone at one time. Take turns. Keep the experience brief and fun. For safety, have an extra adult along.

Summer Smells and Sounds

In July it was such fun feeling summer sensations with wiggly bare toes. Summer comes with special smells, too. *Talk* about the fragrances of summer. The sweetness of warm-weather rain. A whiff of pungent honeysuckle or roses, woods, pine. The sharp smell of gasoline on a hot, hot day. Sun lotion (and bug goo)! A cookout down the street reaching your nose and reminding tummies that it's time for a snack.

Summer speaks out loud in so many ways. Listen. The bell of the ice cream vendor calls out. Shut your eyes. What do the children hear? Locusts hum. Birds clamor. A saw buzzes. A siren sounds. A fountain sings splashy songs. Rain drums. Steal moments for staying still, listening, smelling.

Water Fun

Summer is above all get-wet time. Make it safe and uncomplicated. Put out your splash pool for lots of water fun with little effort. Turn on the sprinkler and play tag in it as it twirls or jerks the water spray. Play the games of winter in the new setting. Simon says, "Jump over the sprinkler . . . stay dry . . . get wet . . . stand still. . . ."

Does anyone in the group have slides of summer adventures from this or other years? Simply set the slides and a hand viewer in a handy spot and preschoolers will go back to look and look again.

Snowballs

Remember how you tried some spring-style treats to make midwinter seem less dreary? Pull a similar switch on a steaming hot day. If you tucked some snowballs into your freezer last January (page 153), pull them out for a snowball "toss" using a tree as a target. The group might just enjoy watching how the sun will melt a snowball—in a little pail of water or on the hot sidewalk.

Catch the spirit of colder weather by beating soapflakes to make winter snow pictures or sculptures (see Whipping Snow, page 168).

Library Offerings

Do not overlook the special summertime activities offered by your community. Libraries have programs planned with preschoolers in mind. They range from simple story hours to sessions with outside entertainers. Sometimes the library is a starting point for a trip.

The children may enjoy perusing the books and making a selection to read at home on another playgroup day.

Each library has its own special atmosphere and set of treasures. You may find a Victorian dollhouse or an array of tropical fish in an enormous tank. Check out what is hanging on the walls. The children can tell you which are their favorite pictures in an exhibition.

Transitions

Back-to-school ads are in the newspapers and fall clothing adorns store windows. Families are planning Labor Day farewells to summer. Some of the children may be graduating from playgroup. The playgroup parents may want to plan a summer's end party.

Consider reserving space at the park for a box supper picnic. Everyone brings a shoebox with the family supper and an extra treat or two tucked inside. It is fun for the children to open the surprise box and for everyone to share. Simple games can be part of the fun. Look to some that are mentioned in the following pages, such as Freeze (page 298).

Summer is never long enough. Somehow you just cannot fit in all the activities that you dreamed of doing during the warm weather. Certainly this is true with plans for your playgroup. You cannot possibly squeeze in everything that seems appealing, from the search for beach treasures to the snowball toss. Be selective, then savor what you choose. You will have lots of happy memories to warm the colder days ahead.

AUGUST ACTIVITIES

◆

ARTS AND CRAFTS

◆ **Painting with Water** *Ages 2 and up*

YOU WILL NEED:
  large paintbrushes
  pails or cans of water

METHOD:
  Children can "paint" the house, garage, car, or sidewalk. This activity might not sound exciting, but it is delightful in hot weather
  and its simplicity absolutely fascinates small children.

◆ **Sandcasting** *Ages 4 and up*

The great results are worth the time and effort.

YOU WILL NEED:
  foil or tin pans of any shape, as deep as the largest shell you will be
    using, 1 per child
  Red Top or other quick plaster of Paris, at least 5 pounds for 4 pans
  damp sand
  large can and stick for mixing plaster
  fish line or heavy string
  scissors
  variety of dried and "de-scented" (page 64) sea creatures or shells
    (starfish, sand dollars, crab, snails, clam, scallops)

METHOD:
  Ahead of Time: This activity is best done outdoors at a picnic table or
  in the kitchen or basement. Set out all the materials in large buckets.

Have the amount of water you need ready for mixing the plaster according to package directions.

With the children: Have the children line the pans with damp sand like a thick pie crust, using their hands to pat it down evenly. Then show them how to push the shells into the sand until the shells are surrounded with but not covered over by the sand "crust." The parts of the shells buried in the sand will be what shows when the plaster has hardened and the pan is removed. When everyone is happy with their arrangement, mix the plaster to the consistency of pancake batter, allowing the children to help stir. Then *quickly* pour the white mixture into the remaining space, like pie filling. Immediately help set both ends of a short piece of fish line or heavy string into the plaster so it will be ready to hang when dry. You might also take a stick and mark the date or the child's name in the plaster.

Even on a very sunny, warm day, it is best to let the sandcasting dry and harden in the pan for at least 12 hours. Then, outdoors or over a wastebasket, the children remove the pan and brush away the excess sand. The result is a most attractive wall plaque with a thin coating of sand covering the plaster and a shell design in relief—a wonderful way to preserve a special beach collection.

◆ Clothespin Sailboat   *Ages 3 and up*

YOU WILL NEED:

spring clip–type clothespins (wooden or plastic), 1 per child
toothpicks
white paper, 9 by 12 inches
glue and brushes
scissors
optional: markers or paint and brushes

METHOD:

Ahead of time: Remove the hinges from the clothespins. Cut a square
of paper (about 2½ inches square) for each child. Make a sample
boat of your own to show the children, using the directions below.
With the children: The children glue the flat pieces of the clothespins
together. This leaves a tiny hole near one end of the "boat." You
insert a toothpick "mast" through each paper square "sail." *Optional:*
The children color the boats. Then the children put glue in the
boat's hole, stand the toothpick mast in it and let dry.

◆ Fossil Art*Ages 3 and up*

YOU WILL NEED:
Best Ever Clay Recipe (page 24)

or

Air-hardening modeling material (from art supply store, hobby
 shop, or educational toy store)
natural materials:

twigs	bones (wishbone, chicken leg)
leaves	feathers
ferns	shells

METHOD:
Ahead of time: Make batch of clay and gather materials for fossil specimens.
With the children: Give each child a chunk of the clay and have him
flatten it to approximately ¼ inch thick (thinner pieces break more
easily). The child then presses an object into the clay base to make
an impression. The delight of this activity is that children can experiment with a variety of imprints before deciding on the one to save.
Leave the clay in a warm, sunny place to harden. The next time you
do fossil art the children might enjoy hunting in the yard for their
own specimens.

◆ Wind Art*Ages 3 and up*

YOU WILL NEED:
fabric strips approximately 12 to 18 inches long and 1 inch wide (use
 lightweight material such as gauze, cheesecloth, bedsheet), 2 to 3
 per child
liquid detergent
food coloring
measuring cup
water
newspaper
large plastic containers (large margarine or deli tubs work well), 1
 per dye color
pipe cleaners or dowels, 6 inches or more in length
stapler
string or fish line

METHOD:
Ahead of time: For each color desired mix 1 cup of water, a few drops
of detergent, and food coloring to the shade desired in a plastic
container.

With the children: The children dip the fabric strips in dye and spread them on newspaper to dry (15 to 20 minutes). Then you staple the strips around dowels or pipe cleaners. Tie on string or fish line and hang the creations outdoors from trees or railings. Children get a sense of wind direction as the colorful art waves in the breeze.

This is easy to do in an assembly line. Dyes are lined up on newspaper beside piles of fabric strips. The children move from dye to dye, dipping a strip and laying it out on newspaper as they go. Or, you can give each child a different color dye and have her dye several strips.

COOKING

◆ Spinach Wrap   *Ages 3 and up*

YOU WILL NEED:
  tub of cream cheese, whipped or soft
  fresh spinach leaves, as flat as possible, 2 to 3 per child
  seasoned salt or other herb seasoning
  plastic knives or spoons
  paper plates

METHOD:
  Children scoop a dollop of cheese onto a spinach leaf. Sprinkle with seasoning. Wrap up. Feast.

VARIATION:
  You can use lettuce or other soft edible leaves, instead of spinach.

◆ "Happle" Bagel Sandwich   *Ages 3 and up*

This is a good cloudy-day project.

YOU WILL NEED:
  mini bagels, 1 per child
  2 to 3 apples
  cheese slices, 1 per child
  cinnamon
  serrated plastic knives
  round cookie cutter or cup
  cookie sheet
  large paper plates

METHOD:

Ahead of time: Cut bagels in half. Halve apples crosswise. Preheat the oven to 350° F.

With the children: Using a plate as a cutting surface, the children cut out a circle of cheese with the cutter or cup. Slice a thin round of apple and remove the center with a knife. Stack the bagel half, cheese, and apple slice. Sprinkle with cinnamon. Top with the other bagel half. Bake on a cookie sheet 5 to 10 minutes or microwave on Medium until cheese is bubbly and bagel is warm.

◆ Fruit Shish Kabob   *Ages 3 and up*

YOU WILL NEED:

choice of fresh fruits (substitute canned if necessary):

melon	pineapple
strawberries	bananas
apples	peaches

knife

serrated plastic knives

bamboo skewers (available in kitchen departments and grocery stores)

paper plates

METHOD:

Ahead of time: Prepare the fruits so they are easy for the children to cut into smaller chunks.

With the children: Using a paper plate as chopping board, each child can cut fruit into chunks and string them onto skewers. Supervise carefully.

DRAMATIC PLAY

◆ Summer Camp-Out   *Ages 3 and up*

Enjoy this outdoor or indoor treat.

YOU WILL NEED:

pup tent with stakes to anchor

or

large sheet, bedspread, or blanket with weights, such as books or bricks, to anchor

sturdy clothesline

METHOD:

Ahead of time: Set up the pup tent, or improvise by stringing a line outside between two trees or inside between two hooks about 3 to 4 feet off the ground. Fold a sheet in half over the line. Pull each side out at an angle, anchor well, and you have a tent just right for preschoolers.

With the children: Play! Some will like the tent for a quiet hideaway with a teddy bear or storybook. Others with family vacation experience might organize "camp-out" play and improvise props for pretend fire, flashlights, or sleeping bags.

SUGGESTION:

Army-navy surplus stores offer a selection of appealing items (mess kits, insignias, and so on) at reasonable prices for older children who interpret a tent as an invitation to boot camp training.

◆ Box Car Train   *Ages 2 and up*

YOU WILL NEED:

cardboard boxes large enough to hold a child, 1 per child
wooden blocks, dolls, or other favorite toys

METHOD:

Ahead of time: Line up the boxes to suggest a train.

With the children: Announce, "Anyone can ride the box car train today." Have everyone select something from the toy supply. Blocks may become cargo, even people or tickets. The play follows the interest of a particular child or of this particular group: breakdown and repair, rescue, a family trip, or just loading and unloading the vehicle. Boxes for each child help them to play side by side and connect through conversation.

SUGGESTION:

Another day, just put out the boxes with no comment. Let the children determine the play. Boxes can become boats, airplanes, cages for animals at the zoo, or a world of other things.

GAMES

♦ **Penny Splash**   *Ages 3 and up*

Cool off on a hot day with this eye-hand coordination game.

YOU WILL NEED:
  pail
  large supply of pennies
  wading pool filled with water
  objects to float:
    sponge   baking pan
    plastic Hula hoop   Frisbee
    toy boat   margarine container

METHOD:
  Put the floating objects in the wading pool. The children take turns
  pitching pennies onto or through the floating objects. Once the pennies have been tossed, everyone helps to collect them from the
  water. Then establish a game line where the preschoolers stand to
  toss. As their accuracy improves, gradually move the line farther
  away from the pool. Be flexible, but encourage the children to test
  their ability with differences in distance. This game will add a carnival touch to outdoor birthday party or neighborhood cookout.

♦ **Kick the Can**   *Ages 4 and up*

YOU WILL NEED:
  plastic or metal can

METHOD:
  Drop the can on the ground. This is best on some hard surface so
  everyone can hear satisfying clanks and bangs. Choose player to be
  "it." "It" stands near the can and closes his eyes, counting until everyone scatters and hides within a designated area. "It" then tries to
  find and tag those who are hiding before they are able to sneak up
  and kick the can. The first person tagged is "it" for the next game.

MUSIC

◆ Rubber Band Guitar   *Ages 3 and up*

YOU WILL NEED:

small, sturdy, low-sided boxes, 1 per child
rubber bands of different lengths and widths

METHOD:

Have the children stretch a variety of rubber bands over their boxes. Let them strum and experiment with the different sounds made. Strum and sing together a familiar song such as "I've Been Working on the Railroad" or let them accompany a recording.

VARIATION:

Tiny boxes that slip into a pocket have great appeal, as do colored rubber bands.

◆ High and Low Sounds #2   *Ages 4 and up*

YOU WILL NEED:

record or tape player
records or tapes—"Do-Re-Mi" from *The Sound of Music* or others
you may choose to fit the activity.

METHOD:

Sing or play the song "Do-Re-Mi" and show the children that your voice goes from low to high. Use your hand to show high and low sounds as you sing. Let the children imitate you with their hands.

PHYSICAL EXERCISE

◆ Freeze   *Ages 2 and up*

Run off some steam with this stop-and-go game when the group gets wild!

YOU WILL NEED:

piano, tape, or record player
lively music

METHOD:

Play the music as the children move freely around the room. When you stop the music say, "Freeze." Everyone freezes like a statue. The children must stay in the positions they were in when the music stopped. Comment on each child's position: "Sarah looks as if she is diving. Peter looks as if he is about to swing at a baseball." The children can help you with ideas. Repeat this routine as long as the children enjoy it. Afterwards, everyone will be ready for something at a slower pace.

◆ Preschoolers' Jump Rope and Chant　　　*Ages 3 and up*

A rainy-day exercise.

YOU WILL NEED:
1 jump rope, long enough for everyone in the group (about 4 feet per person), or individual jump ropes

METHOD:
Extend the rope in a straight line on the floor. Children take their places along the rope. Let them practice jumping from one side of the rope to the other, first on two feet, then hopping on one foot or straddling the rope and shifting from one foot to the other. Once they are familiar with the jump that works best for them, teach them the chant and how to hop or jump to the rain sounds.
Listen to the raindrops

Plop! Plop! Plop!

[Hop . . . 2 . . . 3]

I watch the little raindrops

Drop! Drop! Drop!

[Hop . . . 2 . . . 3]

I want to hear the raindrops

Stop! Stop! Stop!

[Hop . . . 2 . . . 3]

Encourage the children to adapt other chants that they enjoy to jump rope exercise. For additional ideas, see *Jump Rope Jingles*, Ali Reich (New York: Random House, 1983).

SCIENCE

◆ Water Lens Observation   *Ages 3 and up*

YOU WILL NEED:
   plastic pail
   clear plastic wrap
   large rubber band or string large enough to go around the top of
      the pail
   sharp scissors or knife
   pitcher of water
   a selection of objects such as small toy car, shell, bracelet, coin, comb,
      leaf

METHOD:
   Ahead of time: Cut holes in each side of the pail. Cover the top of the
   pail loosely with plastic wrap. Secure it with the rubber band or
   string.
   With the children: Pour water to make a puddle on top of the plastic.
   You may need to loosen the plastic a little so it can hold a good
   puddle. Have a child insert an object through a hole in the side of
   the pail and look down at it through the water. Let the other preschoolers take turns viewing objects this way. As you talk with the
   children about what they are seeing you might ask questions like,
   "How does the bracelet change when you hold it under the water?"
   (It looks bigger.) "Does the twig look the same when you hold it over
   the water? Under the water?" Use the word *magnify.* End the discussion with the idea that water can make things look bigger—it
   magnifies.

◆ Summer Snowstorm   *Ages 2 and up*

YOU WILL NEED:
   any size transparent plastic tube with cap (standard kind used for
      packaging calendars, dish towels or posters)
   small pieces of packaging foam broken up into rice-size pieces

METHOD:
   Place some packaging foam pieces inside the tube and secure the cap
   tightly. The children experiment with static electricity as they rub
   the outside of the tube, which causes the foam pieces to dart around
   on the inside, giving the effect of a snowstorm. Rub slowly and you
   get light snow. Rub quickly and you create a blizzard.

STORYTELLING

◆ Prop Storytelling

Ages 2 and up

YOU WILL NEED:

storybook (simple action story such as *I Can Dress Myself,* by Dick
  Bruna)
props mentioned in the story (example: pieces of clothing
  mentioned in *I Can Dress Myself*)

METHOD:

Be familiar with the story. Tell it as you illustrate it using props. (For
I Can Dress Myself, you would put on each piece of clothing as it is
mentioned in the story.) Leave the book and the props in a special
place so the children can use them when they wish. On other days
repeat the story, and let individual children show the group how
they can do what is told in the book.

SUGGESTION:

Also try *Curious George Goes to the Hospital,* by H. A. Rey: yellow hat,
puzzle piece, stethoscope, nurse's cap, and so on.

TRIPS

◆ Trip to the Ice Cream Store

Ages 2 and up

Everyone has a favorite place for ice cream. Choose one close to your
home—if possible, one where ice cream is being made or ice cream
cakes are being decorated.

METHOD:

Check with the store owner about the best time to have the children
visit. The trip will be extra special if she is able to show them how
she squirts icing from tubes to design and personalize cakes. Plan
enough time so that the group can enjoy an ice cream treat "on
location." You might want to ask for empty gallon ice cream containers, one per child. The children can do an original cut-and-paste
and make wastebaskets another day as mementos of the trip.

WOODWORKING

◆ Rotating Wood Sculpture   *Ages 2 and up*

This is a continuing project for one child or the group as a whole.

YOU WILL NEED:
  a selection of:
    small- to medium-size scraps of wood
    wood turnings (sold by the bag in arts and crafts stores)
    Popsicle sticks, ice cream spoons, clothespins
  fast-drying glue
  cardboard circle, approximately 1 foot in diameter, to use as
    sculpture base
  optional: lazy Susan

METHOD:
  Set the cardboard base on the lazy Susan, if you have one, so the
  sculpture can be turned as the children work. Spread out a generous
  supply of wood pieces. Let the children create a three-dimensional
  design by gluing pieces on top of one another. You will hear lots of
  brainstorming between the children as they help one another glue.
  They will talk about how their work is beginning to look like a city,
  attic, office building, or birthday cake, to mention a few familiar
  favorites. You might do this outside on an especially nice day.

APPENDIX 1

Running Your Playgroup for Profit (Home Day Care)

You may want to consider running a playgroup for profit. It may happen that you and other parents you know are eager for your children to have the playgroup experience, but the others are not available to give their time. Instead they may be willing to pay you to carry on for them. Maybe you have not approached any parents, but you have been thinking about the home playgroup option as an appealing small business for yourself.

PERSONAL CONSIDERATIONS

In either case it is time to do some soul-searching. Is this something you will enjoy doing? Are you relatively easygoing, with a flexible temperament, able to enjoy shaping, planning, and living in the world children can share with you? Are you in good mental and physical health? Taking care of children is strenuous work. Many places will require you, as a day care giver, to have a medical examination and be re-checked every two years.

Are you eager to learn new things to provide more fully for the children? Talk to someone who operates a home day care. There are workshops and support organizations for day care providers that can help someone like you. Check what your community offers. Contact national and state organizations that address themselves to child education and care issues (see pages 308–310 for list of resources).

Are you in a financial position to withstand the initial and continuing costs of running your small business? Find out what minimal changes you need to make in your home and what expenses for basic equipment you might incur. Look into the cost of accident and liability insurance for children and adults. Are you already covered? What kind of income can you expect? Check around to find the going rates locally.

Will your community allow you to do what you have in mind? Check with your town or city hall about local zoning regulations relating to day care operations. Ask what the requirements are regarding water, septic, and heating systems, so you know you are in compliance without incurring backbreaking expenses.

STATE REQUIREMENTS AND GUIDELINES

Obtaining Information from the State

Once you have worked through the preliminaries you will need to find out the state and local requirements for child care. Different states have different names for the office you need to contact. The names have a similar ring. In California it is the Department of Social Services; in Georgia, the Department of Human Resources; in Illinois, the Department of Children and Family Services. Just call the state offices, explain what you want to do, and you will eventually be shuttled to the right source.

Ask the appropriate office to send you the state rules and regulations, along with any additional guidelines for running a small preschool home day care operation. Usually the information will be sent to you free, though some states charge a small fee. Rules, regulations, and licensing requirements vary hugely from state to state. Some are detailed and mandatory, others are voluntary or even nonexistent.

Licensing

When the information comes, check to see if your state asks for registration, certification, or licensing. You may need to do nothing at all. If you do need to obtain a license, keep in mind that processing can take as long as sixty days, so apply quickly and allow ample time before your playgroupers appear for their first day. In some cases you may need to pay a very small licensing fee.

Most often the licensing process includes an application, medical forms to be signed by your doctor, an interview or inspections by a state social worker, and possibly other inspections by a health department official or a fire marshal.

Your Qualifications

If your state has a strong set of regulations, qualifications may cover your age (usually eighteen or older), your previous experience, references, courses you have taken for credit (or the equivalent), first aid training, and financial security for operations. Sometimes the qualification of being a parent is enough.

Caring for the Children

Some states are concerned with every aspect of your care of the children. The specifics vary from state to state, but the states that have the best guidelines and most stringent requirements generally cover similar areas. Below is a list of those areas with some of the most common provisions indicated. This list is a composite drawn from some of the strongest state guidelines, and addresses issues which should be of concern to you if you want to provide what is best for the children, their parents, and yourself.

- ◆ Age range allowed
- ◆ Number of preschoolers in group
- ◆ Days and hours of operation (separate licensing for night care)
- ◆ Records (names, addresses, and phone numbers of parents and child; emergency numbers of parents, doctor, and parent substitute; written instructions for any medication; information regarding any special health problems including allergies; written permission for emergency medical attention; certificates of immunizations; proof of recent medical examinations; ongoing notations on accidents, illness, and progress during playgroup time; signed permission for transportation to activities away from the usual group meeting place; name of a person to whom you may release the child)
- ◆ Transportation (times; safe arrival and departure procedures; seat belts and infant restraints; safety regulations regarding cars and other vehicles)
- ◆ Health and safety (childproofing the home; first aid equipment; continual supervision; illness care: caring for an ill child and separating him from the group; procedures for reporting health-related problems, accidents, abuse, and diseases to parents and the proper authorities). See page 18 for specific health and safety guidelines.
- ◆ Food (meals and snacks; eligibility for child care food programs, nutrition; handling of food)
- ◆ Equipment (adequate supply of toys and materials for participation of all children; a working phone; handy bathroom facilities with toilet and sink; a bed, sleeping bag, or crib for each child)

- Space (square footage requirements: for example, Massachusetts stipulates indoor space of 150 square feet for 1 to 2 children and 225 square feet for 3 to 6 children, outdoor space of 75 square feet per child)
- Discipline (restriction of punishment to positive and timely measures; prohibition of sarcasm, verbal abuse, physical punishment, isolation of a child in closets or unsupervised areas, punishments that interfere with eating, sleeping, and toileting)
- Activities (a variety appropriate to the age and development of the child; regular outdoor play)

Cooperating with the Parents

You may also encounter rules, regulations, and suggestions regarding your responsibility to the parents and their responsibility to you and the children. These usually indicate that parents should be welcome to look at the facilities you have to offer at any time and that you should provide them with information in writing that covers the following:

- Basic enrollment information (age limits, numbers of children, hours and days of operation, cost)
- What information they need to give you for your records
- A description of the program (purpose, kinds of activities, meals, and so on)
- Procedures for safe arrival and departure (including the parents' responsibility for promptness and any penalties for non-compliance, such as payment of extra fees or withdrawal of the child from the program; and alternate care and transportation for a child should his driver arrive under the influence of alcohol or other drugs)
- Policies regarding discipline
- Rules regarding illness care (including separating a sick child from other children)
- A clear understanding that there is an open invitation for parents to visit at any time and to share with you information and feelings regarding their child (contributing to a warm, cooperative atmosphere and protecting against child abuse and liability problems)

When you have the children in your care you should keep regular notations on each child for the parents and for your records regarding any illness, accidents, or other problems that arise during a child's time with you. You will also write up personal progress reports to share with the parents at regular intervals.

The parents need to supply you with:

* All the information needed for your records
* Agreed-upon payments
* A change of clothes, medicine (with written permission for administering), and any other special items necessary for the care of their child

Voluntary Accreditation

Today, child care experts advise parents looking for quality day care to seek a facility that is not only licensed by the state but also accredited by the National Association for Family Day Care (NAFDC) or the National Academy of Early Childhood Programs, an arm of the National Association for the Education of Young Children (NAEYC). The uniform requirements for accreditation by these organizations guarantee a consistent high standard of professional quality.

NAFDC evaluates small home day care operations; NAEYC looks at day care operations where ten or more children are involved, largely outside the home environment. Both organizations offer publications useful to anyone setting up various kinds of playgroups and day care operations.

The National Association for Family Day Care has a practical study guide for caregivers, *Assessment Profile for Family Day Care*. It explains how to achieve a high level of care quality in seven key areas: indoor safety, health, nutrition, interaction of caregiver with parents and children, indoor play environment, outdoor play environment, and professional responsibility of the provider (continuous development of educational skills, business practices, and so on). This guide gives a clear idea of what is expected for accreditation. It is also a sound base for the organization of child care in the home for professionals and nonprofessionals alike.

To begin the accreditation process for family day care, the NAFDC has two criteria. First, you must be in compliance with your own state's requirements. Second, you must have been a care provider for eighteen months. The latter allows time for you to work out some of the initial kinks in your small business and to feel sure this is what you want to do before you go through the accreditation process.

The first part of the process involves a self-assessment, with a list of questions designed to evaluate all aspects of the care you provide. These queries cover the same seven areas discussed in the study guide described above. A parent unaffiliated with your day care operation and another outside person appointed by the NAFDC evaluate your facility by answering the same set of questions. The three question-naires are scored independently.

When this part of the process is complete, the parents currently using your facility fill out another set of questionnaires. Finally, you are asked to write answers to six general questions regarding professional responsibility.

Caregivers who have completed this process generally feel that it is worth the trouble, and parents are universally pleased with the results. Aside from the inner satisfaction of living up to a standard of excellence, care providers find themselves with a well-earned good reputation and a resulting waiting list for their program. They have access to group liability insurance, which saves money, and the accreditation process introduces them to other caregivers in the community who can share advice and support. They also find themselves being held up as shining examples of the best in child care.

Working through the procedures for setting up a day care business is tedious but necessary. Once you have decided that caring for young children in your home is what you really want to do, take a deep breath, plunge in, and systematically go down the list of requirements. Before you know it, you will be spending the bulk of your time with the children. The need for quality day care is enormous, and the rewards are great. You can know that you are giving a special gift of stability to families who leave their children with you. You will become a member of your preschoolers' extended families, and a truly important and loved person in the children's lives.

BASIC RESOURCES TO GET YOU STARTED

National Association for Family Day Care (NAFDC)
725 Fifteenth Street NW, Suite 505
Washington, DC 20005
phone: (202) 347-3356

An organization for family day care providers and consumers. Sets a national standard. Gives a united voice and networking system to professionals. Accredits members who meet a specific set of standards. Publishes *Argus: The Journal of Family Day Care*, a national forum for sharing of information by family day care providers and other professionals. Prints a brochure describing the accreditation process, and a guide, *Assessment Profile for Family Day Care*. One-year Basic Membership, $20; one-year Comprehensive Individual Membership, including subscription to *Argus*, $38.

National Association for the Education of Young Children (NAEYC)
1834 Connecticut Avenue NW
Washington, DC 20009-5789
phone: (202) 232-8777
toll free: (800) 424-2460

An organization of early childhood education professionals. Sponsors conferences, seminars, workshops. Publishes brochures, books, posters, and produces videos. Supplies information on numerous facets of day care. Provides access to support in local areas. A sponsor of the *Early Childhood Research Quarterly*, NAEYC is the parent organization to the National Academy of Early Childhood Programs (see below).

National Academy of Early Childhood Programs (NAEYC Academy)
1834 Connecticut Avenue NW
Washington, DC 20009-5789
phone: (202) 328-2601

Has the only professionally sponsored national, voluntary accreditation system for early childhood centers and schools (programs with ten or more children). Publishes brochures and books including *Guide to Accreditation by the National Academy of Early Childhood Programs* ($37) and a brochure for parents titled *Early Childhood Program Accreditation: A Commitment to Excellence* ($.50).

The Children's Foundation
725 Fifteenth Street NW
Washington, DC 20005
phone: (202) 347-3300

Supplies a range of fact sheets, manuals, newsletters, and training materials for home day care providers, and publishes the *National Directory of Associations and Support Groups*.

Child Care Information Exchange
PO Box 2890
Redmond, WA 98073
phone: (206) 883-9394

This is a rich resource for child care information addressed to child care centers but usable by family day care operations.

Child Welfare League of America (CWLA)
440 First Street NW
Washington, DC 20001
phone: (202) 638-2952

This organization works with state agencies and publishes *Child Welfare League of America Standard for Child Care Services* (revised 1991).

National Association of Child Care Resource and Referral Agencies
(NACCRRA)
2116 Campus Drive SE
Rochester, MN 55904
phone: (507) 287-2220

The NACCRRA can put you in touch with resources and referral agencies that provide help and support to caregivers in your area.

California Child Care Resource and Referral Network
809 Lincoln Way
San Francisco, CA 94122
phone: (415) 661-1714

Publishes a comprehensive guide, *Family Day Care Handbook* (revised 1990), which is California-focused but useful to caregivers anywhere. Covers all aspects of family day care including start up, business details (insurance, contracts, and so on), health and safety (caring for mildly ill children, HIV/AIDS in early childhood settings, nutrition), food, working with parents and children, child development, materials and resources, activities. The handbook ($40) has a three-ring binder format for easy additions.

Toys 'n' Things Press (a division of Resources for Child Caring, Inc.)
450 North Syndicate Street, Suite 5
St. Paul, MN 55104-4127
phone: (800) 423-8309

Publishes and distributes a wide variety of materials for child care providers. Will provide publication list on request.

APPENDIX 2

Nursery Rhymes, Rounds, and Other Familiar Songs

NURSERY RHYMES

"BAA BAA BLACK SHEEP"
Baa, Baa, Black Sheep,
Have you any wool?
Yes sir, yes sir,
Three bags full;
One for my master,
One for my dame,
One for the little boy
Who lives down the lane.

"DO YOU KNOW THE MUFFIN MAN?"
Oh, do you know the muffin man,
the muffin man, the muffin man?
Do you know the muffin man
Who lives down Drury Lane?

Yes, I know the muffin man,
the muffin man, the muffin man.
Yes I know the muffin man
Who lives down Drury Lane.

"FARMER IN THE DELL"

The farmer in the dell,
The farmer in the dell,
Heigh-o the derry-o,
The farmer in the dell.

Repeat, using:
The farmer takes a wife
The wife takes a child
The child takes a nurse
The nurse takes a dog
The dog takes a cat
The cat takes a rat
The rat takes the cheese
The cheese stands alone

"HERE WE GO 'ROUND THE MULBERRY BUSH"

Here we go 'round the mulberry bush,
The mulberry bush, the mulberry bush;
Here we go 'round the mulberry bush,
So early in the morning.

Monday: This is the way we wash our clothes,
Wash our clothes, wash our clothes;
This is the way we wash our clothes,
So early Monday morning.

Repeat, using:
Tuesday—iron our clothes
Wednesday—scrub the floors
Thursday—sew our clothes
Friday—sweep the house
Saturday—bake our bread
Sunday—go to church

"HICKORY DICKORY DOCK"

Hickory, dickory, dock;
The mouse ran up the clock;
The clock struck one,
The mouse ran down;
Hickory, dickory, dock.

"HOT CROSS BUNS"

Hot cross buns,
Hot cross buns;
One a penny, two a penny,
Hot cross buns.

"HUMPTY DUMPTY"
>
> Humpty Dumpty sat on a wall,
> Humpty Dumpty had a great fall.
> All the king's horses
> And all the king's men
> Couldn't put Humpty together again.

"I'M A LITTLE TEAPOT"
>
> I'm a little teapot short and stout
> Here is my handle, here is my spout.
> When I get all steamed up hear me shout,
> Tip me over and pour me out.
>
> I'm a very special pot it's true,
> Here, let me show you what I can do.
> I can change my handle and my spout,
> Tip me over and pour me out.

"JACK AND JILL"
>
> Jack and Jill went up the hill
> To fetch a pail of water;
> Jack fell down
> And broke his crown,
> And Jill came tumbling after.

"LITTLE JACK HORNER"
>
> Little Jack Horner sat in a corner,
> Eating a Christmas pie;
> He put in his thumb, and pulled out a plum,
> And said, "What a good boy am I!"

"LITTLE MISS MUFFET"
>
> Little Miss Muffet sat on a tuffet,
> Eating some curds and whey;
> Along came a great spider,
> Who sat down beside her,
> And frightened Miss Muffet away.

"LONDON BRIDGE"
>
> London Bridge is falling down,
> Falling down, falling down,
> London Bridge is falling down,
> My fair lady.

"MARY HAD A LITTLE LAMB"
>
> Mary had a little lamb,
> Little lamb, little lamb,
> Mary had a little lamb,
> Its fleece was white as snow.

And everywhere that Mary went,
Mary went, Mary went,
And everywhere that Mary went,
The lamb was sure to go.

It followed her to school one day,
School one day, school one day,
It followed her to school one day,
Which was against the rule.

Oh how the children laughed and played
Laughed and played, laughed and played,
How the children laughed and played,
To see a lamb in school.

"OLD KING COLE"
Old King Cole
Was a merry old soul,
And a merry old soul was he.
He called for his pipe
And he called for his bowl
And he called for his fiddlers three.

"OLD MACDONALD HAD A FARM"
Old MacDonald had a farm,
Ee-igh, ee-igh, oh.
And on that farm he had some (chicks).
Ee-igh, ee-igh, oh.

Chorus:
With a (chick, chick) here
And a (chick, chick) there.
Here a (chick).
There a (chick).
Everywhere a (chick, chick).

Repeat, using:
duck—quack
turkey—gobble
pig—oink
cow—moo
donkey—hee-haw

"POP GOES THE WEASEL"
All around the cobbler's bench
The monkey chased the weasel;
The monkey thought t'was all in fun,
Pop! goes the weasel.

"RAIN, RAIN GO AWAY"
Rain, rain, go away.
Come again another day.
Little [*name of child*] wants to play.
Rain, rain, go away.

"RING AROUND THE ROSIE"
Ring around the rosie.
Pocket full of posies.
Ashes, ashes,
We all fall down.

"ROCK-A-BYE BABY"
Rock-a-bye, baby, in the treetop.
When the wind blows, the cradle will rock;
When the bough breaks, the cradle will fall,
And down will come baby, cradle and all.

"SEE-SAW, MARGERY DAW"
See-saw, Margery Daw,
Jacky shall have a new master;
Jacky must have but a penny a day,
Because he can't work any faster.

"SING A SONG OF SIXPENCE"
Sing a song of sixpence,
A pocketful of rye.
Four and twenty black birds
Baked in a pie.
When the pie was opened
The birds began to sing.
Wasn't that a dainty dish
To set before a king?

"TEENSY WEENSY SPIDER"
The teensy weensy spider
Crawled up the water spout.
Down came the rain and washed the spider out.
Out came the sun and dried up all the rain,
So the teensy weensy spider climbed up the spout again.

"TWINKLE, TWINKLE, LITTLE STAR"
Twinkle, twinkle, little star,
How I wonder what you are!
Up above the world so high,
Like a diamond in the sky.

ROUNDS

"ARE YOU SLEEPING?" ("FRÈRE JACQUES")
Are you sleeping, are you sleeping,
Brother John? Brother John?
Morning bells are ringing.
Morning bells are ringing.
Ding, Ding, Dong.
Ding, Ding, Dong.

French version:

Frère Jacques, frère Jacques,
Dormez-vous? Dormez-vous?
Sonnez les matines.
Sonnez les matines.
Din, Din, Don.
Din, Din, Don.

"ROW, ROW, ROW YOUR BOAT"
Row, row, row your boat,
Gently down the stream.
Merrily, merrily, merrily, merrily,
Life is but a dream.

"SWEETLY SINGS THE DONKEY"
Sweetly sings the donkey,
At the break of day.
If you do not feed him,
This is what he'll say:
Hee-haw! Hee-haw!
Hee-haw, hee-haw, hee-haw!

"THREE BLIND MICE"
Three blind mice. Three blind mice.
See how they run. See how they run.
They all ran after the farmer's wife.
She cut off their tails with a carving knife.
Did you ever see such a sight in your life,
As three blind mice?

Note: Preschoolers cannot sing rounds. Sing these and other rounds in unison.

OTHER FAMILIAR SONGS

"DOWN BY THE STATION"

Down by the station early in the morning,
See the empty freight cars all in a row.
Hear the station master shouting "Load 'er up now!
Load the train and off she'll go."

Have you loaded on the coal?
Yes, we've loaded on the coal.

Oh, down by the station early in the morning,
Hear the station master loadin' up the train.
Have you loaded on the trunks?
Yes we've loaded on the trunks.
And the coal?
And the coal.

List—pigs, cows, potatoes, etc.

Oh, down by the station early in the morning,
See the loaded freight cars all in a row.
Hear the station master shoutin' all aboard now,
Chug, chug, toot, toot; off we go.

"I SEE THE MOON"

I see the moon and the moon sees me.
The moon sees the one that I want to see.
God bless the moon and God bless me.
And God bless the one that I want to see.

"IF YOU'RE HAPPY AND YOU KNOW IT CLAP YOUR HANDS"

If you're happy and you know it clap your hands.
If you're happy and you know it clap your hands.
If you're happy and you know it,
Then your face will surely show it.
If you're happy and you know it clap your hands.

Sing again, using substitutes for "clap your hands."
The children can choose:
If you're sad and you know it . . .
If you're angry and you know it . . .

Stamp your feet.
Nod your head.
Tap your toes.

"I'VE BEEN WORKING ON THE RAILROAD"

I've been working on the railroad all the livelong day.
I've been working on the railroad just to pass the time away.
Don't you hear the whistle blowing?
Rise up so early in the morn!
Don't you hear the captain shouting,
"Dinah, blow your horn."
Dinah, won't you blow? Dinah, won't you blow?
Oh, Dinah, won't you blow your horn, your horn.
Dinah, won't you blow? Dinah, won't you blow?
Oh, Dinah, won't you blow your horn?

"JINGLE BELLS"

Jingle Bells. Jingle Bells.
Jingle all the way!
Oh what fun it is to ride in a one-horse open sleigh—
Jingle Bells. Jingle Bells.
Jingle all the way!
Oh what fun it is to ride in a one-horse open sleigh!

"OH, SUSANNA"

Oh, I come from Alabama with my banjo on my knee,
I goin' to Lou'siana my Susanna for to see.
It rained all day the night I left
The weather was so dry.
The sun so hot, I froze myself,
Susanna, don't you cry.

Chorus
Oh, Susanna! Oh don't you cry for me,
For I come from Alabama
With my banjo on my knee.

"PICK A BALE OF COTTON"

You got to jump down, turn around
Pick a bale of cotton.
Jump down, turn around,
Pick a bale a day.

Chorus
Oh lawdy, pick a bale of cotton
Oh lawdy, pick a bale a day.

"PUNCHINELLO"

What can you do, Punchinello funny fellow,
What can you do, Punchinello funny you?
[*Child in center makes a motion, and*

children in the circle copy motion and sing.]
We can do it too, Punchinello funny fellow,
We can do it, too, Punchinello funny you.

"SKIP TO MY LOU"
Flies in the buttermilk, shoo, fly, shoo,
Flies in the buttermilk, shoo, fly, shoo,
Flies in the buttermilk, shoo, fly, shoo,
Skip to my Lou my darling.

Repeat, using (3 times):
Cat's in the cream jar, what'll I do?
Chicken's in the haystack, shoo, shoo, shoo.
Little red wagon painted blue.
Lost my sweetheart, what'll I do?
I'll get another one prettier'n you.
Skip to my Lou my darling.

"TEN LITTLE INDIANS"
There were one, two, three little Indians,
Four, five, six little Indians,
Seven, eight, nine little Indians,
Ten little Indian boys.

Repeat, singing in reverse:
There were ten, nine, eight little Indians, etc.

"THIS OLD MAN"
This old man
He played one.
He played knick knack
On his thumb.
With a knick knack, paddy whack,
Give the dog a bone.
This old man goes rolling home.

Repeat, using:
two—thumb
three—knee
four—door
five—hive
six—sticks
seven—goin' to heaven
eight—on the gate
nine—all the time
ten—over again

"YANKEE DOODLE"
> Yankee Doodle went to town
> A-riding on a pony.
> He stuck a feather in his hat
> And called it macaroni.

> *Chorus*
> Yankee Doodle, keep it up,
> Yankee Doodle dandy,
> Mind the music and the step,
> And with the girls be handy.

APPENDIX 3

List of Activities by Type

ART

COOKING

DRAMATIC PLAY

GAMES

MUSIC

PHYSICAL EXERCISE

SCIENCE

STORYTELLING

TRIPS

WOODWORKING

INDEX

◆

ABOUT THE AUTHORS

◆

Nancy Towner Butterworth received her B.A. from Mount Holyoke College and her M.Ed. from Goucher College. She taught elementary school in Wellesley, Massachusetts. When her children were preschoolers, she was active in the organization and running of playgroups and nursery schools. She and Laura Broad co-authored the first edition of *Playgroup Handbook* and *Kits for Kids*. She has conducted programs and workshops for various parenting organizations covering such topics as "Creativity" and "Holiday Projects for Young Children," and appeared as a guest on the "Phil Donahue Show" for a program regarding the impact of television on young children. She served as a member and as president of the Board of Education in Western Springs, Illinois. More recently she has been involved in drug and alcohol education projects in the schools of Wilbraham, Massachusetts.

Laura Peabody Broad was graduated from Mount Holyoke College and Harvard Graduate School of Education. A former elementary school teacher, playgroup mother, and kindergarten day care leader, Laura has continued her interest in early education by giving in-service training workshops for teacher accreditation, by leading adult education classes, and by presenting quick segments showing activity ideas for children on television.

Laura's research for this edition of *The Playgroup Handbook* was done while teaching at the Congregational Nursery School in Needham, Massachusetts. Currently she is a teacher at the Child Study Center, a laboratory school at Pine Manor College in Chestnut Hill, Massachusetts. In addition she tutors children in grades two through eight and is an instructor at Dean Junior College in Franklin, Massachusetts.